D1475979

Multinationals and Industrial Competitiveness

NEW HORIZONS IN INTERNATIONAL BUSINESS

Series Editor: Peter J. Buckley
Centre for International Business,
University of Leeds (CIBUL), UK

The New Horizons in International Business series has established itself as the world's leading forum for the presentation of new ideas in international business research. It offers pre-eminent contributions in the areas of multinational enterprise – including foreign direct investment, business strategy and corporate alliances, global competitive strategies, and entrepreneurship. In short, this series constitutes essential reading for academics, business strategists and policy makers alike.

Titles in the series include:

The New Economic Analysis of Multinationals
An Agenda for Management, Policy and Research
Edited by Thomas L. Brewer, Stephen Young and Stephen E. Guisinger

Transnational Corporations, Technology and Economic Development
Backward Linkages and Knowledge Transfer in South East Asia
Axèle Giroud

Alliance Capitalism for the New American Economy
Edited by Alan M. Rugman and Gavin Boyd

Alliance Capitalism and Corporate Management
Entrepreneurial Cooperation in Knowledge Based Economies
Edited by John H. Dunning and Gavin Boyd

The Structural Foundations of International Finance
Problems of Growth and Stability
Edited by Pier Carlo Padoan, Paul A. Brenton and Gavin Boyd

The New Competition for Inward Investment
Companies, Institutions and Territorial Development
Edited by Nicholas Phelps and Phil Raines

Multinational Enterprises, Innovative Strategies and Systems of Innovation
Edited by John Cantwell and José Molero

Multinational Firms' Location and the New Economic Geography
Edited by Jean-Louis Mucchielli and Thierry Mayer

Free Trade in the Americas
Economic and Political Issues for Governments and Firms
Edited by Sidney Weintraub, Alan M. Rugman and Gavin Boyd

Economic Integration and Multinational Investment Behaviour
European and East Asian Experiences
Edited by Pierre-Bruno Ruffini

Strategic Business Alliances
An Examination of the Core Dimensions
Keith W. Glaister, Rumy Husan and Peter J. Buckley

Investment Strategies in Emerging Markets
Edited by Saul Estrin and Klaus E. Meyer

Multinationals and Industrial Competitiveness
A New Agenda
John H. Dunning and Rajneesh Narula

Multinationals and Industrial Competitiveness

A New Agenda

John H. Dunning

Emeritus Esmée Fairbairn Professor of International Investment and Business Studies, University of Reading, UK and Emeritus State of New Jersey Professor of International Business, Rutgers University, US

and

Rajneesh Narula

Professor of International Business Regulation, University of Reading, UK

NEW HORIZONS IN INTERNATIONAL BUSINESS

Edward Elgar
Cheltenham, UK • Northampton, MA, USA

Published by
Edward Elgar Publishing Limited
Glensanda House
Montpellier Parade
Cheltenham
Glos GL50 1UA
UK

Edward Elgar Publishing, Inc.
136 West Street
Suite 202
Northampton
Massachusetts 01060
USA

A catalogue record for this book
is available from the British Library

ISBN   1 84376 686 8

Printed and bound in Great Britain by MPG Books Ltd, Bodmin, Cornwall

Contents

Figures

Tables

Acknowledgments

This volume owes much to so many. Each chapter has gone through a serpentine voyage through many a draft to get here, and on the way has benefited from the assistance, advice or comments of many people. To the following people we are certain that we owe a general debt of gratitude: Christine Dunning, H. Peter Gray, John Hagedoorn, Lynn Mytelka, Sanjaya Lall, Luc Soete, Lou Anne Barclay and Jan Fagerberg. Alas, our memories are not quite what they used to be, so if we inexplicably fail to mention certain names, it is without malice or evil intent.

Chapter 4 was originally co-authored with Chang-Su Kim and Jyh-Der Lin. We are grateful for their permission to use this co-authored material here. Gratitude for administrative and secretarial support goes to Jill Turner at Reading University, Nevena Yakova and Phyllis Miller at Rutgers University and Karen Pallisgaard at the Copenhagen Business School. Special mention must be made of the general editorial assistance that Sudha Menon has provided.

Acknowledgment is also due to the copyright holders for permission to reprint the following. Chapter 2 is a revised version of 'Developing countries versus multinationals in a globalising world: the dangers of falling behind', which appeared in *Forum for Development Studies*, 1999, (2), pp. 261–87. Chapter 3 is based on a paper that originally appeared as 'Industrial development, globalisation and multinational enterprises: new realities for developing countries', *Oxford Development Studies*, vol. 28, no. 2, 2000. Chapter 4 was originally published as chapter 7 under the same title in R. Narula (ed.), *Trade and Investment in a Globalising World*, Oxford: Pergamon Press. Chapter 5 was published as 'Regional integration and the strategies of multinational firms', in *Trade and Regional Integration in the Development Agenda*, Washington, DC: IDB, 2002. Chapter 6 is a revised version of 'Explaining international R&D alliances and the role of governments', *International Business Review*, vol. 7, pp. 377–97, 1998.

Chapter 7 is based on 'Explaining strategic R&D alliances by European firms', *Journal of Common Market Studies*, vol. 37, pp. 711–23, 1999. Chapter 8 is based on 'R&D collaboration by SMEs: new opportunities and limitations in the face of globalisation', *Technovation*, 2004, vol. 24, pp. 153–61. Chapter 9 is an extended version of 'Relational assets: the new

competitive advantages of MNEs and countries', in F. Contractor and
P. Lorange (eds), *Cooperative Strategies and Alliances*, Oxford: Pergamon
Press, 2002. Chapter 10 is based on 'Regaining competitiveness for Asian
enterprises', *Journal of International Business and Economy*, vol. 1, 2000.
Chapter 11 is based on 'The role of foreign direct investment in upgrading
China's competitiveness', *Journal of International Business and Economy*,
vol. 3, 2003.

All errors remain our own.

Rajneesh Narula and John Dunning
Copenhagen and Henley-on-Thames

1. The multinational enterprise, industrial development and policy: an introduction to the primary themes of this volume

The essays in this book, part or all of which were originally published between 1998 and 2004, set out the views and opinions of the authors on three main topics. Each of these is a key ingredient in the current debate on the contribution of multinational enterprises (MNE) to economic development in an increasingly globalizing, knowledge-intensive and alliance-based world economy.

The first topic embraces some of the implications of the increasing role played by cross-border trade and foreign direct investment (FDI) for the competitiveness and structural transformation of developing countries. Chapter 2 first offers a brief review of the changing world economic scenario over the past two decades, and how this has affected the locational advantages of developing countries, as perceived by foreign investors, and the ownership advantages of foreign MNEs, as perceived by host countries. In doing so, it emphasizes the need for host governments continually to upgrade the institutional infrastructure underpinning their indigenous resources and capabilities, and their economic policies, if they wish to retain and/or raise their bargaining strengths, and to avoid 'falling behind' in the race to attract foreign investment. We make five main points. First, economic globalization has affected regions and countries unevenly and this is reflected in the configuration of MNE activity. Second, the failure of most of the developing world to catch up is associated with the inadequate level of domestic created assets and the inefficiency of local firms. Third, an important means by which to upgrade their competitiveness has been the importation of technology, skills and organizational capabilities both via FDI and by collaborative arrangements. Fourth, the conditions for catch up are also necessary (but insufficient) conditions to attract FDI. Fifth, there is a threshold level of created assets which determine the ability of domestic firms to benefit from externalities that arise from MNE-related activity, and a threshold level of created assets and industry clusters is also necessary as location advantages to attract such activity in the first place.

Chapter 3 takes these themes and pays more specific attention to the changing economic relationships between MNEs and host developing countries at different stages in the latter's development. We build upon our earlier work (see Dunning and Narula, 1996; Narula, 1996) on the investment development path (IDP) and further develop our understanding of the interactive nature of economic development and foreign direct investment, in this instance focusing on the challenges facing developing countries. We add to our understanding of the intertwined and interdependent nature of development and MNEs by highlighting how motives of investment change with the stages of the IDP. We emphasize that these relationships have been dramatically affected by new technologies, and the renaissance of market-based capitalism; and that, consequentially, host governments have had to re-evaluate not only their micro-management strategies, but also their industrial development options.

The chapter also emphasizes the contextual characteristics of FDI, and the differences in the bargaining power and strategies of the more industrialized vis-à-vis the poorer developing countries. After all, globalization has changed the economic realities of all parties. First, the competences of MNEs are becoming increasingly mobile and knowledge-intensive. MNEs thus give more attention to the availability and quality of the created assets of alternative locations. Second, among developing countries there are now considerable differences between the 'catching up' countries (for example, newly industrializing countries – NICs) and 'falling behind', less-developed countries (LDCs). These developments have helped change the opportunity sets of both MNEs and host countries. FDI-based development strategies are now commonplace among LDCs, but there is also increased competition for the 'right' kinds of investment. In general, the balance in bargaining power has shifted in favour of the MNE, and LDCs increasingly need to provide unique, non-replicable created assets to maintain a successful FDI-assisted development strategy.

In Chapter 4 we extend the principles and predictions of the investment development path (IDP), which has been subject to extensive empirical testing over the past decade, to do two things. The first is to trace the relationship between trade, FDI and economic development; the second is to examine the medium-term impact of both trade and FDI on the changing industrial structure of developing countries. Data from Korea and Taiwan for a 30-year period point to the increased richness of the IDP once these additional variables are taken into account.

The final chapter of Part I considers the impact of regional integration and globalization on FDI flows into developing countries in more detail.

Although FDI has significant influence on economic development, much of the work on regional integration (RI) has focused on trade effects. Chapter 5 seeks to examine the effect of regional integration on MNE strategies while acknowledging other globalization-related developments. In particular, we examine the ways in which various regional integration schemes have affected the strategies of different kinds of MNEs and their subsidiaries *à propos* their value-added activities in developing countries. The chapter distinguishes between two groups of developing countries: the least developed, with little or no domestic industrial capacity, and the rest, with an intermediate level of capacity. We examine MNE strategies in developing countries in four scenarios: (1) in a non-RI, pre-liberalized environment, (2) with RI in a pre-liberalized environment, (3) in a non-RI, post-liberalization scenario, (4) RI in a post-liberalization scenario. We also distinguish between least developed countries (LDCs), and intermediate developing countries, within North–South and South–South RI.

Liberalization and a shift in policy orientation have had a greater effect on MNE strategies than integration. Globalization of MNE activity and liberalization has led to a downgrading of MNE activity in most LDCs. Much of the gains in FDI *flows* have been a result of redistribution, associated with privatization. Countries with a threshold level of domestic capability and more efficient institutions have benefited from increases in the quality of FDI. RI schemes have reinforced these trends, benefiting those countries that have a viable domestic sector, and have created the appropriate multilateral institutions to exploit cross-border efficiencies. In general, South–South RI in a post-liberalized world has had limited benefits for LDCs relative to intermediate developing countries. RI schemes need to be seen as an opportunity to respond gradually to globalization in a controlled and stepwise manner, and not as an alternative to multilateralism.

The second part of the volume addresses three main themes. The first is the growing importance of innovatory activities of firms (and in particular R&D) in promoting economic development and industrial restructuring; and also the role of FDI in furthering this goal. The second is the emergence of cross-border strategic alliances as a means of gaining access by firms domiciled in one country to foreign-based R&D and innovatory systems. The third is the increasingly significant role of national governments in promoting the intellectual capital of their indigenous resources and capabilities, and of inter-firm collaborative alliances.

Chapter 6 first explains the rationale behind the rapid growth and the deepening of cross-border technology-based collaborative ventures over the past two or three decades and how this has been affected by the disinternalization of the value-added chain of many MNEs, and the evolution of quasi-hierarchical modes of corporate activity. National governments have responded to these changes by pursuing policies promoting 'technonationalism' which includes fostering R&D investment by national champions. First, we inquire, from the firm's perspective, why they have an increasing propensity to undertake R&D alliances, with particular focus on international alliances. Second, we try to understand the role of governments in promoting and engaging in the generation and diffusion of intellectual capital in general, and in facilitating inter-firm technological alliances in particular. Third, we evaluate the efficacy of technonationalism, in light of the welfare and social responsibilities of governments, particularly in an age of globalization. We suggest that the role of government is best restricted to L-advantage augmentation, basic research investment and improving international coordination of technology markets. The chapter then goes on to describe and evaluate the response of governments to these events as they attempt to protect or enhance the competitive advantages of their indigenous resources and capabilities, and help their own firms to engage in beneficial strategic partnering or networking with foreign suppliers, competitors or industrial customers.

Chapter 7 then tackles the more specific issue of the impact of the completion of the European internal market on the formation of strategic R&D alliances involving European firms. This chapter first develops an explanation for the increasing popularity of strategic technology alliances, both globally and by EU firms. It then evaluates, using data over the period 1980–94, how private, non-subsidized cooperative agreements in R&D by EU firms have evolved, paying particular attention to the growth of intra-EU activity relative to extra-EU agreements (that is, EU–US and EU–Japan alliances). It finds that, contrary to what might have been expected, those concluded between European and non-European firms have increased relative to inter-European ventures. Essentially, EU firms' partnering habits reflect the need to seek strong partners regardless of nationality within a given industry, although intra-EU partnering enjoyed a brief popularity during the latter half of the 1980s. It suggests that, far from being 'second best', alliances represent the 'first best' alternative to full internalization of intermediate product markets, as they allow both more flexibility and a better economic access to assets complementary to its core competitive advantages.

The advantages of flexibility offered by alliances, and particularly those involving small or medium-size enterprises (SMEs), are further explored in Chapter 8. This chapter asserts that globalization – through the competition it engenders – has not only led to more alliances among large firms, but has created new opportunities and challenges for smaller firms. These opportunities and challenges have been of two main kinds. The first is that some forms of outsourcing or subcontracting, for example in the motor, electronics and garment industries, are best undertaken by SMEs. The second is that, owing to a fall in many spatial transaction costs, the growing opportunities for networking, and the financial and other assistance provided by governments (both in developed and developing countries) for 'seed' and innovatory activities best performed by SMEs, such firms are playing an increasingly pivotal role in the new international division of labour. This state of affairs has altered the *raison d'être* of the SME. On the one hand, SMEs have always sought to specialize in niches, given their limited resources. Consequently, their role as specialized suppliers to large firms has increased. On the other hand, the cross-fertilization of technologies has meant that they also need to span several competences. As will be seen, Chapter 9 illustrates these points by examining two important concurrent dynamics. The first dynamic pertains to the various types of SMEs and how the industrial structure and external environment influence their collaborative activity. The second dynamic is associated with the evolution of technologies, technological paradigms and trajectories. We explain how different types of SMEs tend to dominate the industry structure at a given stage of the evolution of a given core technology. Evidence is presented from a survey on the collaborative activities of one particular form of the SME (the 'stand-alone' SME) in the electronics hardware sector. The analysis is based on in-depth interviews and questionnaire surveys of over a hundred European technology firms and attempts to explain the reasons for the preference of one type of collaboration over another, and the limitations of collaboration as an alternative to in-house R&D.

The three chapters in Part III focus on two main issues. The first describes some of the changing competitive, or ownership (O), advantages of firms and the locational (L) advantages of countries. More specifically, Chapter 9 avers that, alongside the capabilities of MNEs to create and efficiently deploy new knowledge, and those of countries to promote the innovatory capabilities of their indigenous resources in line with their (perceived) long-term dynamic competitive advantage, more attention needs to be given to the institutional framework undergirding these capabilities, and particularly the quality of the relational assets possessed or exploited by both individuals and organizations. Such assets, as Chapter 9 describes, may be either private or socially owned, they may be created or acquired as a result of intraorganizational or interorganizational transactions. In turn, such transactions may be conducted at a dyadic or network level. This chapter (part of which has not been published before) is the first attempt to place these issues firmly in the context of the mainstream explanations of the economic determinants of MNE activity.

Chapters 10 and 11 reproduce the contents of two public lectures given by one of the authors of the volume. Both were presented at international investment fairs – one in Seoul, Korea in 1999, and the other in Xiamen, China in 2002. The subject of both lectures was 'Upgrading the competitiveness of indigenous firms and resources by FDI'; and more particularly, the subject was to describe and evaluate both the forms and the structure of such upgrading. The Seoul lecture was given shortly after the end of the Asian crisis, and it focused primarily on the lessons that Asian businesses and governments might be usefully learning from their US counterparts.

The thoughts expressed in Chapter 11 were prompted by China's accession to the World Trade Organisation (WTO). In this chapter, we pay detailed attention to the specific contributions FDI might make to China's bid to become more competitive as a global player and to the policies and strategies which the Chinese government may consider deploying if it wishes to ensure that such investment best promotes the host countries' structural transformation and its long-term comparative advantage.

Each of the essays in this volume, then, touches upon critical issues now facing the global economy, and of developing countries in particular. We would emphasize three main conclusions. The first is that MNEs have played and are likely to continue to play an important role in the structural upgrading of these countries. However, the extent and pattern of these benefits is strongly dependent on the form of economic and social development desired by the host countries, and on the policies of host governments in pursuing these goals. Although not the only means available, spillovers from FDI are regarded as one of the most practical and efficient means by which industrial development and upgrading can be promoted. While the *potential* for MNE-related spillovers is clear, as are the opportunities for industrial upgrading therefrom, it is increasingly acknowledged that the nature, level and extent of the benefits vary considerably. Furthermore, it is important to realize that MNEs are not in the business of economic development. Even where they do seek to transfer knowledge, they prefer to use technologies that are suited (first and foremost) to their own needs, and the purposes for which they have made the investment. MNEs do not make their proprietary assets available at the whims of governments; rather they tailor their investment decisions to the existing market needs, and the relative quality of location advantages (especially skills and capabilities in which the domestic economy has a comparative advantage). Once the decision to enter a given market through FDI is taken, the kinds of activity and the level of competence of the subsidiary are also co-determined by the nature of the location advantages of the host location. That is to say, while MNE internal factors such as their internationalization strategy, the role of the new location in their global portfolio of subsidiaries and the motivation of their investment are pivotal in the structure of their investment, they are dependent on the available location-specific resources which can be used for that purpose.

MNEs and unrestrained flows of inward FDI may well lead to an increase in productivity and exports, but they do not necessarily result in increased competitiveness of the domestic sector or increased industrial capacity, which ultimately determines economic growth in the long run. FDI per se does not provide growth opportunities unless a domestic industrial sector exists which has the necessary technological capacity to profit from the externalities that derive from MNE activity. To put it simply, FDI is not a *sine qua non* for development (Portelli and Narula, 2004).[1]

The second conclusion is that cross-border strategic alliances are becoming an increasingly important modality by which both firms and countries can enhance their respective O- and L-specific advantages; and that governments need to reappraise, and where appropriate enhance, the innovatory, entrepreneurial and institutional infrastructure to reap the maximum gains from these cooperative ventures. After all, every firm is idiosyncratic in nature, and has distinct technological trajectories. Cooperative arrangements, difficult at the best of times, are made even more complex by the nature of cross-border cooperation. Cooperation between firms of different and distinct technological competences requires some common ground.

Furthermore, the nature of technology development and R&D adds a unique twist. In most cases, these activities are not affected by tariff and non-tariff barriers, since they involve the development and implementation of knowledge, which is highly tacit and embodied in highly skilled personnel.

It is worth noting that globalization is a more powerful force than economic integration within any one region. The fact is that there is a growing convergence of income and consumption patterns, as well as types of technologies used, and this is occurring across all countries within the Triad (North America, Japan and Western Europe). In general, firms are competing and growing in order to compete with other firms in the same industry, regardless of their nationality. The same is true of alliances, where firms are interested in partnering other firms in the same industry, regardless of their nationality, but on their relative qualities as a partner, and the nature of their technological competitiveness.

Globalization has affected the need of firms to collaborate, in that firms now *seek* opportunities to cooperate, rather than identify situations where they can achieve majority control. In addition, the increasing similarity of technologies across countries and cross-fertilization of technology between sectors, coupled with the increasing costs and risks associated with innovation, has led to firms utilizing alliances as a 'first-best' option (see Narula, 2003, for a discussion). Alliances, as with most forms of innovative activity, are primarily concentrated in the Triad countries. However, the propensity of firms of a given nationality to engage in alliances varies according to the characteristics of the country. This is because small and technologically less advanced countries tend to be focused in fewer sectors than large countries, owing, inter alia, to the differences in economic structure and demand.

Government intervention to promote R&D alliances does not, contrary to popular belief, lead to an increase in the overall level of R&D activity in a given location. It should be noted that R&D alliances are even more footloose than traditional majority-owned production or R&D activities, nor, it must be stressed, do R&D alliances provide significant levels of spillovers to the host economies where they might be located. Funds invested in joint research by governments are notoriously hard to track down, in terms of their application, both in a geographic and a technical (that is, project-specific) sense. Furthermore, firms are more interested in establishing themselves near centres of agglomeration, regardless of where these might be located (Narula, 2003). This indicates a very real danger of entering an incentive war, with so many countries willing to subsidize R&D, and with so few obvious spillovers therefrom.

The third conclusion is that globalization and technological advances are reconfiguring the ingredients of the competitiveness of firms and nation states and, in particular, are emphasizing the increasingly important role of both private and social institutions (*à la* Douglass North) as determinants of the success of corporations and of the economic development of societies. Incentive structures and enforcement mechanisms both constrain and pre-determine what firms and governments can and cannot do. Institutional reform may encourage economic restructuring of MNE activity as it is now doing in Central and Eastern Europe. New paradigms of economic development are fully embracing institutions within their purview (Dunning 2004).

At the same time, not only does institutional change usually lag behind technological *et al.* changes, it sometimes is resistant to such changes. All too frequently, economic units will prefer to maintain existing institutions with competitors, customers and external organizations, produce similar products and remain in similar locations, unless an external force is applied (Narula, 2003). That is, they prefer to maintain their current state of equilibrium, if it does not threaten their survival. When an external force is applied – be it because of a new technology, change in the industrial or market structure, legal and governmental fiat – economic units will seek to modify their routines to accommodate this change to create a new 'equilibrium' preferably in close proximity to their existing routines. Firms loathe radical change. Radical change is costly and highly risky and, because routines and institutions develop slowly, radical change that is undertaken rapidly is even more risky.

However, every subsequent change becomes less costly, because the knowledge of developing new markets, technologies and institutions can be applied to future scenarios. That is, the economic unit has acquired the 'technologies of learning' and these can be applied, *ceteris paribus*, to other situations. A US firm's experience of developing its first European affiliate in (say) Germany makes it easier to enter other similar markets such as Denmark and the Netherlands. This line of reasoning has been demonstrated time and time again for firms of all nationalities.[2] The importance of institutions and institution building cannot be overemphasized. If the appropriate institutions and organizations are absent or underdeveloped, economic actors within the system will be unable to absorb and efficiently utilize knowledge that may be made available to them.

NOTES

1. See also special issue of the *European Journal of Development Research*, 2004, vol. 16, issue 3, edited by Sanjaya Lall and Rajneesh Narula.
2. See, for example, Johanson and Vahlne, 1977; Hagedoorn and Narula, 2001; Hogenbirk, 2002.

REFERENCES

Dunning, J.H. (2004), 'Towards a new paradigm of development: implications for the determinants of international business activity', paper presented to UK Chapter of the Academy of International Business, April.
Dunning, J.H., and R. Narula (1996), 'The investment development path revisited: some emerging issues', in J.H. Dunning and R. Narula (eds), *Foreign Direct Investment and Governments: Catalysts for Economic Restructuring*, London: Routledge.
Hagedoorn, J., and R. Narula (2001), 'Evolutionary understanding of corporate foreign investment behaviour: US foreign direct investment in Europe', in R. Narula (ed.), *International Trade, Investment in a Globalising World*, New York: Pergamon.
Hogenbirk, A. (2002), *Determinants of Inward Foreign Direct Investment: The Case of the Netherlands*, Maastricht: Datawyse.
Johanson, J., and J. Vahlne (1977), 'The internationalization process of the firm – a model of knowledge development and increasing foreign market commitments', *Journal of International Business Studies*, **8** (1), 23–32.
Narula, R. (1996), *Multinational Investment and Economic Structure*, London: Routledge.
Narula, R. (2003) *Globalisation and Technology*, Cambridge: Polity Press.
Portelli, B., and R. Narula (2004), 'FDI through acquisitions and implications for industrial upgrading: case evidence from Tanzania', MERIT Research Memorandum 2004–011.

PART I

MNEs and industrial development: issues confronting developing countries

2. Developing countries versus multinationals in a globalizing world: the dangers of falling behind

INTRODUCTION

The nature and extent of the interaction between MNEs and governments of developing countries have undergone several dramatic shifts over the postwar era. Partly, this is a result of fundamental changes in political ideologies and in the economic systems associated with these ideologies. This has led to a wide variety of policies, attitudes and actions by governments towards MNE activity, which has spanned the continuum between the laissez-faire, neoliberal approach maintained by the pre-1997 Hong Kong government and the structural adjustment programmes sponsored by the World Bank, on the one hand, and the centrally-planned administrative systems of Eastern European countries and the People's Republic of China on the other. This heterogeneity of policies is, in itself, unsurprising, given the different stages of development and economic structure of these countries. However, overarching these variables, and influencing them, has been the radical reorientation of development strategies by many developing countries over the past two decades from those of an import-substituting and inward-looking variety towards those geared towards outward-looking and export-oriented goals. These have led to an even wider variety of policy orientations as countries have undertaken structural adjustment programmes, while preserving certain elements of their former regimes.

The present thrust towards MNE-friendly attitudes by governments dates back to the early 1980s, and can be ascribed to broad changes in the world economy which have been generically (although not always appropriately) described as 'globalization'. Economic globalization, as used here, refers to the increasing cross-border interdependence and integration of production and markets for goods, services and capital. This process leads to a widening of the extent and form of international transactions, and to a deepening of the interdependence between the actions of economic actors located in one country and those located in others (Dunning, 1997). It is important to stress that globalization is a process and not an event. The primary determinants of globalization have been (1) the rapid development of information and computer technologies (ICT) and the continued fall in real transport and transaction costs; and (2) the renaissance of democratic capitalism and the free market system of allocating scarce resources. However, globalization has not affected all countries and regions to the same extent, especially in the developing world. While a small handful of developing countries have prospered, a vast majority have experienced a corresponding divergence of their income levels and consumption patterns away from their counterparts in the industrialized world.

This has resulted in what is essentially a dichotomy of countries, namely, a widening in the income levels of the wealthiest industrialized countries (and a handful of wealthier developing countries) at one extreme and the poorest countries at the other. Indeed, as argued by Gray (1996), globalization, while benefiting the middle-income developing countries, has so far brought relatively few economic gains to the least developed countries, for example, most of sub-Saharan Africa.

These related processes have fundamentally altered the relationship between MNEs and governments, as both entities have adjusted their strategies and policies to the realities of the new global environment. Although a growing number of developing countries have adopted development strategies that increasingly rely on inbound foreign direct investment (FDI) to upgrade their indigenous resources and improve the competitiveness of their domestic industries, most have been unable to replicate the success stories of the Asian newly industrializing countries (NICs). Essentially these countries are stuck in a vicious circle, which, in great measure, is due to their failure to improve their human and technological infrastructure, macroeconomic policies and institutional frameworks. This vicious circle is also exacerbated by the increased competition for FDI inflows among the developing countries, which has led to a dissipation of potential net benefits from MNE activities through a series of locational tournaments (Mytelka, 1999, 2002).

This chapter is organized as follows. The next section traces the changing geographical configuration of MNE activity and of economic growth over the past two decades, and the changes in the nature of interaction between governments and MNEs. We go on to suggest reasons for the widening of income gaps in a globalizing world and evaluate the respective roles which MNEs and governments may play in reducing them. The chapter then ties the competitive position of countries to the role of MNE activity. The last section presents some policy implications for developing economies, emphasizing the need for MNEs and governments to view each other's roles as complementary, since the upgrading of resources and capabilities of countries improves the net benefits to both parties.

ECONOMIC GLOBALIZATION, ECONOMIC GROWTH AND GOVERNMENTS

The relationship between MNEs and democratic national governments is governed by a fundamental difference in the objectives of each. The MNE, as with most private economic entities, desires to maximize the welfare of its owners,[1] while the national government wishes to do the same for its citizens. Although not a zero-sum game (even where the relationship is not confrontational) the failure to find common ground often results in a suboptimal outcome for both parties. Indeed, in the 1970s, most governments viewed MNEs with a certain amount of hostility. Since that time much has changed, with both MNEs and governments coming to realize that each has much to offer the other, and that a cooperative rather than an adversarial association may best promote mutual interests. In the 1990s, both players took a more systemic and integrated approach towards upgrading their resource creation and usage, and maintaining their long-term competitiveness. This has led to a more pragmatic approach by national governments to MNE activity. Such a shift in approach and attitude, especially among developing countries, which hitherto had adopted a confrontational approach to inbound FDI, must be seen in the light of dramatic events that have taken place in the world economy.

Before examining the changes that have occurred in the government–MNE interface, it is important to understand the underlying reasons behind these changes, not just in the interaction between these two sets of actors, but within each set of players. While there has been a tendency to classify many of the changes of the past 20–25 years under the heading of 'globalization', this entails a simplification of several complex phenomena which, together, have fashioned a reconfiguration of the world economy and the way in which it is organized. In particular the last decade of the 20th century has seen a reorientation in the socio-institutional structure of democratic capitalism from hierarchical to alliance capitalism (Dunning, 1994, 1997) and an increasing rapidity of technological change. The latter factor has increased the threshold of location-specific assets needed to sustain economic growth (Cappelen and Fagerberg, 1995).

Despite this new era of economic pragmatism and the increased cooperation between MNEs and national governments, globalization has not occurred evenly across industries and countries. Indeed, there has been an increased economic segregation of countries into three broad categories. The first consists of the wealthy industrialized countries which, over the past few decades, have experienced a convergence in income levels, consumption patterns and technological capabilities. The second comprises the (primarily Asian) NICs, which are also catching up and converging on the first group. The third category is made up of a large number of developing countries which, far from converging on the first and second group, are in fact diverging from them, either because they have 'stayed behind' relative to the first group, or because they have 'stumbled back' in both a relative and absolute sense (Hikino and Amsden, 1994). Put another way, the homogeneity among markets that is associated with globalization has occurred on a regional, rather than a global, basis. These processes have been the subject of considerable research, which has tried to explain the slowdown of productivity growth amongst the industrialized countries, as well as the long-run tendency for income levels and productivity levels to converge in the long-run with that of the lead country. The main thesis of the convergence theory is that the lead country possesses the largest capital stock and the highest level of technology and knowledge. The greater the gap between the lag and the lead country, the larger is the pool of potential created assets[2] the follower country may acquire and (provided it possesses the capabilities to harness these assets) the greater the potential for economic growth.[3]

The divergence of the majority of the lower-income developing countries has been illustrated by Dowrick and Gemmell (1991) and Alam and Naseer (1992), among others. This divergence has occurred despite technological catch-up due to the proliferation of the activities of MNEs, the integration of world markets and the emergence of new technologies, each of which should, in theory at least, increase spillovers of wealth-creating assets to lagging countries. This convergence of income, technological and knowledge levels of the middle- and higher-income countries has furthered the homogeneity of their consumption patterns and markets. It has led to a sort of de facto integration amongst the countries of the Triad, in addition to the de jure integration within subgroups such as the European Union and North American Free Trade Agreement (Narula, 1993, 1996). It is important to note that the process of catch-up and convergence is a dynamic one, and membership of these three groups is, by definition, unstable. Some developing countries have experienced technological learning and catch-up reversing the process of divergence, most notably China and India.

The simultaneous divergence of the growth and income levels between richer and poorer economies, and the convergence amongst industrial (and rich) economies, harkens back to the vicious cycle of poverty. The inability of the least developed countries to escape from the vicious cycle, and therefore to converge, can be explained by the absence of the same conditions that underlie convergence within the developed countries. In particular, while technological spillovers assist productivity growth in industrialized economies, non-industrialized, poorer economies are unable to utilize such spillovers either because they are not available to them or because the countries do not have the appropriate social–institutional systems and the necessary technological and organizational capability.[4]

GLOBALIZATION AND MNE ACTIVITY: REVIEWING THE EVIDENCE

MNE activity, by its very definition, implies cross-border activity, and it is self-evident that this trend towards homogeneity of incomes and consumption patterns has been considerably assisted by the activities of MNEs. Indeed, the growth of MNE activity in all its forms has been unprecedented over the past 15 years, growing faster than trading activities or overall economic growth (Table 2.1). Other research by the current authors (Narula, 1996; Dunning and Narula, 1994, 1996) suggests that, with the exception of China,[5] MNE activity has become more concentrated among the higher- and middle-income countries.

Table 2.1 Selected indicators of FDI and international production, 1986–95 (billions of US dollars and percentages)

Indicator	Value at current prices, 1995[a]	Annual growth rate (per cent) 1986–90	Annual growth rate (per cent) 1991–4
FDI inflows	315	24.7	12.7
FDI outward stock	2730[b]	19.8	8.8
Sales of foreign affiliates of MNEs	6022	17.4	5.4
Royalties and fees receipts	41[d]	21.8	10.1
GDP at factor costs	24948[d]	10.8	4.3
Gross product of foreign affiliates	1410[e]	10.8	11.4[g]
Gross fixed capital formation	5681[d]	11.0[f]	4.0
Exports of goods and services	4707[b]	14.3	3.8[c]

Note: [a]estimates, [b]1993, [c]1991–3, [d]1994, [e]1991, [f]1982–9, [g]1989–91.

Source: UNCTAD (1996).

Among other features of FDI trends in recent years, one might highlight the following:

1. Both inbound and outbound FDI as a percentage of GDP have substantially increased for almost all countries.

2. The primary source of outbound FDI continues to be the industrialized countries. These countries accounted for 95.0 per cent of such investment in the period 1980–90, 89.4 per cent in the period 1990–94, having increased their share of outward FDI stock between 1980 and 1993, from 79.1 per cent to 79.4 per cent.
3. Though there has been a marked increase in the total outward FDI from developing countries,[6] developing countries accounted for just 0.3 per cent of annual average FDI outflows worldwide during the period 1970–79, and 10.1 per cent between 1990 and 1994. At the same time, just 14 countries[7] continue to account for well over 90 per cent of all developing country outward FDI stocks (Dunning *et al.*, 1998).
4. Around 70 per cent of FDI from the Triad countries is being directed towards other Triad countries. Although, as Table 2.2 shows, there has been an increase in the share of inward FDI to developing countries, this increase almost entirely represents an increase to a small group of developing countries which primarily includes the Asian NICs and China. Thus, between 1980 and 1993, China and the Asian NICs increased their share of total worldwide inward FDI stocks from 2.4 per cent and 0.7 per cent to 3.9 per cent and 2.7 per cent, respectively.
5. Of the 'new' outward investors from developing countries, an increasing share of the investment is being made in industrialized countries rather than in other developing countries (Dunning *et al.*, 1998).
6. Once the oil-exporting countries are excluded, Asia would appear to be the only continent (Table 2.2) which has experienced an increase in its share of inward FDI. Although Asia has experienced a marginal increase in its share of worldwide GDP, this is primarily due to the NICs.
7. The ratio of inward FDI stock to GDP, which is a proxy for the role of MNE activity in the host economy, has increased significantly for non-oil-exporting developing countries, from 5.24 per cent in 1980 to 12.25 per cent in 1993. More interestingly, a similar trend is observable in Africa and Latin America.
8. An increasing amount of FDI (over 50 per cent) is being allocated to the tertiary sector.
9. The growth of strategic alliances and other quasi-market forms of activity remains primarily an industrialized country MNE phenomenon (Freeman and Hagedoorn, 1995).

In the context of the present chapter, the increasing share of FDI stocks relative to GDP across all developing countries is particularly relevant. Even among the low-income countries, only seven of the 24 non-oil-exporting, low-income countries experienced a decline in their FDI to GDP ratio. In the case of the lower middle-income countries, only three experienced a

Table 2.2 Significance of regions in world GDP and inward FDI stocks, 1980 and 1993

	1980				1993			
	IFDI stock (US$ mn)	FDI share in total (%)	GDP share in total (%)	FDI/GDP (%)	IFDI stock (US$ mn)	FDI share in total (%)	GDP share in total (%)	FDI/GDP (%)
Developed countries	372252	77.5	79.1	4.8	1564661	75.2	82.5	8.5
Developing countries	108272	22.5	20.9	5.3	500896	24.1	15.9	14.2
Latin America	48031	10.0	8.6	5.8	167599	8.1	6.0	12.6
Africa	20816	4.3	2.5	8.6	50182	2.4	1.0	21.9
Asia	37961	7.9	9.7	4.0	279417	13.4	8.6	14.6
Total	480611	100.0	100.0	4.9	2079538	100.0	100.0	9.3
Developing countries less oil exporters								
Developing less oil exporting countries	66377	13.8	13.0	5.2	315707	15.2	11.6	12.3
Latin America	35319	7.3	5.1	7.1	113579	5.5	4.1	12.5
Africa	13077	2.7	0.9	14.5	17359	0.8	0.4	19.2
Asia	16517	3.4	6.8	2.5	181070	8.7	6.8	11.9
Asian NICs	11477	2.4	1.5	7.8	81880	3.9	3.0	12.4
China	3444	0.7	2.7	1.3	57172	2.7	1.9	13.4
Asia, less China and NICs	1596	0.3	2.6	0.6	42018	2.0	2.0	9.7

Note: GDP data are based on sample of 91 countries for which both FDI and GDP data are available for both periods; the GDP share of China is considerably underestimated owing to exchange rate fluctuations.

Sources: UNCTAD (1995), World Bank (1995).

decline in this ratio.[8] This increase in significance can partly be explained by the decline in the GDP levels due to the economic and technological divergence of a majority of these countries. Nonetheless, there has also been an increase in FDI flows to a number of developing countries, not all of whom have experienced catching up. For instance, Argentina received 5.5 per cent of all inflows to developing countries over the period 1990–94, twice that of Hong Kong in the same period. In part, this increased inflow to developing countries has been in response to privatization programmes amongst countries undertaking structural adjustment programmes: for example 7.6 per cent of inflows to developing countries between 1989 and 1993 represented FDI from privatization (UNCTAD, 1996).

Thus the evidence would suggest that the role of MNEs in the diverging economies not only continues to be significant, but has actually increased over the past decade. Indeed, as Table 2.2 shows, this role is much greater in the developing countries than in the industrialized countries. For low-income countries, the ratio of FDI to GDP had increased from an average of 8.7 per cent in 1980 to 10.2 per cent in 1993, while, for low middle-income countries, this ratio had increased from 10.0 per cent to 12.2 per cent in the same years. Indeed, we would venture to suggest that, had MNEs not maintained their investment (and in some cases increased it), the divergence of these countries might have been considerably greater.

With ten developing host countries accounting for 67 per cent of inward FDI stock and 79 per cent of inward FDI flows in 1993, this would suggest that, with the increasing reliance of less developed countries on FDI as a source of capital, technology and knowledge, there is increasing likelihood that there will be further polarization of the world economy and widening of the gap between the Triad and the bulk of developing countries. However, despite the fact that the role of MNEs in these countries has increased, opportunities for sequential investments are considerably limited, especially in higher value added activities and sectors which provide significant potential spillovers. In an analysis of the effects of global integration on development, Gray (1996) suggests that the benefits of globalization are self-reinforcing: the inability of these countries to attract inward FDI that results in positive spillover effects is likely to offer few opportunities for exports and inflows of portfolio capital.

Underlying the relative decline of interest by MNEs in the diverging countries are three interrelated phenomena. First, there has been a significant reconfiguration in the ways MNEs both conduct and coordinate their international operations. Second, there has been a fundamental change in the nature and type of immobile location-specific created assets to which MNEs are interested in acquiring access. Third, there has been a significant shift in the expectations of countries from MNE activity.

These underlying determinants have each affected the strategies and activities of MNEs differently, and the consequences and nature of these changes will be examined throughout the remainder of this chapter. Not coincidentally, these changes are directly linked to the economic changes associated with the advent of globalization, and can be broadly traced back to two fundamental changes in the world economy: (i) developments associated with the introduction and adoption of new technologies, which have drastically reduced real transport and transaction costs; and (ii) the renaissance of capitalism and the end of the Cold War.

New Technologies

The growth of new technologies has had a significant impact on the means by which MNEs view country-specific advantages. Central among these have been a series of spectacular advances in information and computer technologies (ICTs), which some scholars believe are initiating a new technological paradigm around which a new Kondratieff cycle of economic change will cluster (Freeman, 1987; Freeman and Perez, 1988). ICTs have dramatically shrunk the economic distance between countries, and have facilitated a series of generic productivity improvements. Needless to say, their rapid development over the past two decades has further enhanced the process of globalization, of both countries and firms. They have done so through at least three means.

First, new technologies have led to *improved coordination of cross-border activities*. It is a fundamental feature of MNE activity that cross-border market failure exists in the supply of intermediate products, and especially intangible assets. ICT has reduced both the costs of acquiring and disseminating information and the transaction and coordination costs associated with cross-border activity has done so on at least two levels. First, information about both input and output markets is more easily accessible. This allows firms which previously could not engage in international business transactions now to do so. Indeed, a UN study (1993) has indicated that there is a greater number of small and medium enterprises engaging in international activity than was hitherto the case. Second, MNEs are better able to integrate the activities of their various affiliates through the use of these technologies and to respond more quickly to changing conditions in the countries in which they operate. Taken together, these transaction cost-reducing processes have enabled MNE activity to be much more efficiently organized across borders. They have also facilitated a shift towards more rationalized and strategic asset-seeking MNE activity, and away from the more multi-domestic approach which was more prevalent prior to the 1970s.[9]

While the decline of transaction and coordinating costs has led to an increased efficiency of *intra-firm* networks, there have also been substantial cost savings in the coordination and monitoring costs associated with *inter-firm* networks. This growing use of networks, both intra- and inter-firm, is one of the primary features of the age of alliance capitalism (Dunning, 1997). The use of strategic alliances, joint ventures, R&D consortia and the like has experienced rapid growth, both within and between countries (Hagedoorn and Narula, 1996). Indeed, the growing use of organizational modalities which permit firms to engage in quasi-internalized arrangements is attributable, at least in part, to the ease with which collaborators and competitors may be monitored, and the extent to which the risks of shirking have declined. In the case of the converging and catching-up economies, larger markets for similar products and the ability of MNEs to organize production activities on a rationalized basis has led, *ceteris paribus*, to higher rents, allowing a better exploitation of the economies of scale, since similar products may be sold in several countries at the same time.

The failure of the majority of the developing countries to develop the necessary created assets, especially those of skilled human capital and infrastructural facilities, underlies the limited extent to which affiliates in developing countries have been involved in the process of rationalization. Nonetheless, there are some benefits of reduced transaction costs from ICT for developing countries. First, information about policies, incentives and procedures are much more widely disseminated. Second, countries are able to compete more effectively with other locations for investment. Third, they are better able to coordinate activities within the country (between, say, regions that are competing for investment) and between various arms of policy makers and agencies through one-stop shopping (Wells and Wint, 1993).

A second feature of new technologies has been the *emergence and development of entirely new industries*, which have generated entirely new sources of employment in both the manufacturing and the services sectors. Indeed, the mushrooming of new industries has been attributed to the productivity paradox (Freeman and Soete, 1994; OECD, 1996). Despite the growth and proliferation of ICT, there has been a marked lack of improvement in the overall productivity statistics of most countries. The fact that the productivity growth in the manufacturing sector due to new technologies has been 'averaged' out by growth in the 'service' part of manufacturing has been postulated as one of the primary explanations for the productivity paradox. As noted by Woodall, 70 per cent of the revenues in the computer industry come from products that did not exist two years earlier (Woodall, 1996). The difference in the extent to which these developments have affected the converging and diverging countries is not as acute as elsewhere for the simple reason that, because these are new technologies, there is not likely to be as large a 'gap' between the lead and lag countries. Indeed, developing countries have attempted a 'niche' strategy in developing created assets by specializing in particular new technologies as a way of achieving competitiveness; the often cited examples are of India's burgeoning software sector and the focus of other nations on biotechnology (Acharya, 1996). However, the failure of the majority of developing countries to exploit these new technologies has acted as a centripetal force, encouraging centralization of production within the Triad by MNEs.

Third, new technologies have led to *truncated product life cycles* which have led to new or modified products which are more rapidly developed and manufactured. Firms are able to undertake technological developments and are able to bring them to market much more rapidly than was previously the case. Computer-aided design (CAD) as well as developments in 'flexible' manufacturing systems and computer-aided manufacturing has further reduced the set-up costs and time taken to bring a new product to market. Although this has led to a reduction in fixed costs associated with new products, these technologies are not costless. First, rapid product life cycles imply a relatively high R&D intensity if firms need to remain competitive. They also suggest that an innovating firm needs to recoup quickly these high fixed costs, before its technology becomes redundant, especially if a rival firm wins the 'race' to innovate the next generation product.[10] It must therefore (a) sell at a relatively high cost per unit, and/or (b) develop a production process with a low minimum efficient scale and/or (c) recoup its investment by acquiring a large market for its products so as to spread its fixed costs. However, whichever strategy a firm undertakes, it generally increases the need for it to seek and expand overseas markets. Once again, target markets tend to be those with similar income and consumption patterns, rather than the diverging developing countries, where multi-domestic strategies still prevail. In these markets MNEs tend to supply products for which the R&D costs have already been amortized.

Renaissance of Market-based Capitalism and Economic Liberalization

The 1980s were a decade of considerable ideological and economic upheaval. In particular, we would mention three events which, although separate, have common roots. First, the Cold War ended. Since 1989 more than 30 countries have abandoned central planning as the main mode of allocating scarce resources. Second, over 80 developing countries have liberalized their economic policies from inward-looking, import-substituting regimes towards export-oriented, outward-looking policy frameworks (UNCTAD, 1995). Between them, these two developments have led to a liberalization of attitudes of national governments towards inward FDI, the privatization of state-owned enterprises, and the reduction of structural market distortions. This trend continued and deepened during the 1990s.

Third, there has been an across-the-board liberalization of a variety of cross-border markets due to (i) regional and interregional free trade agreements and protocols, for example the completion of the European single market, NAFTA and MERCOSUR,[11] (ii) a range of bilateral arrangements; and (iii) multilateral, binding arrangements such as the establishment of the World Trade Organization (WTO) and the completion of the Uruguay round of GATT. Each of these agreements has contributed towards a reduction in barriers to trade. In addition, in recent years increasing attention has been paid to agreements which liberalize the flow of FDI and other forms of MNE activity, such as the General Agreement on Trade in Services (GATS), the Trade Related Investment Measures agreement (TRIMs) and the Trade Related Intellectual Property Rights agreement (TRIPs). Although some of these agreements, such as TRIMs and TRIPs, existed prior to the establishment of WTO, they have become much more specific, and are explicitly aimed at being upgradable. Furthermore, FDI-related disputes can now be brought directly into the WTO disputes settlement process (Brewer, 1996).

What has this meant for FDI and MNE activity and MNE–government relations? Privatization, in particular, has allowed MNEs to acquire, in one fell swoop, fully operational (albeit inefficient) firms in countries with relatively low levels of domestic competition but significant market potential, and, thanks to overvalued exchange rates, at relatively low cost. Over the period 1989–93, FDI from privatization accounted for $12.2 billion or 7.6 per cent of all inflows to developing countries. Over 75 per cent of this was directed towards Latin America and the Caribbean, where privatization accounted for 16.9 per cent of all inflows to the region. In the case of central and eastern Europe, FDI inflows to privatization schemes amounted to $7.5 billion, or 59.7 per cent of the total FDI inflows to the region. Average tariffs and non-tariff barriers have fallen considerably, and affiliates of MNEs are increasingly given national treatment.

However, the news is not as good for emerging economies. The increased competition between countries offering favourable investment climates for both domestic and foreign investment has increased significantly. While the amount of total FDI stock directed towards developing countries may have increased, an increasing proportion of new investment is of a kind that *requires* the use of specialized created assets, and therefore tends to be directed to the developed and wealthier developing countries with the necessary level of technological assets. Liberalization, on the other hand, has meant that a much larger pool of countries (possibly twice as many as two decades earlier) offer 'generic' location advantages such as access to natural assets and basic infrastructure. The problem of too many countries chasing too little FDI is exacerbated by the competition between provinces and regions within countries which offer their own set of incentive schemes to funnel scarce investments to their locations. Countries and provinces are therefore under pressure to 'give away' bigger investment incentives in order to attract the FDI that is often central to their development strategies. Furthermore, inflows from privatization represent a single, one-off phenomenon: MNE acquisitions through privatization schemes may generate a large initial infusion of capital, but subsequent inflows are by no means guaranteed. Indeed, because MNEs intend to generate some rents from these investments, the net inflows can be expected to be significantly smaller in subsequent years.

THE COMPETITIVE POSITION OF COUNTRIES AND THE ROLE OF MNE ACTIVITY

The decline and/or stagnation in the economic development of the diverging (and poorer) countries directly affects the competitiveness of these countries and that of their firms. Competitiveness is increasingly determined by a country's location-specific advantages, and particularly the mechanisms and institutions that encourage the evolution of created assets from natural assets (see, for example, Narula, 1993, 1996; Dunning, 1993; Narula and Wakelin, 1998).

Abramovitz (1990) suggests a similar argument, that the tendency to converge depends on the countries in question having similar *social capability* and *technological congruence*. By social capability, he means the political, cultural, and economic and social infrastructure associated with a country. The second condition, that of technological congruence, is a function of the capability of a country to benefit from technological spillovers from leading countries, and its ability to accumulate technology. Not all countries will be equally able to catch up in all industries; the extent to which this is possible will depend on the nature and level of its created and natural assets as well as the characteristics of its markets. Neither will every country be able to exploit its full potential for rapid growth because of resource constraints and limited or underdeveloped markets. This situation is bound to get worse with divergence: as the economic distance between a diverging economy and the lead countries increases, the product overlap decreases, therefore inhibiting the laggard country's ability to catch up with the lead country because of the reduced opportunities for technological spillovers. Hansson and Henrekson (1995) have also suggested that, in addition to these two factors, increased trade intensity and an outward looking policy orientation significantly facilitate the convergence process.

Indeed, the failure of countries to improve the quality of their immobile resources and capabilities emphasizes the role of governments in overcoming the failure of markets to do so. The development and maintenance of a country's created assets is crucial because, not only are they a basis for encouraging entrepreneurship and the growth of domestic enterprises, but they also determine the ability of firms to harness new technologies and skills through, inter alia, the availability of skilled human capital. Nonetheless, if firms are to generate competitive ownership advantages that allow them to compete in international markets (and which is increasingly the case as a result of the wholesale liberalization of markets) they must acquire or develop these over a period of time. It is important to emphasize that ownership advantages include not just technology in a traditional sense, but also (i) the organizational skills to coordinate intra-firm activities (ii) the knowledge of from where to acquire inputs efficiently from suppliers, (iii) familiarity with markets to sell their outputs efficiently and (iv) the ability to utilize efficiently information about technology, markets and organizations that is specific to another firm, to a group of individuals or to a location. The last point needs further clarification. Created assets such as information are generally context-specific,[12] inasmuch as they are specific to the firm which is currently utilizing it, and cannot be used efficiently by another individual or firm unless the technology is 'learnt' (that is, made firm-specific) by the recipient firm. This also applies to information that is embodied in skills possessed by human capital in a given location. Since such learning is a gradual process, it is by no means costless, and the efficiency with which a given firm can make a given technology firm-specific determines the actual cost. This argument is similar to the thesis advanced by Stiglitz (1987) that firms must 'learn to learn'. According to Nelson and Pack (1995) the ability of learning to learn is an important determinant of the success of the Asian NICs.

In order to catch up, then, a country must enhance the ability of its firms to have access to, and effectively utilize, the stock of knowledge available to the firms in countries which are economically and technologically more advanced than itself. Put another way, domestic firms must have the opportunity to combine their own competitive advantages and the location-specific assets of their home country with those of their counterparts in foreign countries. As governments have come to a 'new' realization regarding the fundamental need to enhance the ownership advantages of their firms, further encouraged by the much-publicized successes of the East Asian newly industrializing economies, they have increasingly sought out MNEs. Indeed, as Sanjaya Lall (1995, p. 5) has cogently expressed it,

Transnational corporations are amongst the most powerful means available for transferring modern technologies by developing countries and overcoming obstacles to their utilisation. By virtue of their large internal markets for capital, skills and technology and information, they face fewer market failures than local firms. In most circumstances, therefore, there is no reason to restrict entry – their presence can only benefit local productivity and competitiveness. Moreover, since TNCs are at the forefront of innovation, their presence provides an effective means of keeping up with technical progress. Their established brand names, global marketing presence and international flows of information all add to their technological advantages.

Indeed, the use of MNEs as a source of technology, information and human resource development has been a primary strategy of many NICs, although some countries (for example, Korea) have preferred to use market and quasi-market mechanisms such as licensing, joint ventures and turnkey projects to obtain such assets, while others, such as Taiwan, have encouraged MNEs to engage in FDI (Lall, 1996; van Hoesel, 1999). However, firms cannot rely on purely market forms of technology transfer, because, as the technology level rises, the information becomes more idiosyncratic and firm-specific, and less easily transferable at arm's length. Consequently, the role of location advantages is twofold: first, as the basis for the growth of domestic enterprises, and second, as a means to attract MNEs to engage in value-adding activities.

What form should the government intervention to enhance created assets take? It is by now generally agreed that MNE-specific created assets cannot be diffused costlessly or instantly to the host country's domestic economy (see, for example, Teece, 1977; Amsden, 1992) and it is one of the tasks of government to manipulate these to improve the competitiveness of its firms. The extent of government intervention depends on several factors. The exact nature of policies is outside the scope of the present chapter, but some broad objectives of government intervention can be stated here, depending on the overall long-term economic strategy of the country.

First, even where the MNE is willing to utilize its competitive advantages in conjunction with the immobile created assets of countries, there need to be domestic firms that both have the access to the complementary assets and possess the competitive advantages necessary to take advantage of spillovers. These include, not just firms in the same industry, but those in related industries such as supplier firms. For instance, were, say, Ghana to attract investment in the aerospace industry, the absence of domestic firms with the complementary assets to utilize efficiently the externalities from the direct and indirect technology spillovers would lead to minimal benefits for the host country. Second, the competitive assets of both domestic and foreign-owned firms need to be sustained in the face of international competition using supporting institutions. These institutions include the legal infrastructure to protect existing assets through strong (and enforceable) patent laws, and the ability to develop new assets. In a dynamic economy, firms have to invest continually in innovatory and training activities in order to maintain their competitive advantages, but these require the use of country-specific created assets, such as an adequate supply of skilled labour and appropriate macro-organizational policies, R&D subsidies, and so on. Third, domestic firms must have some incentive to reinforce their technological assets and competitive advantages over time, through exposure to international competition. Captive markets and oligopolistic positions do not act as an incentive to upgrade created assets, as was shown by the state of the Indian manufacturing industry prior to liberalization. Fourth, MNEs must have some incentive to allow for a deliberate attrition of their competitive advantages. This may take the form of (privileged) access to domestic markets (for example, auto firms in China), or subsidized or exclusive rights to certain natural assets (Aramco in Saudi Arabia). These issues have been studied in greater detail elsewhere by several other scholars (see Lall, 1990, 1996, 1997; Amsden, 1992, Hikino and Amsden, 1994; Wade, 1988; Ozawa, 1995) and will not be re-examined here.

DIVERGING ECONOMIES AND FDI: SOME POLICY IMPLICATIONS

The preceding discussion would seem to suggest the following conclusions. First, the growing interdependence of countries and their convergence of income and technological levels and consumption patterns is peculiar to the wealthier industrial countries and a minority of developing countries, for example NICs and China. Second, the failure of the rest of the developing world to achieve convergence and catch-up is associated with the inadequate (and often declining) level of domestic created assets and the inefficiency of local firms. Third, although the involvement of MNEs in the diverging economies appears to have increased over the last decade, this may be attributable to their economic decline as well as to one-off increases due to privatization, without which divergence might have been even more pronounced. Fourth, an increasingly important means by which to upgrade their competitiveness has been the importation of technology, skills and organizational capabilities, and the access to foreign markets provided by foreign firms, both via FDI and by collaborative arrangements of one kind or another. Fifth, the conditions for catch-up and convergence are also the necessary (but not sufficient) conditions to attract FDI. That is, there is a certain threshold level of created assets associated with a given location and its resident firms which determines the ability of these firms to benefit from externalities that arise from MNE-related activity, and a threshold level of created assets and industry clusters is also necessary as presenting location advantages to attract such activity in the same place.

Herein lies the chicken-and-egg dilemma that faces countries that wish to replicate the success of the Asian NICs. Countries clearly need to improve their location advantages, primarily through the growth of their created assets, if their firms are to become more competitive. One source of capital and created assets to achieve this is through MNE activity, which prefers to invest where such location advantages already exist. It is also clear from recent evidence[13] that simple prescriptions which address macroeconomic restructuring such as those associated with the World Bank programmes are insufficient by themselves: Amsden and van der Hoeven (1996) review evidence that indicates that most non-Asian developing countries that engaged in restructuring in the 1980s have experienced a collapse in investment as their competitiveness seems to have been built on lower wage costs rather than on higher productivity.

It is also clear that there are no guarantees that policies that have worked for one country will necessarily work for another, given the path dependence and idiosyncratic nature of each country and its firms, and the diverse range of policies that each country has followed. Nor, indeed, have all countries benefited equally from the vagaries of international politics. For example, it is no secret that countries such as Korea and Taiwan benefited enormously from Cold War politics, and were able to capitalize on it, as had Japan and much of Europe a decade earlier.

It would seem, nonetheless, that countries have at their disposal three tools in attracting FDI activity, the first two of which at the same time improve the competitiveness of their own firms. Each of these issues deserves considerable attention and study; we can only offer a few thoughts here.[14] The first is that of providing and upgrading its created assets both of a general variety, and at a more industry-specific level. These include the improvement of infrastructure, such as roads, electricity and telephones. Created assets also depend on the development of institutions to support the acquisition and creation of knowledge and wealth-creating assets. These include the training of skilled human resources through educational and training schemes, intellectual property rights protection, and so on. These can lead to significant improvements in the transaction costs and productivity levels of domestic and foreign firms.

Second, MNE activity may be attracted through the use of appropriate macro-organizational policies, such as encouraging inward FDI into those sectors in which the country already possesses a comparative advantage in natural and created assets and industrial clusters. Such a distinction is not entirely a matter of guesswork. Ozawa (1996) has postulated that countries at earlier stages of their investment development paths tend to follow a relatively predictable process of industrial development from Heckscher–Ohlin labour intensive industries to undifferentiated Smithian and on towards differentiated Smithian (assembly-type) sectors. It is only as countries proceed towards Stage 4 and towards their technology frontier that 'picking winners' becomes a risky strategy. It is important to match the structural upgrading of sectors and location advantages with the activities of MNEs and the evolution of the ownership advantages of domestic firms (as best exemplified by Japan and Korea[15]). Another area of macro-organizational policy worth more attention is that of coordinating trade and FDI policies (Graham, 1996).[16]

The third tool at the disposal of governments is that of financial and fiscal incentives. However, the increasing interest in FDI as a positive economic force due to economic liberalization, discussed earlier, has also led to increased competition for what is relatively the same share of FDI. This has led to a sort of 'incentive war' with a record number of regions and countries competing to attract foreign investors: UNCTAD (1995) indicates that financial and fiscal incentives increased in 93 countries between the mid-1980s and the early 1990s. However, research by Mudambi (1995) suggests that, while incentives are not in themselves effective, the longer these incentives persist, the more likely it is that they will have a positive effect. This leads us to an important caveat worthy of note. FDI flows are not determined primarily by regulatory factors once an enabling framework is in place (UNCTAD, 1996). Difficult conditions and limited incentives do not, by themselves, determine investment. What matters most is that regulation needs to be consistent over time, rather than the regulations or incentives per se.

At the same time, there is a danger that, because of the increased competition, countries may give away more than the potential benefits that accrue from the MNE activity (McIntyre *et al.*, 1996). This is all the more so since developing countries must compete with backward regions from industrialized countries and former centrally planned economies whose infrastructure tends to be far superior, and whose pockets are far deeper than those of most developing countries. For instance, the Mercedes Benz plant in Alabama, USA attracted US$250 million in incentives for an MNE investment of $300 million, working out to be about $166 000 per worker. An even higher incentive figure of $254 000 per employee is estimated for the Volkswagen plant in Portugal (UNCTAD, 1995).

Needless to say, the aim of such large subsidies is long-term.[17] The objectives of policy makers in giving such incentives are twofold. First, there is the hope that the positive externalities to the local industry through indirect and direct means will resuscitate the local economy. Second, the presence of such a significant investor will act as the 'seed' investment in what governments hope will result in a healthy cluster of firms. That is, additional firms in a particular industry might be persuaded to invest in the same location either because they wish for close geographic proximity to the 'seed' firm in order to act as suppliers and/or exploit externalities therefrom, or because its presence acts as a signal of the level of created assets in the region, or simply as an oligopolistic reaction in a follow-my-leader strategy. Such clustering may result in additional economies of agglomeration, if a critical mass of firms in a given industry establish themselves. Should such a critical mass of firms develop, it represents significant location advantages in its own right. Indeed, a study by Head *et al.* (1994) would suggest that agglomeration is determined less by differences in resources, labour and infrastructure than by the presence of other firms.[18]

This sort of footloose behaviour would seem to be typical in this age of alliance capitalism and rationalized production by MNEs. However, the increasing mobility of MNEs is a double-edged sword. While it is the goal of such incentive schemes (including export processing zones – EPZs) to create such a clustering of activity, this is not always a success, as affiliates can also as easily be relocated. McIntyre *et al.* (1996) list several cases of EPZs which have only succeeded in attracting a minimal amount of investment. The problem, it would seem, is not just how to attract initial investments, but how to ensure sequential investments and, more importantly, how to make them 'sticky'. Furthermore, how much investment leads to a critical mass of firms such that economies of agglomeration are achieved? These are important and crucial questions that deserve further study.

What our arguments here propose is a variation on the traditional infant industry theme. Countries require externalities to promote economic growth, and these spillovers may most efficiently be achieved through inward FDI. The provision of subsidies, incentives and investments in infrastructure is justifiable only where a net positive benefit (in terms of spillovers) results over the long term. Investment promotion measures are by no means foolproof and, particularly in the case of the least developed countries, take considerable time to bear fruit. It must be said that the forecast for the diverging economies is not good, as they are endowed with neither the time nor the capital to experiment with policy options; divergence leads to a continuing shrinking of market size in real terms and a growing technological gap, which also results in the gradual loss of interest in these markets by MNEs as potential economies of scale and scope are eroded. Furthermore, diverging economies themselves are not a homogeneous group, some of them being relatively well endowed with certain kinds of created assets, and in a better position than others both strategically and economically, to catch up.

One of the principal points that we have tried to raise in this chapter is that the traditional infant industry creation and development remains a central objective in economic development and industrial upgrading for developing countries. Indeed, our policy recommendations, in this broader sense, are not new. However, globalization has altered economic realities, and the means by which infant industries may be made competitive has fundamentally changed. Liberalization and new technologies mean that traditional policy instruments and interventions are no longer effective. In addition, industrial and economic policy can no longer be developed in isolation from the global economic environment. Membership of organizations such as WTO, WIPO (World Intellectual Property Organization) and the like requires a certain compliance with international standards, and makes certain traditional infant industry instruments actionable by other member countries. Several types of policy instruments hitherto used by developing countries to encourage MNEs to transfer skills and technology are either illegal (such as local content regulations, under the TRIMs agreement) or are time-restricted (for example, certain kinds of subsidies under the Subsidies and Countervailing Measures – SCM – agreements). This is not to say that these tools are completely useless, since least developed countries are granted numerous exceptions. For instance, least developed countries have seven years from 1 January 1995 to eliminate illegal TRIMs, although extensions may be granted to the use of TRIMs to safeguard balance of payments or to protect an infant industry. In addition, TRIMs do not cover specification of a minimum level of local employment or a minimum level of local equity participation. There are other exceptions: SCM agreements cover loans, grants and tax credits, but not pre-competitive R&D or assistance to disadvantaged regions. In addition, SCM covers only those subsidies that are specific to elected enterprises, and not when applied to an industry in general (Brewer and Young, 1998).

Thus, while diverging countries can continue to build up infant industries using some traditional policy instruments, there are now considerable caveats to their application. In addition, policy makers need to be proactive and implement the three tools outlined here systemically, since the exceptions made for the least developed countries have to be phased out over a relatively short period.

It is germane to add a note of caution to this discussion. The increased role of MNEs in the least developed countries has meant that MNEs are increasingly significant players in the economic development of these countries, and can directly influence the direction and nature of structural adjustment, given their economic clout. There is little or no basis for assuming that MNEs will use or have used their privileged position to affect decisions that will necessarily increase economic development. Whether, or to what extent, MNEs have resulted in structural maladjustment is not known, but there certainly exists considerable potential for such effects to occur. This forms an important area for further study.

There are also other unanswered questions about the mechanisms by which a pareto-optimal outcome might be achieved from both an economic development and the MNE profit-optimizing perspective. Numerous studies on FDI have been conducted trying to ascertain the net benefits of FDI, and there seems to be a consensus that, in general, FDI has beneficial effects on the economy at large, but that the level of the benefits varies with the type of investment. However, determining the nature of these benefits requires an in-depth case study approach to understand the nature of linkages that are generated by firms, and the extent to which interventions by governments (through subsidies and local content requirements), as well as institutional infrastructural issues (such as the availability of electricity, support institutions and training) have affected the linkages created by foreign-owned firms.

A third area that deserves more attention is the role of MNEs in creating agglomerative effects or clusters. Although the issue of clustering has received considerable attention from economic geographers, little of this work tends to focus on the pivotal role of the MNE. A number of developing countries have established industrial and science parks, with the express objective of creating clusters. In order for these industrial parks to succeed, the presence of a certain minimum level of location-specific advantages (infrastructure and skilled labour) is essential as a catalyst to attract these firms to establish themselves in a given spatial area; and, most important, so is the presence of domestic firms with the technological capabilities to absorb the spillovers pertaining from the activities of these firms. We do not know if MNEs can be used to seed clusters of economic activity, or to what extent MNEs act as 'magnets' to other firms.

NOTES

1. This is used in the sense suggested by Nelson and Winter (1982); that is, that firms can in reality only 'satisfice': since they are boundedly rational, they maximize within the constraints imposed by their lack of perfect information.
2. The distinction between natural and created assets is an important one. Natural assets may be defined as fruits of the earth and include the stock of untrained labour and resource endowments. Created assets are those that derive from the upgrading of these natural assets. They may be tangible (for example, the stock of physical and financial assets) or intangible (for example, technological knowhow, goodwill, managerial and entrepreneurial skills, interpersonal relationships, forged by individuals, and culture and organizational structure of institutions).

3. The arguments regarding catch-up and convergence and the fundamental role of technological change amalgamate views that are most often identified with Gerschenkron (1962), but are also embraced by new growth theories. See, for example, Cappelen and Fagerberg (1995) for a discussion.
4. However, the divergence trend of productivity growth is true only of the industrial sector, while in agriculture there has been catch-up by poorer economies (Dowrick, 1992). Therefore a second explanation for the divergence may be the failure of non-industrialized economies to restructure their economic structure away from an agricultural base to an industrial one.
5. Which between 1990 and 1994 accounted for 8.4 per cent of all inward FDI.
6. From an annual average of $49.5 billion in 1980–84 to $215.5 billion in 1990–94.
7. These countries are China, India, Brazil, Colombia, Philippines, Thailand, Mexico, Chile, Venezuela, Hong Kong, Korea, Malaysia, Singapore and Taiwan.
8. Income level classifications are based on those used by the *World Development Report*.
9. Firms that operate in several markets but maintain each individual region or country as essentially independent operations are referred to as having a 'multi-domestic' strategy.
10. Patent protection is a highly imperfect tool to protect an inventor from competition, especially in industries where technological change is rapid and competition high. Consequently, an innovating firm's only way of maintaining its competitive advantage may be by being 'first', and remaining in the lead in subsequent rounds of innovation (Levin *et al.*, 1987).
11. There are also non-binding agreements and protocols such as the OECD code of liberalization of capital movements (which are binding upon member states, but not on non-members) and guidelines for multinational enterprises.
12. Owing to the path dependency of information and the bounded rationality of firms, learning is a localized procedure.
13. See, for instance, two special issues, *Journal of International Development*, vol. 7, no. 5, 1995 (edited by Sanjaya Lall) and *World Development*, vol. 22, no. 4, 1994 (edited by Alice Amsden).
14. And indeed has received greater attention in the work of, among others, Wade (1988, 1990), Amsden (1989, 1992) and Lall (1990).
15. See, for instance, the work of Ozawa (for example, 1995, 1996) and Amsden (1989, 1992).
16. This issue has been explored by UNCTAD (1996).
17. However, there are some restrictions on the continued use of large subsidies within the framework of the Subsidies and Countervailing Measures (SCM) agreement of the WTO, which restrict the level of specific subsidies (albeit with numerous caveats).
18. It should be noted that most successful centres of agglomeration have resulted from an increasing pattern of specialization over a long period; that is, they have 'historical' origins.

REFERENCES

Abramovitz, M. (1990), 'The catch-up factor in postwar economic growth', *Economic Inquiry*, **28**, January, 1–18.

Acharya, R. (1996), *The Biotechnology Revolution*, Cheltenham, UK and Brookfield, USA: Edward Elgar.

Alam, M., and A. Naseer (1992), 'Convergence and polarisation: testing for an inverted-u relation between growth rates and GDP per capita', *Applied Economics*, **24**, 363–6 .

Amsden, A. (1989), *Asia's Next Giant*, New York: Oxford University Press.

Amsden, A. (1992), 'A theory of government intervention in late industrialisation', in L. Putterman and D. Rueschemeyer (eds), *State and Market: Rivalry or Synergy?*, Boulder, CO: Lynne Rienner.

Amsden, A., and R. van der Hoeven (1996), 'Manufacturing output, employment and real wages in the 1980s: labour's loss until the century's end', *Journal of Development Studies*, **32** (4), 506–30.

Brewer, T. (1996), 'Multilateral investment agreements in the new era of foreign direct investment: implications for India and other emerging market economies', *Foreign Trade Review*, **29**, 265–76.

Brewer, T., and S. Young (1998), *The Multilateral Investment System and Multinational Enterprises*, Oxford: Oxford University Press.

Cappelen, A. and J. Fagerberg (1995), 'East Asian growth: a critical assessment', *Forum for Development Studies*, **2**, 175–95.

Dowrick, S. (1992), 'Technological catch up and diverging incomes: patterns of economic growth 1960–88', *The Economic Journal*, **102**, May, 600–610.

Dowrick, S., and N. Gemmell (1991), 'Industrialisation, catching up and economic growth: a comparative study across the world's capitalist economies', *The Economic Journal*, **101**, March, 263–75.

Dunning, J.H. (1993), *Multinational Enterprises and the Global Economy*, Wokingham: Addison-Wesley.

Dunning, J.H. (1994), 'Globalisation, economic restructuring and development', The Raul Prebisch Lectures, Geneva: UNCTAD.

Dunning, J.H. (1997), *Alliance Capitalism and Global Business,* London: Routledge.

Dunning, J.H., and R. Narula (1994), 'Transpacific direct investment and the investment development path: the record assessed', *Essays in International Business*, March.

Dunning, J.H., and R. Narula (1996), 'The investment development path revisited: some emerging issues', in J.H. Dunning and R. Narula (eds), *Foreign Direct Investment and Governments: Catalysts for Economic Restructuring*, London: Routledge, pp. 1–41.

Dunning, J.H., R. van Hoesel and R. Narula (1998), 'Third world multinationals revisited: new developments and theoretical implications', in J. Dunning (ed.), *Globalization, Trade and Foreign Direct Investment*, Oxford: Pergamon, pp. 255–86.

Freeman, C. (1987), 'The challenge of new technologies in interdependence and cooperation', *Tomorrow's World*, 123–56, Paris: OECD.

Freeman, C., and J. Hagedoorn (1995), 'Convergence and divergence in the internationalisation of technology', in J. Hagedoorn (ed.), *Technical Change and the World Economy*, Aldershot: Edward Elgar.

Freeman, C., and C. Perez (1988), 'Structural crises of adjustment, business cycles and investment behaviour', in G. Dosi, K. Pavitt and L. Soete (eds), *Technical Change and Economic Theory*, London: Pinter.

Freeman C., and L. Soete (1994), *Work for All or Mass Unemployment*, London: Pinter.

Gerschenkron, A. (1962), *Economic Backwardness in Historical Perspective*, Cambridge, MA: Belknap Press.

Graham, E. (1996), *Global Corporations and National Governments*, Washington, DC: Institute for International Economics.

Gray, H.P. (1996), 'Globalization and economic development', mimeo, Rutgers University, Newark, NJ.

Hagedoorn, J., and R. Narula (1996), 'Choosing modes of governance for strategic technology partnering: international and sectoral differences', *Journal of International Business Studies*, **27**, 265–84.

Hansson, P., and M. Henrekson (1995), 'What makes a country socially capable of catching up?', *Weltwirtschaftlisches Archiv*, 760–83.

Head, K., J. Ries and D. Swenson (1994), 'Agglomeration benefits and location choice: Evidence from Japanese manufacturing investment in the United States', NBER working paper no. 4767.

Hikino, T., and A. Amsden (1994), 'Staying behind, stumbling back, sneaking up, soaring ahead: late industrialization in historical perspective', in W. Baumol, R. Nelson and E. Wolff (eds), *Convergence of Productivity: Cross Country Studies and Historical Evidence*, New York: Oxford University Press.

Hoesel, R. van (1999), *New Multinational Enterprises from Korea and Taiwan*, London: Routledge.

Lall, S. (1990), *Building Industrial Competitiveness in Developing Countries*, Paris: OECD.

Lall, S. (1995), 'Industrial strategy and policies on foreign direct investment in East Asia', *Transnational Corporations*, **4**, December, 1–26.

Lall, S. (1996), 'The investment development path: some conclusions', in J.H. Dunning and R. Narula (eds), *Foreign Direct Investment and Governments: Catalysts for Economic Restructuring*, London: Routledge, pp. 423–41.

Lall, S. (1997), 'East Asia', in J.H. Dunning (ed.), *Governments, Globalisation and International Business*, Oxford: Oxford University Press, pp. 407–30.

Levin, R., A. Klevorick, R. Nelson and S. Winter (1987), 'Appropriating the returns from industrial research and development', *Brookings Papers on Economics Activity*, **3**, 783–820.

McIntyre, J., R. Narula and L. Trevino (1996), 'The role of export processing zones for host countries and multinationals: a mutually beneficial relationship?', *International Trade Journal*, **10**, Winter, 435–66.

Mudambi, R. (1995), 'The MNE investment location decision: some empirical evidence', *Managerial and Decision Economics*, **16**, 249–57.

Mytelka, L. (1999), 'Locational tournaments for FDI: inward investment into Europe in a global world', in Neil Hood and Stephen Young (eds), *The Globalization of Multinational Enterprise Activity and Economic Development*, London and New York: Macmillan/St Martins Press, pp. 278–302.

Mytelka, L. (2002), 'Locational tournaments, strategic partnerships and the state', in David Wolfe and Meric Gertler (eds), *Innovation and Social Learning: Institutional Adaptation in an Era of Technological Change*, London: Palgrave/Macmillan, pp. 89–110.

Narula, R. (1993), 'Technology, international business and Porter's "diamond": synthesising a dynamic competitive development model', *Management International Review*, **33**, 85–107.

Narula, R. (1996), *Multinational Investment and Economic Structure*, London: Routledge.

Narula, R., and K. Wakelin (1998), 'Technological competitiveness, FDI and trade', *Structural Change and Economic Dynamics*, **9**, 373–87.

Nelson, R., and H. Pack (1995), 'The Asian growth miracle and modern growth theory', mimeo, Columbia University, New York.

OECD (1996), *Technology, Productivity and Job Creation*, Paris: OECD.

Ozawa, T. (1995), 'Structural upgrading and concatenated integration', in D. Simon (ed.), *Corporate Strategies in the Pacific Rim: Global versus Regional Trends*, London: Routledge, pp. 215–46.

Ozawa, T. (1996), 'Japan: the macro-IDP, meso-IDPs and the technology development path (TDP)', in J.H. Dunning and R. Narula (eds), *Foreign Direct Investment and Governments: Catalysts for Economic Restructuring*, London: Routledge, pp. 143–73.

Stiglitz, J. (1987), 'Learning to learn, localised learning, and technical progress', in P. Dasgupta and P. Stoneman (eds), *Economic Policy and Technological Progress*, Cambridge: Cambridge University Press.

Teece, D.J. (1977), 'Technology transfer by multinational firms: the resource cost of transferring technological knowhow', *Economic Journal*, **22**, 242–61.

UN (1993), *Small and Medium-Sized Transnational Corporations*, New York: United Nations.

UNCTAD (1995), *World Investment Report 1995*, Geneva: United Nations.

UNCTAD (1996), *World Investment Report 1996*, Geneva: United Nations.

Wade, R. (1988), 'The role of government in overcoming market failure in Taiwan, Republic of Korea and Japan', in H. Hughes (ed.), *Achieving Industrialization in East Asia*, Cambridge: Cambridge University Press.

Wade, R. (1990), *Governing the Market: Economic Theory and the Role of Government in East Asian Industrialization*, Princeton, NJ: Princeton University Press.

Wells, L.T., and A. Wint (1993), 'Don't stop with the one-stop shop: foreign investment in a liberalising third world', *International Executive*, **35**, 367–84.

Woodall, P. (1996), 'A survey of the world economy', *The Economist*, 28 September–4 October.

World Bank (v.d.), *The World Development Report*, Oxford: Oxford University Press.

3. Industrial development, globalization and multinational enterprises: new realities for developing countries

INTRODUCTION

Fundamental changes in political ideologies and economic systems among a large number of developing countries have led to dramatic shifts in the way governments of these countries perceive their interests and those of their constituents. As a result, there are now a wide variety of attitudes and policies of national governments towards the activities of multinational enterprises (MNEs). This heterogeneity of responses is not, in itself, surprising, given the different stages of development, political ideologies, cultural norms, history and institutional infrastructure of countries. It is, nonetheless, possible to generalize that the relations between national governments and MNEs in the 1990s, if still uneasy, are more favourable than they have been for many years (Dunning, 1998).

The present thrust towards MNE-friendly attitudes by governments dates back to the early 1980s, and corresponds to a variety of changes in the world economy which have been generically (although not always appropriately) described as 'globalization'. Economic globalization refers to the increasing cross-border interdependence and integration of production and markets for goods, services and capital. This process leads to a widening of the extent and form of international transactions, and to a deepening of the interdependence between the actions of economic actors located in one country and those located in others (Dunning 1997a). It is perhaps best demonstrated by the huge increases in the transnational flows of both portfolio and direct investment, and in the number of cross-border strategic alliances.[1]

One of the primary consequences of globalization has been the growing convergence of income levels, consumption patterns and institutional structures, both among the industrialized countries and between them and the more advanced developing countries, and also the increasing significance of their intra-firm trade in goods and services (Fukuyama, 1995; Landes,

1998). The two primary determinants of globalization have been, (i) the rapid and widespread implementation of new technologies, particularly information and computer technologies (ICTs), and the consequential fall in cross-border communication and organizational costs; and (ii) the renaissance of democratic capitalism and the liberalization of many domestic and international markets.

Globalization has influenced both the nature of the comparative or location-specific (L) advantages of countries and the competitive or ownership specific (O) advantages of corporations, and also the opportunity sets facing the governments of the former and the managers of the latter. Inter alia, value-adding activities have become increasingly knowledge- or information-intensive, not just in high-technology sectors, but also in those that were previously regarded as natural resource- or labour-intensive. Both firms and governments have thus adjusted their strategies and policies to the realities of the new global environment. First, the nature and content of MNE activity has undergone a marked shift, as MNE's firm-specific intangible assets (especially intellectual capital) have become more mobile. Second, national governments now increasingly compete with each other to attract mobile investment. As the significance of immobile created assets[2] in influencing the competitive position of MNEs has increased, so too have the bargaining stakes of the two parties.

However, globalization has not affected all countries and regions to the same extent or in the same way. Indeed, it has resulted in a widening in the created assets and income gap between the industrialized countries and a handful of wealthier developing countries on the one hand, and the poorer developing countries on the other. The focus of this chapter is on the latter group of countries which have 'fallen behind'. One of the consequences of this economic polarization is that the bargaining position (and the opportunity costs) of national governments vis-à-vis foreign direct investors has become more variable. For example, different kinds of L and O advantages are associated with inward MNE activity in (say) Taiwan, compared to Bangladesh. In addition, the motives, modes and extent of MNE involvement vary considerably as countries move along their development paths (Dunning and Narula, 1994, 1996; Ozawa, 1995, 1996). Such lacunae need to be examined more closely.

FDI-based development strategies are now commonplace among developing countries. Although there has been a growth in the global FDI flows, there is also increased competition among governments for such investment and, particularly, that which provides opportunities for indigenous spillovers of technology and organizational capability. In a global world, competition between core and peripheral economies for a finite number of discrete investment projects will, if the L advantages of the competing entities are similar, be 'won' by the government with the biggest financial incentives and subsidies. Moreover, such tournaments have the potential to dissipate the net benefits to countries. The improvement of relatively immobile L advantages is the only feasible means of maintaining a sustainable FDI-assisted development strategy. This can be done by optimizing the intra-country spatial distribution of economic activity, and by encouraging agglomeration of related activity to attract mobile investment. MNEs, in turn, are also looking for specialized locations that provide particular kinds of scarce assets to advance their own competitiveness.

This chapter is organized as follows. The following section places this chapter in context, by examining the need for and plausibility of different frameworks for different groups of countries. We then discuss the relationship between the motives for foreign production and the changes in opportunity costs from the viewpoint of both developing host country governments and MNEs. Next, we proceed to explain how globalization has influenced the comparative advantages of firms and the locational attractions of countries, or regions within countries. The final section presents some policy implications and conclusions.

ANALYTICAL FRAMEWORK

The economic relationship between MNEs and democratic national governments is governed by a fundamental difference in the objectives of each. The primary goal of MNEs, as with most private economic entities, is the maximization of the welfare of their owners (wherever they may be located) while national governments wish to do the same for the constituents within their jurisdiction. Although this is not a zero-sum game – even where the relationship is not a confrontational one – the failure to find common ground often results in a suboptimal outcome for both parties. Nonetheless, there is a greater alignment in the interests of the two parties than there used to be. As both countries and firms seek to upgrade their resources and capabilities, by and large, the only real disagreements that remain concern the distribution of the costs and benefits of inbound FDI, including those of increased interdependence with the rest of the world. This remains a thorny issue which, to some degree, is determined through negotiations between the two parties, and their relative opportunity sets.

It is obvious that these issues go well beyond those of economics and business; and must necessarily include sociopolitical considerations as well. This is particularly the case with globalization, which has increased the vulnerability of hitherto relatively closed economies to the external shocks and influences from the world economy at large. This has long been the case for most Triad countries (North America, Japan and Western Europe), and is becoming increasingly so for developing countries. In addition, as Stopford and Strange (1991) well illustrate, firm–government interaction is also influenced by the dynamics of government–government and firm–firm relationships.

It is not our intention here to review the literature pertaining to the shifting political economy of MNE–government relations: this has been tackled elsewhere.[3] In this chapter, we are primarily interested in probing how globalization has changed the way in which developing country governments interact with MNEs, as the latter play an increasingly significant role in their economies (UNCTAD, 1998). For example, the share of outbound FDI stock directed to developing countries increased from 20.6 per cent in 1990 to 30.2 per cent in 1996, while the ratio of inbound FDI flows to gross fixed capital formation (GFCF) in developing countries rose from 3.2 per cent to 8.7 per cent over the same period (UNCTAD, 1998).[4]

Several attempts have been made to explain the bargaining relationship between MNEs and governments, the two most notable being Lecraw and Morrison (1991) and Rugman and Verbeke (1998).[5] Essentially, the concept is that relative bargaining positions of the two parties are based on the opportunity costs as perceived by the MNEs of their O advantages, and that of the L advantages offered by the countries in which they are contemplating an investment; and that of host countries of their L advantages and that of the O advantages offered by the foreign investors. The primary aspects of the relationship as proposed by Lecraw and Morrison are laid out in Figure 3.1. This model is not a dynamic one, in the sense that it does not examine the path of the changing opportunity sets of either party. For example, the liberalization of markets has had a particularly dramatic effect on most countries, both developing and developed, which have experienced massive deregulation, privatization and the reduction of trade and investment barriers over a span of a decade (or less). Nor does the model dwell on a second dynamic, namely, the differences in the opportunity sets of countries as their economic structures and living standards change.

The point we wish to emphasize here is that the development path of a developing country is strongly dependent on the specific resources, institutions, economic structure and political ideologies, and social and cultural fabric of countries. The kind of FDI activity it might attract (or wish to attract), too, at different stages of development, is different. Indeed, these two issues are closely related. Globalization has made the differences between groups of countries become more rather than less noticeable, even though simultaneously they are becoming increasingly interdependent. Although every individual negotiation is a unique event, both the type of investment and the stage of economic development of the host country allow

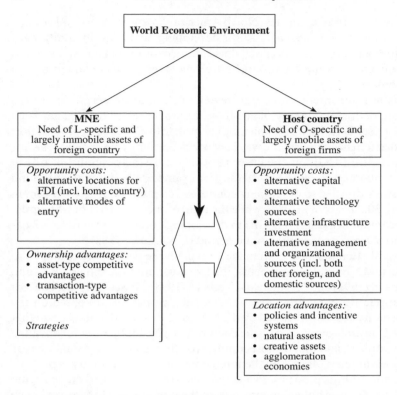

Source: Adapted from Dunning (1993) and Lecraw and Morrison (1991).

Figure 3.1   Host countries and MNEs: a static view of bargaining issues

us to generalize that the situation currently faced by the least developed countries is fundamentally different from the catching-up countries such as the newly industrializing countries (NICs). The opportunity sets faced by the latter group, while similar to the Triad countries (and from whose perspective the bargaining framework was originally developed), also remains distinct.

We develop our argument regarding the existence of three distinct groups by relating it to the investment development path (IDP), a paradigm which postulates that the relationship between FDI and economic development of countries can be usefully analysed by categorizing their evolution through five stages (for example, Narula 1993, 1996; Dunning and Narula, 1994, 1996). Our primary interest throughout this chapter will be the developing countries, with particular focus on the stage 1 and 2 countries of the IDP that have 'fallen behind'. Throughout the rest of this chapter, references to 'falling behind' countries, 'least developed' countries and 'stage 1 and 2' countries will be used interchangeably.

Understanding the Heterogeneity of Developing Countries and its Influence on their L Advantages

In Figure 3.2 we present some bullet points regarding the way the MNE/ country bargaining situation has changed with globalization and how this has affected different countries. Developing countries do not represent a homogeneous group, and this situation has been exacerbated by the effects of globalization. The heterogeneity and uneven development of countries may be explored from several perspectives. The literature on economic catch-up and convergence,[6] for instance, tends to classify countries into three broad groups. The first consists of the wealthy industrialized countries which, over the last two decades, have experienced a convergence in their income levels, consumption patterns and technological capabilities. The second comprises the more advanced industrialized developing countries (primarily the Asian NICs), which are catching up and converging on the first group. The third category is made up of a large number of poorer developing countries which, far from converging on the first and second group, are diverging from them, either because they have 'fallen behind' relative to the first group, or because they have 'stumbled back' in both a relative and absolute sense (Hikino and Amsden, 1994). Put another way, the rising income levels usually associated with globalization have occurred only partially, and in a very selective way.

Similar trends have been noted in the case of FDI. Studies on the relationship between inward and outward FDI and the economic development of a country suggest five stages of development, a brief description of which is given in Figure 3.3. At a micro level, it is now axiomatic that different motives underlie FDI, and that this is associated with the industrial restructuring process, which also follows a distinct pattern.[7] Despite FDI flows to developing countries having grown several-fold over the past two decades, the relative share to developing countries (if one excludes the petroleum-exporting countries) increased from 13.8 per cent of the world total to 15.2 per cent.[8] Table 3.1 sets out some details of the changes in the GDP per capita and inward FDI stock per capita of countries, classified according to the World Bank income groups. Although this classification is not entirely consistent with the IDP stages, there is considerable overlap, sufficient to illustrate our thesis. These data confirm work (for example, Narula 1996, Dunning *et al.*, 1998) on the convergence and divergence phenomena in the case of FDI. While the inward FDI stock per capita of

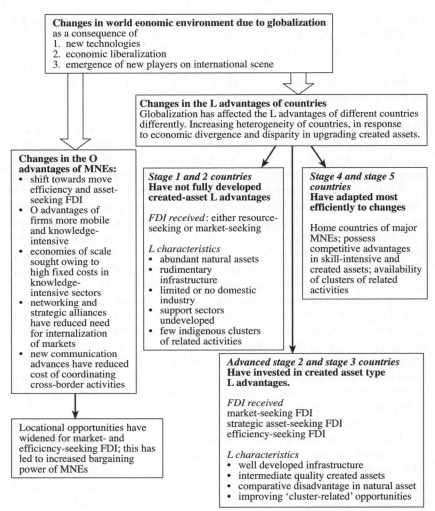

Figure 3.2   Changing bargaining positions between groups of countries

the low-income and lower-middle income countries increased by a factor
of 3.6 between 1980 and 1995, that of the upper-middle and high-income
groups rose by a factor of about 4.4 over the same period. As a result,
the gap between the poorest countries and the high income countries has
increased: for example, the ratio of their average FDI stocks increased from
259 in 1980 to 308 in 1995 (Table 3.1). A similar trend is noted for the lower-
middle income group. The majority of these countries are in stage 1 and

stage 2. In addition, they have diverged as a group from the industrialized countries (stage 4 and 5: high-income countries in Table 3.1) with only a handful of countries at stage 3 (upper-middle income countries in Table 3.1) experiencing convergence and catch-up, in terms of both income levels and FDI stocks.

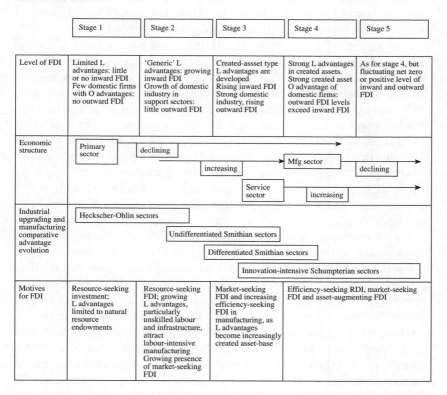

Figure 3.3   Primary relationships underlying the investment development path

With the increasing reliance of less developed countries on FDI as a source of capital, technology and knowledge (UNCTAD, 1998), further polarization of the world economy and widening of the gap between the Triad and the bulk of developing countries seems likely. In addition, despite the fact that the role of MNEs in some of the stage 1 and 2 countries is increasing, notably in South East Asia (Mason, 1998), opportunities for sequential investments are limited, especially in higher value-added activities and sectors which provide the most significant potential spillovers (Blomstrom, 1989). In an analysis of the effects of global integration on development, Gray (1996) predicts that, as globalization proceeds, the marginal net benefits derived by the least developed countries from international involvement will decline. He suggests that the costs of marginalization are self-reinforcing as much as the inability of these countries to attract the kinds of inward FDI which result in positive spillover effects, and this is also accompanied by fewer opportunities for exports and inflows of portfolio capital.

It is important to note that the IDP is used here only as a general framework for identifying and evaluating the linkages between motives, different kinds of FDI and the economic structures of countries, and the differences between the bargaining positions of countries. Essentially, globalization has made many of the L advantages of countries and the O advantages of firms increasingly knowledge-intensive. Some of these advantages have become more mobile, others less so. Moreover, it would seem that these advantages have become more interdependent. For example, a firm's O advantages in time $t+1$ may be dependent on the locational profile of its assets in time t, while a country's L advantages in time $t+1$ may be influenced by its ability to attract the O advantages of foreign firms in time t (Narula, 1996). While it is true that there is considerable variation in the international investment position of countries at the same stage of development, there are broad similarities that allow us to generalize.

It is to be noted, nonetheless, that these development stages may overlap, precisely because of the various economic and industrial policy options implemented by governments. Industrial policy which concentrates on selected industries for growth by means of intensive investment in created assets (for example, education and technological capacity) can and does accelerate the movement of countries through the IDP (van Hoesel, 1999). Attracting specialized FDI to a particular sector can alter the sequence of industrial upgrading (Williamson and Hu, 1994), because specialized FDI may help improve the created assets associated with a sector. Moreover, created assets in any one sector (for example, consumer electronics) may have significant knowledge flows externalities in another (say microelectronics design), which, in turn, may represent significant input to another sector (say software development). But this presumes the presence of a virtuous circle, and the development of appropriate clusters.

We accept, of course, that inbound FDI does not always play a decisive role in this process of industrial upgrading, or in the development of clusters. Clusters may develop without significant MNE intervention. The case of Korea illustrates this, where the large domestic conglomerates have acted as the main engine of growth. Similarly, in Sialkot, Pakistan, clusters of indigenous small firms supplying surgical and clinical instruments to world markets have evolved without FDI-based knowledge inflows (Nadvi, 1996).[9]

Table 3.1 Changes in GDP and inward FDI stock per capita, 1980 and 1995: evidence of divergence

	GDP per capita			Inward FDI stock per capita		
	1980	1995	1995÷1980	1980	1995	1995÷1980
Low income countries (n = 42)						
mean	435.2	357.4	0.8	1.4	4.9	3.6
SD	320.1	163.9		1.7	6.1	
Low-middle income countries (n = 36)						
mean	1 219.1	1 818.3	1.5	10.4	37.4	3.6
SD	618.7	720.3		12.2	39.3	
Upper-middle income countries (n = 20)						
mean	3 898.3	5 340.2	1.4	40.4	179.5	4.4
SD	3 576.6	1 813.6		33.5	182.7	
High income countries (n = 32)						
mean	11 780.3	22 081.8	1.9	353.7	1 520.9	4.3
SD	7 254.5	8 381.4		1 643.9	6 777.0	
Ratio of high income countries FDI p.c. to that of low income countries				259.0	307.5	
Ratio of high income countries FDI p.c. to that of low-middle income countries				34.0	40.7	
Ratio of high income countries FDI p.c. to that of upper-middle income countries				8.8	8.5	

Notes: All countries for which GDP was unavailable for 1980 and 1995 (or close proxy) were excluded; this excludes all former Soviet bloc countries, but includes Vietnam and China; countries were classified according to World Bank criteria for 1995: low income < $765 GDP per capita, low-middle income, $766–3035, upper-middle income, $3036–9385, high income > $9386.

Sources: GDP and population based on World Develoment Indicators CD-ROM, World Bank (1997), inward FDI stock based on UN (1997).

However, although inward FDI does not represent the only option available to developing countries, it may represent the most *efficient* option. This is for at least four reasons. First, the costs of acquiring technological and organizational knowhow through markets is an expensive undertaking and, given the shortage of domestic capital, this option is not open to many developing countries. Second, liberalized markets mean that firms, *ceteris paribus*, are likely to be more eager to maintain control of their competitive advantages, either through the establishment of wholly owned subsidiaries or through joint ventures. There are exceptions, but generally only where strong strategic reasons and/or structural distortions exist: for instance, where the host country has a strong bargaining position,[10] or where the technology has reached the status of a commodity. Third, infant industry protection is *de rigueur* in creating a domestic sector from scratch, but protected markets are a limited option within the framework of the World Trade Organization (WTO). Fourth, the complementary resources necessary to support a viable and strong domestic sector are usually capital- and knowledge-intensive.

We wish to emphasize that the availability of foreign-owned capital (either portfolio or direct) for developing countries is not at issue here. There have been capital flows of both kinds to viable projects in the less developed countries, particularly in extractive industries, and through privatization programmes. In addition, there have been some low value-adding, labour-intensive activities such as garment assembly, which come from attempts to circumvent the multi-fibre agreement. Nonetheless, these activities do not, in general, provide much opportunity for technological spillovers and beneficial externalities. In other words, it is not FDI per se that is hard to attract, but rather the right kind of FDI. The next section discusses this assertion in some detail.

FDI, MOTIVES AND OPPORTUNITY COSTS

It is generally acknowledged that there are four main motives for investment: to seek natural resources, to seek new markets, to restructure existing foreign production through rationalization, and to seek strategically related created assets. These, in turn, can be broadly divided into two types. The first three represent motives which are primarily *asset-exploiting* in nature: that is, the investing company's primary purpose is to generate economic rent through the use of its existing firm-specific assets. The last is a case of *asset-augmenting activity,* whereby the investing firm wishes to add to its existing assets.

Figure 3.3 suggests that countries in stages 1 and 2 of their IDP are unlikely to attract much asset-augmenting FDI. Such investment is primarily an activity undertaken in stage 4 and 5 countries and, to a lesser extent, stage 3 countries. While there has been an increase in asset-seeking FDI in some developing countries during the last decade, this continues to be the exception rather than the rule. This is simply because the human resources, technological capabilities and organizational skills that these countries (or their firms) possess tend to be in relatively low-technology and/or natural resource-intensive sectors which have become 'generic' over time. In the case of strategic technology partnering (an important means by which asset augmentation is undertaken) Freeman and Hagedoorn (1994) and Narula and Sadowski (2002) both show that, with the exception of a few developing countries in stage 3 of their IDP – notably the Asian NICs and China – relatively little technology partnering involves developing country firms. Asset-augmenting MNE activities in stage 1 and stage 2 countries tend to be confined to adaptive R&D, except where the product or process is host country-specific. There are exceptions to this generalization: for instance, where a MNE has established a location as a regional centre (such as Unilever's use of Thailand as a specialist regional R&D centre for personal products) or, in rare cases, where immobile L advantages take the form of a cluster of highly skilled but relatively inexpensive labour, as in the case of Bangalore in India for software design.

Let us now briefly describe the main kinds of FDI currently directed at the developing countries in stage 1 and 2 of their IDPs.

Resource-seeking FDI

One of the most significant kinds of FDI for developing countries continues to be natural resource-seeking FDI. Resource-seeking FDI is a case where created asset type L advantages do not play a significant role in determining FDI inflows. Simply put, where a region or country possesses an absolute advantage in a particular scarce resource, the government of that region or country is in a strong bargaining position. Where the resource sought is a natural one, the marginal cost of its extraction to both parties is close to zero. Consequently, the location is able to generate economic rent depending on the resource's rarity and accessibility in other locations. Most other resources, where the advantage is a comparative one, do not maintain a low marginal cost to governments over time as the cost of utilizing such resources rises as the country moves along its IDP. Thus they do not attract inward FDI with the same interest at all stages of the IDP. The case of unskilled labour is one example. The siting of labour-intensive production becomes gradually less attractive to potential foreign investors as the costs of this input rise, and this is particularly so where productivity improvements fail to match wage cost increases. The leverage in such cases lies increasingly with MNEs, as inter alia cross-market liberalization has compelled governments in several countries to offer similar 'generic' and (easily) replicable L advantages (McIntyre *et al.*, 1996).

Its international nature means that, as far as resource-seeking FDI per se is concerned, there is relatively little difference in the bargaining positions between developing and developed countries. However, since resource-seeking investment generally (but not always) implies low value-adding activity and low capital expenditure on plant and equipment (extractive industries being the exception), FDI is less 'sticky', that is, more footloose. In general, a purely resource-seeking investment is not normally tightly integrated into the investing firm's global strategy. Indeed, MNEs rarely engage in complete internalization of raw material markets, preferring instead to conclude long-term contractual agreements with suppliers, or to purchase their inputs at arm's-length prices.

In general, FDI in stage 1 countries is likely to be almost entirely resource-seeking, and this remains as true today as it did 30 years ago. Since there are few other L advantages to offer MNEs, this is often the only kind of FDI likely to occur. Where vertical forward integration and further value adding does occur (perhaps because of developments in L advantages as the country moves to stage 2), the 'stickiness' of the investment increases, which strengthens the bargaining position of the host government. Both market-seeking and efficiency-seeking investment imply higher integration within the MNE, and a higher level of commitment as well as a higher degree of embeddedness.

Market-seeking FDI

Market-seeking FDI becomes significant either where there are substantial barriers to exporting from the home country or where the local or adjacent markets offer potential investors significant opportunities to achieve production economies of scale. This situation is most often experienced in the latter part of stage 1 and from stage 2 of their IDPs. This requires not only a sizable population, but also the ability of the market to support (within a reasonable time frame) the expected demand on which the investment is based. In addition, though, there is often a 'follow-my-leader' strategic response by other firms, whereby a market that might have supported two or three competitors is inundated by a larger number of new entrants than the market can efficiently support. The case of both the Chinese and the Indian car markets are examples of such a scenario, where, despite the potential for high demand levels, few participants are actually able to make a profit. This is not the case with all sectors; investments in food and personal products, for instance, are much more likely to achieve economies of scale, since these products have a relatively low income elasticity of demand. Indeed, the motor industry may represent a special case in these countries, for what is now described as aggressive market-seeking investments in developing countries in many cases began life as defensive import-substituting investments. These were only permitted under certain stringent conditions, but the MNE normally expected to have access to a captive protected market in return.

Market-seeking FDI, by its nature, is based on a single central L advantage. Its presence or absence is partly stage-dependent, but is essentially an exogenous event, with one exception. Membership of a free trade area allows countries that have small domestic markets to expand their de facto market size. In such situations, however, several formerly sovereign markets become integrated, and the choice of location then rests on other L advantages. This may have detrimental effects too: for example, once sanctions against South Africa were lifted, a certain hollowing out of market-seeking FDI in neighbouring countries was observed, as a result of their free trade agreements with South Africa.

Efficiency-seeking and Strategic Asset-seeking FDI

These two types of investment are similar, in that they both normally require a certain threshold level of created assets in the host country; and both tend to be fostered by the process of globalization. It is no surprise, then, that they are generally associated with countries at the latter end of stage 2 onwards and, especially in the case of asset-seeking FDI, with the more advanced industrialized countries.

Efficiency-seeking investment in the least developed countries is an ambiguous concept, although, for many years, MNEs have engaged in export-oriented resource-seeking investment, which is, de facto, efficiency-seeking FDI. Moreover, such investment, in the sense that different aspects of manufacturing activity are located in particular locations to exploit the economies of cross-border specialization and the uneven distribution of immobile created assets, is a relatively new phenomenon.

In both efficiency- and asset-seeking investments, the role of subnational clusters and the agglomeration of related activities is particularly significant. The bargaining positions of countries that are home to centres of agglomeration or, indeed, possess the science and technology infrastructure necessary to attract asset-augmenting FDI, are considerably different from those of countries which primarily attract asset-exploiting FDI. It is to be noted that, even where centres of excellence or agglomeration exist in a given industry, this does not imply that further knowledge-intensive investments will be attracted to the same location, unless clear spillovers or externalities exist. Nonetheless, countries (or regions within countries) that have (the basis for) agglomerative economies are the ones likely to be in a strong bargaining position. This was originally the case for export processing zones (EPZs). It now applies to higher value adding activities – even in stage 2 countries such as India – but only where such L advantages are perceived by MNEs to complement their own core competences efficiently.

HOW GLOBALIZATION AFFECTS O AND L ADVANTAGES

In developing a clearer understanding of the changes deriving from globalization per se, it is necessary for us to highlight how the phenomenon has affected the L advantages of countries (both developing and industrialized), and the nature of the opportunity sets available to developing countries in general. At the same time, these same forces have influenced the nature of the O advantages of firms and their need and willingness to internalize these markets for them. To some extent, at least, the adoption of outward-looking, export-oriented policy stances by developing countries has been inspired by the success of relatively rapid industrialization by the Asian NICs. However, the circumstances under which these countries achieved their rapid growth are closely related to the geopolitical and economic situation of the post-Second World War era. These circumstances cannot be easily replicated in this age of globalization and the current international political and economic climate.

The shift in the bargaining power of national governments vis-à-vis foreign MNEs concerns two interrelated phenomena directly associated with the economic changes associated with globalization, and especially with the introduction and adoption of new technologies, as well as the renaissance of market-based capitalism. Table 3.2 and Table 3.3 summarize how these changes in the world economic environment are likely to have influenced the opportunity sets facing both MNEs and governments. However, as we have already emphasized, the heterogeneity of developing countries implies that the general picture set out in these tables disguises some important nuances pertaining to the changes in the nature of opportunity costs that have special reference to the least developed countries.

New Technologies

The growth of new technologies has had a significant impact on the locational preferences of MNEs. Of particular note are developments in the fields of new materials, biotechnology, aerospace technologies and optical technologies. Information and communication technologies (ICTs)[11] have dramatically shrunk the economic distance between nation states, and have fostered a series of generic productivity improvements. We outline below some of the ways in which these technologies have influenced and are influencing the competitive advantages of firms and countries.

New technologies and the O advantages of firms

Table 3.2 presents some of the primary effects of new technologies on the competitive advantages of firms. In particular, we would highlight two main consequences.

Improved coordination of intra-firm and inter-firm activities It is a fundamental feature of international production that cross-border market failure exists in the supply of intermediate goods and services, especially intangible assets. New advances in ICTs have reduced the cost of acquiring and disseminating knowledge and information in two main ways. First, information about both input and output markets is more easily accessible. This allows firms which previously could not engage in international business transactions to do so.[12] Second, MNEs are better able to integrate the activities of their foreign affiliates through the use of these technologies, and to respond more quickly to changing demand and supply conditions in the countries in which they operate. Taken together, these transaction cost-reducing processes are enabling international production to be more efficiently organized. They are also prompting more rationalized and strategic asset-seeking FDI.

While these new economies of common governance are of particular reference to MNEs which pursue global strategies (Porter, 1986), multi-domestic MNEs[13] are also able to utilize regional similarities and develop 'hub and spoke' approaches, and to exploit scale and scope economies between and within regions (Buckley and Casson, 1998). Such options allow firms to hedge investments, but are only possible as a result of the reduced monitoring costs associated with ICTs.

There have also been substantial cost savings in the coordination and monitoring of costs arising from managing inter-firm networks. This growing use of networks, both intra- and inter-firm, is one of the primary features of modern capitalism (Dunning, 1995). The number of strategic alliances, joint ventures, R&D consortia and the like has experienced rapid growth over the last two decades, both within and between countries (Hagedoorn and Narula, 1996), but mainly among the Triad countries. One of the main advantages of improved intra- and inter-firm collaboration and coordination is the ease with which MNEs are able to respond to changes in both demand and supply conditions. In general, this has meant that firms pursuing multi-domestic strategies can now practise a policy of regional rationalization, which, in principle, should benefit both the participating countries and the MNE.

Table 3.2   The changing nature of the world economic environment and the opportunity sets of MNEs

| | | Triad-based MNEs | |
	Alternatives in location	Mode of investment	Asset-type ownership advantages	Transaction-type ownership advantages
Liberalization	Growing use of efficiency-seeking investment, as MNEs locate to better exploit economies of scale and scope More options for location of labour and resource-intensive investment because of liberalization Limited or no change in options for knowledge-intensive sectors, and for asset-augmenting activities	Easier to enforce non-equity agreements as well as arm's-length transactions, especially within Triad	Improved property rights protection for firms due to WTO, WIPO Overall growth of created asset-based O advantages	Improved Ot advantages for firms that have rationalized within economic blocs (EU, NAFTA) relative to those which have not
New technologies	Improved access to information leads to more efficient choice of location Need to be in closer proximity to related industries to reduce spatial transaction costs	Truncated product life cycles; need for multi-technology competencies also lead to increased use of alliances	Increasing mobility of Oa advantages New industries have in some instances provided an opportunity to extend product life cycle Higher share of knowledge content in O advantages	Improved cross-border communication results in more optimal intra-firm coordination and integration

Rapidity of innovation in new technologies   This has led to truncated product life cycles as new or modified products are more speedily innovated and manufactured. Firms need both to be able to undertake technological developments and to bring them to market much more quickly than was previously the case. Computer-aided design, 'flexible' manufacturing systems and computer-aided manufacturing have further reduced the set-up costs and time taken to bring to market a new product. Although this has led to a reduction in fixed costs, these technologies are not costless. Shortened product life cycles, for example, often require a relatively high R&D expenditure if firms are to remain competitive. They also suggest that innovating firms need to recoup these fixed costs, before their new products and processes become redundant,[14] by expanding their markets. Once again, the target foreign markets tend to be the industrializing and industrial economies, rather than the poorer developing countries. In their penetration of these latter markets, MNEs may still pursue multi-domestic strategies and supply products for which R&D costs have already been amortized.

New technologies and the L advantages of countries

Table 3.3 sets out some of the likely effects of new technologies on the L advantages of countries. Our objective here is to focus on the special case of the poorer developing countries, and we highlight some of these differences here.

One of the primary means by which the L advantages have been affected by new technologies has been the *emergence and development of entirely new industries*, which have generated new sources and kinds of employment. The extent to which these developments have affected the ability of developing country firms to catch up is not as acute as with more established sectors. This is because, in fundamentally new technologies, there is not likely to be as large a 'gap' between the lead and lag countries. Indeed, some stage 2 countries, like most of the stage 3 countries, have successfully engaged in a 'niche' strategy by specializing in the production of very specific new technologies as a way of upgrading their competitiveness. The often cited example of India's burgeoning software sector is one such case, and the focus of other nations (for example, Cuba) on biotechnology is another (Acharya, 1996). However, the failure of the majority of developing countries to exploit these new technologies has acted as a centripetal force, and encouraged the centralization of high-value production by MNEs. It should be noted, however, that the opportunity costs of national governments in pursuing a strategy of promoting new technologies are quite high, in terms both of creating the necessary infrastructure, including clusters of related activities, and of sustaining the requisite macro-organizational policies and financial

Table 3.3 The changing nature of the world economic environment and the opportunity sets of host countries

	Alternatives for technology and capital systems	Policies and incentive	Natural assets	Created assets
Liberalization	More alternatives in terms of technology, as well as increased modes of transfer	Policies become increasingly standardized among countries Subsidy limits from WTO membership reduce O advantages of domestic firms	Natural assets increasingly a commodity, except where substantial comparative or absolute advantage exists	Increasing mobility of highly skilled workforce Created assets increasingly firm-specific
New technologies	Opportunity for leapfrogging: smaller stock of knowledge Improved ability to find alternatives, thanks to ICTs	More inter-country and inter-region competition on incentive schemes Easier for firms to transfer price, thanks to ICTs, and reduce tax burden		Truncated life cycles mean that L advantages may become obsolete High fixed cost in upgrading technological infrastructure and national systems of innovation regularly

incentives over an extended period of time. In the main, the smaller and/ or poorer developing countries cannot afford to invest in several niches simultaneously, and consequently the question of technological target selection (that is, picking the 'right' sectors) becomes critical.

The relatively low costs to entry are not uniform for all new technologies, however. Most subsectors of ICTs, for instance, are highly capital-intensive, and are built on well established and highly competitive technologies. Indeed, these are the types of sectors which developing countries are keen to develop, and to do so by attracting inward FDI. Triad-based MNEs continue to dominate such sectors, and although such firms do engage in value-added activities in developing countries, they tend to concentrate these in a few locations where the appropriate infrastructure and created assets are available. The failure of the majority of the stage 1 and 2 countries to supply the kinds of support facilities which MNEs need to complement their own O advantages underlies the limited extent to which affiliates in these countries have attracted efficiency-seeking FDI.

Reduced transaction costs due to ICTs have had a limited effect on the L advantages of the least developed countries. Much of the FDI in stage 1 countries tends to be natural resource-seeking. These sectors have not benefited greatly from advances in communications technologies. Nonetheless, there are some such benefits. First, information about policies, incentives and procedures are much more widely disseminated. Second, they are better able to coordinate activities within their countries and between various arms of policy makers and agencies through 'one-stop shopping' (Wells and Wint, 1993).

The truncation of life cycles has meant that the least developed countries that have made investments in certain specific types of created assets may not be able to achieve a realistic return on their high fixed costs by the time (or if) the technology becomes obsolete. Furthermore, shifting to a new technological paradigm may take several years, as country-specific changes must be made at all levels, from macro-organizational policy to educational systems, and the high fixed costs involved may not be a realistic option for developing countries.

Renaissance of Market-based Capitalism and Economic Liberalization

The 1980s were a decade of considerable ideological and economic upheaval. In particular, we would emphasize three interconnected events. First, the cold war ended. Since 1989, more than 30 countries have abandoned central planning as the main mode of allocating scarce resources. Second, over 80 developing countries have liberalized their economic policies from inward-looking, import-substituting regimes towards outward-looking, export-oriented policy regimes (UNCTAD, 1997). Between them, these two developments have led to a softening of attitudes of national governments towards inbound FDI, the privatization of state-owned enterprises and the reduction of cross-border structural market distortions. MNEs are now actively involved in, and have access to, an unprecedented number of countries. This trend is a continuing one that deepened throughout the 1990s.

Third, there has been an across-the-board liberalization of cross-border markets due to the growth of regional and interregional free trade agreements and protocols, a range of bilateral arrangements and the establishment of new multilateral agencies such as the WTO. As a consequence, all forms of international transactions have increased markedly over the last decade. In addition, increasing attention is now being given to the establishment of a multilateral framework which will ensure a liberalized environment for the flow of FDI and for other forms of MNE activity.

Liberalization and O advantages
Table 3.2 presents a list of the main benefits which MNEs have gained from the renaissance of the market economy. Overall, liberalization has been very beneficial to MNEs. Privatization, in particular, has allowed foreign investors to acquire fully operational (albeit often inefficient) firms in countries at relatively low cost, thanks inter alia, to depreciation of exchange rates of the recipient economies.[15] At the same time, the foreign affiliates of MNEs are increasingly being accorded national treatment by their host governments. In addition, liberalization, the establishment of WTO and new protocols on intellectual property rights have improved the appropriability of intangible assets by MNEs. *Inter alia*, they have helped corporations to undertake and enforce more cross-border arm's-length, non-equity-type agreements. In addition, however, these developments have allowed MNEs to enter markets using equity that was previously restricted to FDI.

Liberalization and L advantages
Although the effects of liberalization (some of which are set out in Table 3.3) are easily observed, the news is not as good for stage 1 and 2 economies as it is for industrial and converging countries. Saeger (1997) observes that trade liberalization has had a deindustrialization effect on the South. Competition between countries and regions to attract mobile investment has increased significantly. Technology-intensive and knowledge-augmenting investment flows seek out complementary created and immobile assets in the recipient countries (Teece, 1992; Dunning, 1995). It therefore tends to be directed to the technologically more advanced developed and developing countries.

In general the L advantages of the least developed countries have been reduced, both because of absolute changes within countries, and because of relative changes between countries. This is for several reasons. First, because of the widespread liberalization of foreign trade and investment regimes, so many more developing countries offer 'generic' location-specific advantages such as access to natural assets, basic educational provisions and infrastructure. Furthermore, there is a growing tendency for these natural assets to be marginally priced. Second, national and subnational governments are under pressure to offer ever-increasing incentives to attract the kind of FDI that they perceive will advance their development strategies (Mytelka, 1999, 2002). Given the financial limits these countries face as it is, this reduces the opportunities to invest in the upgrading of their assets, and to overcome market failure. Third, several types of policy instruments used by developing countries to encourage MNEs to transfer skills and technology are either illegal (such as local content regulations, under the TRIMs agreement) or time-restricted (for example, certain kinds of subsidies under the SCM agreements, implementation of the TRIPs agreement). Fourth, it is increasingly difficult to determine whether the financial subsidies given by governments to MNEs are utilized for the purposes for which they are intended. Subsidies are more easily rerouted by global firms, and are hard to monitor, often defeating the objectives of governments.

This is not to say that there are no benefits of the WTO era. First, it has facilitated an increased flow of technology and knowledge, and more alternative sources. Second, firms situated in LDCs potentially have greater (and less impeded) access to important markets such as those of the OECD countries (Lall, 1997a). Third, there is the opportunity for binding arbitration and redress through the WTO. Brewer and Young (1999) point out that dispute settlement through the WTO is a preferable alternative to 'the uncertainties of unilateralism', particularly for developing countries. They note that 60 per cent of requests for arbitration involved developing countries during its initial four years.

It would seem that an overhaul of regional free trade and bilateral agreements represents a necessary complement to global liberalization, and may, in certain instances, improve the L advantages of countries (such as de facto market size), and bargaining position vis-à-vis important economic blocs. However, there is a vast difference in the benefits that accrue from (say) the Association of Southeast Asian Nations (ASEAN) and NAFTA (Baldwin, 1997).

It is also important to realize that the process of liberalization is increasingly an event over which governments of individual developing countries have less and less control. Let us elucidate. First, the deregulation or liberalization of any particular market in a country represents an *endogenous* event. However, the resulting benefit that accrues to the country is a function of how many other countries have also liberalized. Second, membership of supranational institutions such as the WTO (as well as free trade areas, and other forms of economic integration) obliges the participating countries to conform their liberalization policies to a common standard. Third, membership of de facto trade and investment blocs can effect a change in policy since, with fewer and fewer countries still operating within a command economy or an import-substituting regime, the opportunities for engaging in economically sound non-market arrangements are reduced.

This erosion of the kind of L advantages associated with protected trade and investment regimes may have far-reaching consequences, particularly for industries not yet able to compete in world markets. Although the benefits of liberalization arising from increased inward FDI have been notable, some divestment has also occurred where the initial MNE activity was prompted by tariff and non-tariff barriers. Since the conclusion of NAFTA, for example, defensive import-substituting FDI in Canada has fallen sharply. Although there are few data on divestment in developing countries, it is likely that, since proportionally more FDI prior to liberalization was defensive market-seeking, this phenomenon might be a significant one.

Although liberalization should not, in principle, lead to a trade-off between the O advantages of firms and the L advantages of countries, this seems to be the case, or at least is the perception of many developing country policy makers. Thus, for example, the OECD-sponsored Multilateral Agreement on Investment (MAI), is regarded by a number of developing country governments as being too focused on the needs of the investors, and not sufficiently so on the development needs of the host countries (Ganesan, 1997).

POLICY IMPLICATIONS AND CONCLUSIONS

Globalization has fundamentally changed economic realities. Thirty years ago, a general approach towards understanding the bargaining relationship between countries and MNEs made a good deal of sense. This, we believe, is no longer the case. One of the primary effects of globalization has been a reconfiguration of countries into three groups: the least developed countries which have 'fallen behind', the catching-up developing countries, and the developed or 'converged' countries. The process whereby this has happened is a complex one. We have tried to outline some of the dynamics and what it has meant for the relationship between MNEs and developing country governments, and particularly to those of the 'falling-behind' countries. We have explained how changes in L and O advantages, due to globalization, have influenced the nature and context of MNE–government relations, and why a distinction can and should be made between these groups of countries.

Over the last two decades, the opportunity costs of FDI for both host country governments and MNEs have significantly changed. From an MNE perspective, globalization has considerably influenced the nature and composition of the core competences of firms. In particular, these are more mobile, knowledge-intensive and geographically dispersed than they used to be. Moreover, MNEs are increasingly seeking to consolidate or advance their global competitive positions, by rationalizing their cross-border value-added activities. Inter alia, this is shown by the continuing rise in intra-firm trade (UNCTAD, 1997). This has been helped, in no small measure, by the reduction in their cross-border transaction and coordination costs which itself has been fostered by trade and investment liberalization.

In pursuing these objectives, MNEs – and particularly those within the knowledge-intensive sectors – are being forced to pay more attention to the availability and quality of the largely L-specific created assets of alternative investment sites. Indeed, choosing a 'right' portfolio of locations for their value added activities is a competitive advantage in its own right. Michael Porter has gone as far as to say that 'anything that can be moved or sourced from a distance is no longer a competitive advantage' and that 'the true advantages today are things which are sticky, that is not easily moveable' (Porter, 1998, p. 29). Moreover, it is important to note that not all industries have become equally mobile or globalized. As Stopford (1997) notes, while the optimum size of production may have risen in some industries, making global integration desirable, in other cases, new technologies have reduced the minimum efficient scale. This has meant that MNEs (particularly in industries where external economies through spatial linkages are critical) are becoming more embedded in local and regional milieus than was previously the case, and, in consequence, they have become *less* mobile.

From a national government perspective, exogenous and endogenous changes in the global economic and political environment have necessitated a reappraisal of the benefits of openness. Indeed, over the last two decades, there has been an ideological shift away from the traditional inward-looking import-substituting model adopted by many developing countries, where the state was perceived to be the primary force behind the creation, utilization and dissemination of knowledge (Frischtak, 1997). At the same time, although the change in policy orientation and the subsequent privatization of state-owned enterprises has reduced the interventionist role of governments, their role as market facilitator and provider of complementary created asset-based location-specific advantages has become more critical (Dunning, 1997b; Stopford, 1997).

Industrial development options for the least developed countries hinge increasingly on leveraging foreign investment as a means of promoting technological upgrading. This requires that countries attract the right kind of FDI. Specifically, these countries need to shift the emphasis of their inward FDI away from resource-seeking activities to market seeking and other asset-exploiting activities. Breaking away from natural asset-based activity and encouraging MNEs to invest in higher value-adding activities can only be achieved by improving their country-specific L advantages. A certain level of immobile created assets is an essential catalyst to the attraction of mobile investment. Even more so is the presence of domestic firms with the technological capabilities to absorb the spillovers pertaining to the activities of these firms. Governments have, sometimes passively, resorted to attracting inbound investment in two major ways, neither of which has necessarily improved their L advantages.

The first has been to step up, or offer a new range of fiscal and other incentives. But simply to offer incentives is no substitute for the development of created assets which may be beneficial to the domestic sector as well. Indeed, such incentives offered in isolation of other L advantages are not effective (Mudambi, 1995), although they may have an effect if they persist over time. At the same time, there is a danger that, owing to the increased competition to attract MNEs, governments may give away more than the potential benefits that accrue from the MNE activity (Mytelka, 1999, 2002). This is all the more so since governments of developing countries (or regions within these countries) are increasingly competing with less prosperous regions in industrialized countries and with those of the former centrally planned economies, whose infrastructure tends to be far superior, and whose pockets are much deeper than those of most developing countries. Given the costs of providing these incentives, and the profusion of locations offering them, there is a danger that, in an attempt to attract new 'desirable' investors, not only may net benefits to countries become negative, but the new investors may be treated preferentially relative to existing (and embedded) firms (Mudambi, 1998). The limited resources of developing countries mean that this does not represent a desirable long-term option.[16]

A second passive option that countries have embraced, often as a condition for debt relief or rescheduling, has been the World Bank-administered structural adjustment programmes, which have tended to focus on the sudden and wholesale liberalization of markets, and other macroeconomic cures. The success of these programmes has been mixed at best, as is now acknowledged by the chief economist of the World Bank, Joe Stiglitz. He has said that World Bank policies have hitherto been too much emphasis on macroeconomic stabilization at the expense of institution building.[17] In a seminal paper, Rodríguez and Rodrik (1999) have argued that open trade policies, such as lower tariff and non-tariff barriers, by themselves are not a primary determinant of economic growth. They demonstrate that, up to a certain point, growth may actually be *enhanced* by barriers to trade, especially when countries are technological laggards and have comparative advantages in non-dynamic sectors.

On its own, liberalization, as with excessive protectionism, is insufficient as a driver of growth. The work of Lall (see especially 1997a, 1997b) points to the need for a holistic approach in selecting and leveraging sectors for dynamic growth, for stable governments, transparent policies and the provision of basic infrastructure and skills. We will not reproduce his arguments here, but simply underline his main point that the presence of a certain minimum level of L-specific advantages is an essential catalyst to the attraction of mobile investment, as is the presence of domestic firms with the technological capabilities to absorb the spillovers pertaining from the activities of these firms. Although some of the 'traditional' means used by the NICs to encourage backward and forward linkages from FDI are no longer legal under the various multilateral agreements, there are nonetheless several exceptions made for the least developed countries.[18] The use of incentives and subsidies is no substitute for the presence of created assets, not just because of the inability to absorb spillovers, but also because, in locational tournaments involving richer countries, the poorer developing countries are almost certainly bound to lose. In any case, incentives, performance requirements and subsidies (whatever their legal status) have had a limited effect on encouraging actual technological transfer and creation of domestic capabilities. Local content rules, for instance, do not by themselves result in backward linkages, because learning requires domestic firms with the appropriate skills to internalize them, and the conditions which make this necessary. The use of FDI as a means to transfer technology is efficient only as long as sufficient absorptive capability of the technologies exists locally (Borensztein *et al.*, 1998). In addition, though, the 'right' market conditions must exist for domestic firms to learn. Mytelka (1985) illustrates that, where domestic firms have access to subsidized capital and privileged access to resources, they are less likely to adapt imported technological inputs.

But the shortage of domestic capital (both financial and intellectual) and the need to develop assets which are by definition knowledge- (and often capital-) intensive points to the dilemma of limited resources. The creation of enclaves and clusters provides the answer to this, although such solutions are rife with political ramifications. By 'enclaves' we mean selective and limited upgrading of the L advantages of countries, in terms both of particular industrial sectors, and (more contentiously) of particular geographical regions. Since countries have limited resources, it makes sense to develop and upgrade their immobile assets, using their limited resources, in enclaves, with an eye to particular sectors. Providing the necessary infrastructure to all parts of a country may be politically optimal, but economically inefficient. One alternative (or complement) to this is to consider FDI in infrastructural projects, under a BOT (build–operate–transfer) basis. The fact that enclaves such as EPZs have not always been successful reflects the failure of host governments properly to appreciate the order in which events should have taken place, namely, the development of clusters of economic activity, from which might come welfare benefits, rather than vice versa. The limited nature of the L advantages offered to MNEs, and the high costs of establishing these zones in remote areas, where the necessary support industries were absent, underlay their failure (McIntyre *et al.*, 1996).

But simply to offer the kinds of advantages (for example, in respect of education and transport infrastructure) made available by competitive governments is not enough. What is needed is the provision of immobile created assets which are 'custom made' for the incoming investors (Peck, 1996) or are specific to the country and region seeking the investment (Dunning, 1998). Often such assets are complementary to each other and need to be spatially clustered if they are to be deployed with optimum efficiency (Storper and Scott, 1995). In pursuance of this kind of strategy, national governments such as Singapore and Ireland and subnational governments, for example, Wales, Northern Ireland, Shanghai, Bangalore, New South Wales, Baden-Württenberg and Piedmont – to name just a few – have met with a great deal of success.

The basic idea of building enclaves is a sound one. After all, developing countries have limited resources to plough into created asset enhancement, and a selective locational strategy for this task makes sense. Once countries have progressed beyond the threshold of their L-specific advantages, the gradual development of high-grade clusters of economic activity becomes a high priority. Selecting sectors is a task fraught with pitfalls, not least because selecting the 'right' industry as a target becomes more difficult the closer the country is to the technological frontier. When governments attempt to select preferred industries on which to focus some distance away from the technological frontier (say, in differentiated Smithian sectors, see Figure 3.3), the direction in which investment is to be made is fairly obvious since firms at the frontier (that is, the technology leaders) have already done so[19] in the past (Narula and Dunning, 1998). That is to say, the further a country is from the technological frontier, the easier it is to 'pick' industries that will be successful. The relative success of MITI in picking winners in the 1950s and 1960s, and their subsequent less successful interventions in the 1980s and 1990s, well illustrates this point. Although there is a danger in investing limited resources in niche sectors which become obsolete, or are replaced by a new technological paradigm, this need not happen if broader sectors are targeted that are complementary to, and help upgrade, existing competencies and skills. The development of Singapore's biotechnology sector illustrates this well (Lall, 1997a). As Stopford (1997, p. 473) explains,

> To nurture clusters, work needs to be done to identify specific technologies that can reinforce the position of existing leaders, or that suit the skills of the workforce or even that satisfy the demand that is particularly sophisticated in the nation. Investment in 'market-friendly' aspects of the underlying technologies can, as in Singapore, create a vital base for the building of firm-specific advantages by either local or foreign firms.

On the other hand, in the era of globalized production, it is easier to create production clusters from scratch. Because of the abilities of MNEs to locate different parts of their value-added chain in several locations to achieve global efficiency, there is an increased opportunity to specialize, and to attract inbound FDI in niche areas. A complementary approach to improving L advantages is to engage in some form of economic integration on a regional basis. However, as Baldwin (1997) notes, with a few exceptions (for example, MERCOSUR), most regional trade blocs and other forms of economic integration among developing countries have remained very much a matter of organization rather than substance.

It is clear that developing countries have evolved a myriad set of industrial strategies. However, since the economic structure of each country is very path-dependent and idiosyncratic, it is difficult to suggest any one 'best' solution. Given the stakes involved, and the pressures on developing countries to develop unique location-specific advantages to attract the kind of FDI they need, some sort of interventionist approach seems to be necessary. No self-evident solution exists, because the changing world economic environment makes some of these options impractical, or invalid for particular countries at particular stages of their IDP.

A central assumption to any economic prescription is the need for good governance and political stability. Political stability implies long-term continuance of economic policy. As Freeman and Lindauer (1999, p. 20) note, 'The reason returns to schooling are low in Africa, that capital flight is high and the shift towards free trade has not created growth miracles is that schooling, investment and trade operate successfully only in a peaceful, stable, environment for economic activity.' In many cases, it has not necessarily been strong regulation that has detracted FDI, but the lack of consistent regulation.

The challenge to national governments lies in providing the 'right' kind of immobile assets, and to encourage mobile investments to be locked into these assets. It should be said, however, that for LDCs the question is more urgent, since there is a threshold level of assets (including institutional infrastructure) which is required to attract even the most basic forms of FDI. In addition, though, if externalities are to accrue from FDI, these are most likely associated with those market or efficiency-seeking investments which need to be spatially linked to location-bound complementary activities.

NOTES

1. These features are described in various publications, including UNCTAD (1997), Perraton *et al.* (1997) and OECD (1997).
2. Notably all kinds of knowledge, organizational and institutional capital.
3. Dunning (1993) charts the evolution of MNE–government interaction over a 30-year period, and in so doing demonstrates the way in which economic forces are influenced by, and influence, the nature of government–MNE relationships. See also Dunning and Narula (1994).
4. Where the inbound FDI stock as a percentage of gross domestic product (GDP) rose from 8.3 per cent to 15.4 per cent over the same period (UNCTAD, 1997).
5. The methodology proposed by Rugman and Verbeke (1998) focuses more on the strategic aspects of the relationship. It encompasses a broader analysis that provides the basis for a more dynamic approach, although it is a general model in that it does not address either developing country-specific issues or how the situation varies between countries. Essentially, this model argues that the relationship between MNE and governments is determined inter alia by the degree of symmetry between inward and outward FDI in a given country, the dispersion of firm-specific advantages within MNEs, the strategic approach by MNEs to government policy and the congruence between MNE and home and host country goals. The authors include the net direct investment position as a determinant, but do not consider the influence of the absolute levels.
6. See, for example, Dowrick and Gemmell (1991), Dowrick (1992), Verspagen (1993).
7. See, for example, Dunning and Narula (1994, 1996), Narula (1993, 1996), Ozawa (1995, 1996), van Hoesel (1999).
8. Africa and Latin America fell from 7.3 per cent and 2.7 per cent in 1980 to 5.5 per cent and 0.8 per cent, respectively, in 1993.
9. They supply 10–15 per cent of the world market for high quality surgical instruments, and 50 per cent of the market in low-quality clinical instruments. For further examples, see Nadvi and Schmitz (1994).
10. For instance, where the local market is large and the MNE can only get access to other sectors in exchange for technology, or lucrative turnkey or other subcontracts are included.
11. Some scholars believe ICTs are initiating a new technological paradigm (see, for example, Freeman and Perez, 1988).
12. Several recent UN studies (for example, UN, 1993; UNCTAD, 1997) have indicated that an increasing number of small and medium enterprises are engaging in FDI.
13. Firms that operate in several markets, but maintain each individual region or country as essentially independent operations are referred to as having a 'multi-domestic' strategy.
14. It can either (a) sell at a relatively high cost per unit, and/or (b) develop a production process with a low minimum efficient scale of production, and/or (c) recoup its investment by acquiring a large market for its products so as to spread its fixed costs, and/or (d)

engage in an alliance with another firm (or firms) to speed up, and share the costs of, the innovatory process.

15. Over the period 1989–93, FDI from privatization accounted for $12.2 billion or 7.6 per cent of all inflows to developing countries (UNCTAD, 1996). Over 75 per cent of this was directed towards Latin America and the Caribbean, where privatization accounted for 16.9 per cent of all inflows to the region. In the case of Central and Eastern Europe, FDI inflows to privatization schemes amounted to $7.5 billion, or 59.7 per cent of the total FDI inflows to the region.

16. One of the benefits of the stalled MAI would have been a cap on such locational tournaments. However, the SCM agreement does provide some quantitative limits on these. For instance, subsidies cannot account for more than 15 per cent of the value of a new plant, although there are a number of caveats and restrictions that apply (see Brewer and Young, 1998, for more details).

17. *The Economist*, 'Sick Patients, Warring Doctors', 18–25 September 1999.

18. For instance, LDCs have seven years from 1 January 1995 to eliminate illegal TRIMs, and extensions may be granted to the use of TRIMs to safeguard balance of payments or to protect an infant industry. TRIMs do not cover specification of a minimum level of local employment, or a minimum level of local equity participation. LDCs also have until 2006 to implement TRIPs. Likewise, the SCM agreement covers loans, grants and tax credits, but not pre-competitive R&D, or assistance to disadvantaged regions. In addition, SCM covers only those subsidies that are specific to elected enterprises, and not if applied to an industry in general. For countries below a $1000 per capita GDP level, export subsidies will not be countervailed. For more details, see Brewer and Young (1998).

19. It is, necessary however, to emphasize the difference between firms that are a distance from the technology frontier and those that are simply experiencing X-inefficiency. The latter group are simply using an inferior technology, while the former are operating at an earlier stage of the product life cycle.

REFERENCES

Acharya, R. (1996), *The Biotechnology Revolution*, Cheltenham, UK and Brookfield, USA: Edward Elgar.

Baldwin, R. (1997), 'The causes of regionalism', *World Economy*, **3**, 865–88.

Blomstrom, M. (1989), *Foreign Investment and Spillovers: A Study of Technology Transfer to Mexico*, London: Routledge.

Borenszstein, E., J. De Gregorio and J.-W Lee (1998), 'How does foreign direct investment affect economic growth?', *Journal of International Economics*, **45**, 115–35.

Brewer, T.L., and S. Young (1998), *The Multilateral Investment System and Multinational Enterprises*, Oxford: Oxford University Press.

Brewer, T.L., and S. Young (1999), 'WTO disputes and developing countries', *Journal of World Trade*, **23**, October, 169–82.

Buckley, P., and M. Casson (1998), 'Models of the multinational enterprise', *Journal of International Business Studies*, **29** (1), 21–44.

Dowrick, S. (1992), 'Technological catch up and diverging incomes: patterns of economic growth 1960–88', *The Economic Journal*, **102**, 600–610.

Dowrick, S., and N. Gemmell (1991), 'Industrialisation, catching up and economic growth: A comparative study across the world's capitalist economies', *The Economic Journal*, **101**, 263–75.

Dunning, J.H. (1993), *Multinational Enterprises and the Global Economy*, Wokingham: Addison-Wesley.

Dunning, J.H. (1995), 'Reappraising the eclectic paradigm in an age of alliance capitalism', *Journal of International Business Studies*, **26** (3), 461–91.

Dunning, J.H. (1997a), *Alliance Capitalism and Global Business*, London: Routledge.

Dunning, J.H. (1997b), 'A business analytic approach to governments and globalisation', in J.H. Dunning (ed.), *Governments, Globalisation and International Business*, Oxford: Oxford University Press, pp. 114–31.

Dunning, J.H. (1998), 'Transnational corporations: an overview of relations with national governments', *New Political Economy*, **3** (2), 280–84.

Dunning, J.H., and R. Narula (1994), 'Transpacific direct investment and the investment development path: the record assessed', *Essays in International Business*, no. 10, March.

Dunning, J.H., and R. Narula (1996), 'The investment development path revisited: some emerging issues', in J. Dunning and R. Narula (eds), *Foreign Direct Investment and Governments: Catalysts for Economic Restructuring*, London: Routledge, pp. 1–41.

Dunning, J.H., R. van Hoesel and R. Narula (1998), 'Third World multinationals revisited: new developments and theoretical implications', in J. Dunning (ed.), *Globalization, Trade and Foreign Direct Investment*, Oxford: Pergamon, pp. 255–86.

Freeman, C., and J. Hagedoorn (1994), 'Catching up of falling behind: patterns in international inter-firm technology partnering', *World Development*, **22**, 771–80.

Freeman, Richard, and David L. Lindauer (1999), 'Why Not Africa?', NBER working paper no. 6942.

Freeman, C., and C. Perez (1988), 'Structural crises of adjustment, business cycles and investment behaviour', in G. Dosi *et al.* (eds), *Technical Change and Economic Theory*, London: Pinter.

Frischtak, C. (1997), 'Latin America', in J.H. Dunning (ed.), *Governments, Globalisation and International Business*, Oxford: Oxford University Press, pp. 431–54.

Fukuyama, F. (1995), *Trust: The Social Virtues and the Creation of Prosperity*, London: Hamish Hamilton.

Ganesan, A.V. (1997), 'Development-friendliness criteria for a multilateral investment agreement', *Transnational Corporations*, **6** (3), 135–42.

Gray, H.P. (1996), 'Globalization and economic development', mimeo, Rutgers University, Newark, NJ.

Hagedoorn, John, and R. Narula (1996), 'Choosing modes of governance for strategic technology partnering: international and sectoral differences', *Journal of International Business Studies*, **27** (2), 265–84.

Hikino, T., and A. Amsden (1994), 'Staying behind, stumbling back, sneaking up, soaring ahead: late industrialization in historical perspective', in W. Baumol, R. Nelson and E. Wolff (eds), *Convergence of Productivity: Cross Country Studies and Historical Evidence*, New York: Oxford University Press.

Hoesel, R. van (1999), *New Multinational Enterprises from Korea and Taiwan*, London: Routledge.

Lall, Sanjaya (1997a), 'East Asia', in J.H. Dunning (ed.), *Governments, Globalisation and International Business*, Oxford: Oxford University Press, pp. 407–30.

Lall, Sanjaya (1997b), 'Policies for industrial competitiveness in developing countries: learning from Asia', report prepared for the Commonwealth Secretariat, Oxford.

Landes, David (1998), *The Wealth and Poverty of Nations*, London: Little, Brown and Company.

Lecraw, D., and A. Morrison (1991), 'Transnational corporation–host country relations: a framework for analysis', *Essays in International Business*, no. 9, September.

Mason, Mark (1998), 'FDI in the Mekong Delta', paper presented to a conference on FDI in Asia, Macau, Institute of European Studies, April.

McIntyre, J., R. Narula and L. Trevino (1996), 'The role of export processing zones for host countries and multinationals: a mutually beneficial relationship?', *International Trade Journal*, **10**, 435–66.

Mudambi, Ram (1995), 'The MNE investment location decision: some empirical evidence', *Managerial and Decision Economics*, **16**, 249–57.

Mudambi, Ram (1998), 'The role of duration in MNE investment attraction strategies', *Journal of International Business Studies*, **29** (2), 239–62.

Mytelka, L. (1985), 'Stimulating effective technological transfer: the case of textiles in Africa', in N. Rosenberg and C. Frischtak (eds), *International Technology Transfer*, New York: Praeger.

Mytelka, L. (1999), 'Locational tournaments for FDI: inward investment into Europe in a global world', in Neil Hood and Stephen Young (eds), *The Globalization of Multinational Enterprise Activity and Economic Development*, London and New York: Macmillan/St Martins Press, pp. 278–302.

Mytelka, L. (2002), 'Locational tournaments, strategic partnerships and the state', in David Wolfe and Meric Gertler (eds), *Innovation and Social Learning: Institutional Adaptation in an Era of Technological Change*, London: Palgrave/Macmillan, pp. 89–110.

Nadvi, K. (1996), 'Small firm industrial districts in Pakistan', unpublished PhD thesis, University of Sussex, Brighton.

Nadvi, K., and H. Schmitz (1994), 'Industrial clusters in less developed countries: review of experiences and research agenda', Institute of Development Studies discussion paper 339, University of Sussex, Brighton.

Narula, R. (1993), 'Technology, international business and Porter's "diamond": Synthesising a dynamic competitive development model', *Management International Review*, **33**, 85–107.

Narula, R. (1996), *Multinational Investment and Economic Structure*, London: Routledge.

Narula, R., and J.H. Dunning (1998), 'Explaining international R&D alliances and the role of governments', *International Business Review*, **7**, 377–97.

Narula, R., and Bert Sadowski (2002), 'Technological catch-up and strategic technology partnering in developing countries', *International Journal of Technology Management*, **23**, 599–617.

OECD (1997), *The World in 2020: Towards a New Global Age*, Paris: OECD.

Ozawa, T. (1995), 'Structural upgrading and concatenated integration', in D. Simon (ed.), *Corporate Strategies in the Pacific Rim: Global versus Regional Trends*, London: Routledge, pp. 215–46.

Ozawa, T. (1996), 'Japan: The macro-IDP, meso-IDPs and the technology development path (TDP)', in J. Dunning and R. Narula (eds), *Foreign Direct*

Investment and Governments: Catalysts for Economic Restructuring, London: Routledge, pp. 423–41.

Peck, F.W. (1996), 'Regional development and the production of space: the role of infrastructure in the attraction of new inward investment', *Environment and Planning*, **28**, 327–39.

Perraton, J., D. Goldblatt, D., Held and A. McGrew (1997), 'The globalisation of economic activity', *New Political Economy*, **2** (2), 257–77.

Porter, M.E. (ed.) (1986), *Competition in Global Industries*, Cambridge, MA: Harvard Business School Press.

Porter, M.E. (1998), 'Location, clusters and the new macro-economics of competition', *Journal of Business Economics*, **33**, 7–13.

Rodríguez, Francisco, and Dani Rodrik (1999), 'Trade policy and economic growth: a skeptic's guide to the cross-national evidence', NBER working paper no. 7081.

Rugman, A., and A. Verbeke (1998), 'Multinational enterprises and public policy', *Journal of International Business Studies*, **29** (1), 115–36.

Saegar, S. (1997), 'Globalization and deindustrialization: myth and reality', *Weltwirtschaftliches Archiv*, **133**, 579–607.

Stopford, J. (1997), 'Implications for national governments', in J.H. Dunning (ed.), *Governments, Globalisation and International Business*, Oxford: Oxford University Press, pp. 457–80.

Stopford, J., and Susan Strange (1991), *Rival States, Rival Firms. Competition for World Market Shares*, Cambridge: Cambridge University Press.

Storper, M., and A. Scott (1995), 'The wealth of regions', *Futures*, **27** (5), 505–26.

Teece, D.J. (1992), 'Competition, cooperation and innovation: organisational arrangements for routines and rapid technological progress', *Journal of Economic Behaviour and Organization*, **18**, 1–25.

UN (1993), *Small and Medium-Sized Transnational Corporations*, New York: United Nations.

UN (1997), *World Investment Report 1997: Transnational Corporations, Market Structure and Competition Policy*, Geneva: United Nations.

UNCTAD (1996), *World Investment Report 1995: Transnational Corporations and Competitiveness,* Geneva and New York: United Nations.

UNCTAD (1997), *World Investment Report 1997: Transnational Corporations, Market Structure and Competition Policy*, Geneva and New York: United Nations.

UNCTAD (1998), *World Investment Report 1998: Trends and Determinants*, Geneva and New York: United Nations.

Verspagen, B. (1993), *Uneven Growth Between Interdependent Economies. An Evolutionary View on Technology Gaps, Trade and Growth*, Aldershot: Avebury.

Wells, L.T., and A. Wint (1993), 'Don't stop with the one-stop shop: foreign investment in a liberalising third world', *International Executive*, **35**, 367–84.

Williamson, P., and Q. Hu (1994), *Managing the Global Frontier*, London: Pitman Publishing.

World Bank (1997), *The World Development Report*, Oxford: Oxford University Press.

4. Incorporating trade into the investment development path

INTRODUCTION

This chapter[1] has an explicit purpose. It is to take a first step in incorporating trade levels and patterns into the notion of the investment development path (IDP), a notion which seeks to relate the stock of inward and outward direct investment (inward FDI and outward FDI) position of countries to their stages of development and economic structures.

The chapter proceeds as follows. In the following section, we present a truncated overview of the IDP, and why we believe that, by relating its trajectory to the changing level and patterns of trade, namely the trade development path (TDP), we may better understand the combined interaction between the two modes of cross-border transactions and the pace and pattern of economic development. We briefly describe the contents of the IDP and TDP and formulate a number of general propositions. Then we set out some specific hypotheses, which seek to relate the changing sectoral structure of trade and FDI in Korea and Taiwan over the last 30 years to the growth of their gross national product (GNP) per capita. The last part briefly summarizes our conclusions.

SOME ANALYTICAL ISSUES

The IDP

The IDP seeks to explain the international direct investment position of a country in terms of the juxtaposition between the locational attractions of its endogenous resources, capabilities and markets, vis-à-vis those of other countries, and the ownership or competitive advantages of its firms vis-à-vis those of other nationalities.[2] More specifically, it avers that, as countries increase their gross national product (GNP) per capita and the created asset component of their resources and capabilities,[3] so the level, significance and pattern of their inward FDI and outward FDI, and the relationship between them, display a systematic change.

In their earliest stage of economic development (stage 1), countries have few location-specific (L) advantages to attract inward FDI, and their firms possess virtually no ownership-specific (O) advantages to engage in outward FDI. As countries begin to industrialize – and the focus of this chapter is on two industrializing countries – the quality of their indigenous and immobile resources and capabilities, including their institutional capabilities and social infrastructure, improves, as does their domestic spending power. This starts to attract inward FDI, but, at this stage (stage 2), apart from a limited amount of natural resource and created asset-seeking investment, outward FDI is still minimal. This, however, changes in stage 3, as indigenous firms start to generate their own O-specific advantages. They tend to exploit these firstly by exports, and then, as their foreign markets expand and/or the costs of home-based production rise, by outward FDI. At this stage, too, in order to become global players, industrializing country firms begin to seek out foreign technology, management skills and organizational expertise, by means of mergers and acquisitions (M&As) or strategic alliances,[4] particularly with firms from the more industrialized countries. Eventually, in the later stages of the IDP,[5] outward FDI might well exceed inward FDI – at least for a time – after which there is a tendency for *net* outward FDI to gravitate towards, and fluctuate around, zero, or at very low levels relative to the total value of inward and outward FDI.[6]

The countries we are considering in this chapter would appear to be entering stage 4 of their IDPs, inasmuch as, in the 1990s, outward FDI of both Korea and Taiwan began to exceed inward FDI (see Table 4.3). Notwithstanding the fact that the Asian crisis of the mid-1990s caused a reconfiguration of their international direct investment positions, notably by raising the L advantages of both countries and lowering the O advantages of Korean and Taiwanese firms (and/or their ability to acquire foreign created-assets) there is no doubt that the time span of their transition from stage 1, or early stage 2 to stage 4 has been considerably shorter than that of their earlier counterparts in Europe and the USA. Inter alia, the emergence of the global innovating economy, and the increasing speed at which technological and organizational advances can be transferred across national boundaries, have helped speed up the process of industrialization. Government policy towards inbound and outbound FDI has also played an important role. For example, for most of the period under review, the Korean government restricted, by one means or another, the amount and/or type of inward FDI allowed, while, in the case of Taiwan, no outward FDI was allowed in mainland China until the late 1980s.

In addition to the general proposition that the nature of trajectory of a country's IDP will be related to its GNP per capita and to such location-specific variables as size, economic structure, absorptive capacity, openness and government policy towards FDI,[7] the character and composition of both inward FDI and outward FDI are also likely to change as development proceeds. In stages 1 and 2 of the IDP, for example, both inward and outward FDI flows are predominantly of the natural resource and market-seeking type.[8] At the same time, both inward FDI and outward FDI are likely to be between different industrial sectors, that is, FDI will be *inter*-industry in character. In stages 3 and 4, as the economic structure of countries is increasingly directed towards the production of Schumpeterian (S) goods and services,[9] and tends to converge with that of more advanced industrial countries, FDI flows become more of the efficiency and strategic asset-seeking variety. Moving through these stages, the composition of inward FDI and outward FDI then becomes increasingly *intra*-industry,[10] and less *inter*-industry in character. It also tends to become knowledge and/or information-intensive.

The TDP

The relationship between trade and economic development is a well-researched topic.[11] In this chapter, we are primarily concerned with the product composition of manufacturing imports (M) and exports (X); and how these change, particularly in their created asset intensity, as development proceeds. Our general proposition is that, at relatively low levels of GNP per capita, an industrializing country will engage primarily in *inter*-industry trade, importing products with a higher created asset content than those they export. As development proceeds, the created asset intensity of both M and X increases, with that of X lagging that of M. As this occurs, the proportion of intra-industry trade to total trade increases, and particularly so in the case of those products which are themselves created asset-intensive.

For the most part, scholarly research on the determinants of the TDP and IDP has proceeded independently, although in a schema introduced in 1986, and revised in 1995 (see Dunning and Norman, 1986; Dunning, 1995), an attempt was made to show how, as countries proceeded along their development paths, and as technological progress and human resource development led to an intensification of the created asset component of all products,[12] the relative significance of both intra-industry trade and intra-industry FDI would rise. At the same time, the schema suggested that, as a result of inter-industry, inbound FDI (which, almost by definition, is created asset-intensive[13]), the created asset intensity of the host country's exports is accelerated, and with it, the growth of *intra*-industry trade. Finally, as a country becomes fully industrialized (that is, it reaches stages 4 or 5 of its IDP), much of its efficiency and strategic asset-seeking FDI is with other industrialized, or rapidly industrializing, nations; hence is of an intra-industry FDI kind.

The above paragraphs therefore suggest that there is likely to be some interface between the TDP and the IDP both at a macro level, with both trade and FDI increasing their significance relative to the GNP of countries, and at a sectoral level. Part of this interaction may be sequential (and it is a hypothesis of this chapter that changes in the industrial structure of the IDP generally lag those of the TDP) and part may occur simultaneously, as FDI and trade either complement or substitute for each other.[14] But, whatever the case, the paradigm underpinning the explanation of trade, FDI and economic development is that of dynamic comparative advantage, suitably modified from its initial formulation to include (a) created immobile assets and (b) the ownership-specific advantages of particular firms.

In the following section, we seek to test empirically some of these ideas, from the experience of the Korean and Taiwanese economies between 1968 and 1997. However, prior to this, in Figure 4.1 we summarize the kinds of interaction which we might expect to find between the created asset intensity of imports and exports and that of inward and outward direct investment flows, as development proceeds; and also how we might expect the IDPs and the TDPs of countries to interact with each other. As a proxy for created asset intensity, we have taken the FDI intensity of each of the manufacturing sectors in Korea and Taiwan (at a 2, 3 or 4 digit level, depending on the data available)[15] and classified these into three groups: above FDI intensity (A sectors), average FDI intensity (O sectors) and below average intensity (B sectors). Further details of this procedure are set out in Appendix 4.1 and Appendix 4.2.

SOME SPECIFIC HYPOTHESES

The first hypothesis (H1) relates to the nature of the TDP. H1 consists of two parts. H1a is that the *proportion of total manufactured imports accounted for by average or above average FDI intensive goods (A and O goods) will rise quite sharply in the first two stages of Korean and Taiwanese IDP, but in the third phase it will rise less sharply or even fall.* This slowing down phase reflects the fact that imports of less FDI-intensive goods are likely to rise, as the domestic production of these becomes less competitive in Korea and Taiwan.

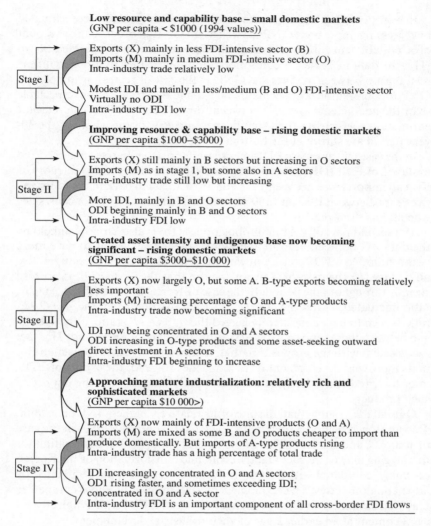

Low resource and capability base – small domestic markets
(GNP per capita < $1000 (1994 values))

Exports (X) mainly in less FDI-intensive sector (B)
Imports (M) mainly in medium FDI-intensive sector (O)
Intra-industry trade relatively low

Stage I

Modest IDI and mainly in less/medium (B and O) FDI-intensive sector
Virtually no ODI
Intra-industry FDI low

Improving resource & capability base – rising domestic markets
(GNP per capita $1000–$3000)

Exports (X) still mainly in B sectors but increasing in O sectors
Imports (M) as in stage 1, but some also in A sectors
Intra-industry trade still low but increasing

Stage II

More IDI, mainly in B and O sectors
ODI beginning mainly in B and O sectors
Intra-industry FDI low

**Created asset intensity and indigenous base now becoming
significant – rising domestic markets**
(GNP per capita $3000–$10 000)

Exports (X) now largely O, but some A. B-type exports becoming relatively
less important
Imports (M) increasing percentage of O and A-type products
Intra-industry trade now becoming significant

Stage III

IDI now being concentrated in O and A sectors
ODI increasing in O-type products and some asset-seeking outward
direct investment in A sectors
Intra-industry FDI beginning to increase

**Approaching mature industrialization: relatively rich and
sophisticated markets**
(GNP per capita $10 000>)

Exports (X) now mainly of FDI-intensive products (O and A)
Imports (M) are mixed as some B and O products cheaper to import than
produce domestically. But imports of A-type products rising
Intra-industry trade has a high percentage of total trade

Stage IV

IDI increasingly concentrated in O and A sectors
OD1 rising faster, and sometimes exceeding IDI;
concentrated in O and A sector
Intra-industry FDI is an important component of all cross-border FDI flows

Note: These stages, and the GNP per capita data, assume that there are no, or relatively
few, restrictions on either inward or outward FDI and trade flows.

*Figure 4.1   Four stages in the IDPs and TDPs of industrializing developing
countries*

The second part of H1 (H1b) is that *the proportion of manufactured exports
accounted for by A and O goods will accelerate as economic development
proceeds, but will lag that of imports.*

In respect of H1a, the respective coefficients and R^2 values were estimated by regressing imports on GNP^2 as well as on GNP, in order to take account of a possible curvilinear relationship between the two variables. As to H1a, the data in Table 4.1 confirm a monotonic rather than a curvilinear relationship between imports and GNP. In the case of regressing imports on GNP, the correlation coefficients are higher and the R^2s are more respectable than the coefficients and R^2s between imports and GNP^2. The relevant correlation coefficients, their significance and R^2s for the whole of the 30-year period are shown at the bottom of the table.

In the case of Taiwanese FDI-intensive imports, the sharpest rise occurred in stage 2 of their IDP, that is, during the 1980s. The share of this category of Korean imports rose between 1968 and 1976, then fell back in the following five years. Between 1982 and 1995 it fluctuated around 60–70 per cent, since when it has risen sharply.

The second part of the first proposition (H1b) is also broadly upheld by the data. As between Taiwan and Korea, the former seems to have more clearly followed a TDP consistent with the principle of dynamic comparative advantage. In the case of Taiwan, we see that the $A_x + O_x/T_x$ ratio rose steadily throughout the period. In the case of Korea, however, the $A_x + O_x/T_x$ ratio fluctuated, as did the $A_m + O_m/T_m$ ratio. As predicted, the $A_x + O_x/T_x$ ratio is seen to have consistently lagged the $A_m + O_m/T_m$ ratio, although the gap between these ratios narrowed steadily throughout the period. This fact is consistent with the proposition that, as a country reaches some maturity in its industrial development (that is, reaches stage 4), the export of FDI-intensive products is likely to rise much more quickly than the import of such products.

Our data also show that, in spite of its relatively higher GNP per capita, Taiwan lagged behind Korea in its $A + O/T$ ratio until the 1990s in the case of imports, and the late 1990s in the case of exports. One explanation for this lagging may be the fact that the economic transformation of the Korean economy, compared with that of Taiwan, has tended to be dominated by large conglomerates. The economies of size enjoyed by these companies may well have enabled them to engage in trade and FDI with a high created asset content at an earlier stage of their industrial development.

In Table 4.2 we set out some details of the changing industrial structure of Korean and Taiwanese imports and exports between 1968 and 1997. We find, as predicted, that the coefficients of correlation between the most FDI-intensive imports and exports (A-type goods) and GNP per capita are strong and positive at a 1 per cent or 5 per cent level, and that – again as predicted – the correlation between the least FDI-intensive imports and exports (B-type goods) were strongly negative, again at a 1 per cent or 5 per cent level. The relationship between goods of average FDI intensity (O goods) and GNP per capita was shown to be more mixed.

Table 4.1 The FDI intensity of Korean and Taiwanese imports and exports and GNP per capita

		GNP per capita ($)		Imports $((A_m+O_m)/T_m)$		Exports $((A_x+O_x)/T_x)$	
		Korea	Taiwan	Korea	Taiwan	Korea	Taiwan
S1	1968	54	304	55.8	33.2	10.1	13.6
	1969	68	345	57.0	32.0	10.6	22.6
S2	1970	85	389	51.1	33.0	5.2	11.1
	1971	103	443	54.6	29.3	7.3	10.7
	1972	124	522	63.9	27.1	37.1	10.5
	1973	158	695	62.2	25.2	38.9	10.2
	1974	216	920	65.3	27.9	36.3	15.7
	1975	285	964	64.6	32.8	38.3	15.9
	1976	385	1 132	69.1	32.9	32.4	13.6
	1977	489	1 301	56.7	34.4	18.3	15.6
	1978	649	1 577	60.4	52.7	18.1	22.2
	1979	821	1 920	61.8	52.6	21.0	22.8
	1980	964	2 344	54.4	51.3	19.3	25.1
	1981	1 176	2 669	59.2	51.9	17.9	25.2
	1982	1 327	2 635	62.1	50.9	15.0	24.8
	1983	1 556	2 823	64.7	53.0	17.7	26.7
	1984	1 758	3 167	65.5	57.4	20.7	29.3
	1985	1 943	3 297	68.7	56.7	21.6	30.5
S3	1986	2 255	3 993	66.1	60.0	25.6	31.8
	1987	2 636	5 275	64.0	61.5	34.1	34.3
	1988	3 126	6 333	65.1	61.5	36.1	38.8
	1989	3 485	7 512	63.3	62.4	35.4	40.2
	1990	4 158	7 954	61.7	62.8	36.4	43.8
	1991	4 948	8 815	60.4	62.9	37.9	45.8
S4	1992	5 457	10 470	60.4	63.5	40.2	48.6
	1993	6 009	10 852	66.0	61.8	42.4	51.4
	1994	6 805	11 597	65.4	64.1	46.8	53.3
	1995	7 740	12 396	63.9	65.9	53.2	57.9
	1996	8 486	12 872	74.8	68.8	56.3	59.3
	1997	9 046	13 198	74.7	67.9	58.2	60.9
Coefficients	GNP			0.0012**	0.0026*	0.0038**	0.0035***
R^2				0.4254	0.4687	0.5967	0.9213
Coefficients	GNP^2			0.0015**	0.0011*		
R^2				0.2287	0.1107		

Table 4.1   continued

Notes:
1.   * significant at 0.1 level, ** 0.05 level, *** 0.01 level
2.   The relevant equations for imports (*Im*) and exports (*Ex*) were as follows: $Im = a+b^*GNP$, $Im = a+b^*GNP^2$, $Ex = a+b^*GNP$.
3.   The coefficients and R^2 for the imports were estimated by regressing imports on GNP^2 as well as GNP in order to examine the curvilinear relationship between imports and GNP.
4.   It is difficult to identify precisely the span of each of the stages of development based upon *the international investment position* of the two countries, as their GNPs per capita and policies towards inward and outward FDI in any given year differ from each other. But very roughly, and in both cases, stage 1 lasted between 1968 and 1969; stage 2, which, in fact, can be broken down into two subperiods (1970–78 and 1979–85), from 1970 to 1985; stage 3 from 1986 to 1991; stage 4 from 1992 to 1997.

The second hypothesis (H2) relates to the relationship between the IDP and the level and structure of a country's economic development. As with H1, H2 is subdivided into two parts. H2a avers that *both inward and outward FDI will be positively correlated to the level of economic development (that is GNP per capita) and that, initially, outward FDI will lag inward FDI, but later will rise more rapidly than it, before settling into a 'fluctuating equilibrium'*.[16]

H2b relates the IDP to the structure of economic development. It suggests that *the proportion of FDI directed to the production of above-average or average FDI-intensive (A+O/T) goods will rise as countries move along their IDPs, but with the proportion of FDI-intensive goods accounted for by outward FDI lagging that of inward FDI.*

The data on inward FDI and outward FDI, as set out in Table 4.3, though less detailed or comprehensive than those on trade, support H2a. The correlation coefficients between manufacturing inward FDI and outward FDI for Korea and Taiwan and GNP per capita are positive and significant at a 1 per cent level. The respective coefficients for the proportion of outward FDI to inward FDI are less buoyant, though still significant. This is partly because, in the early part of the period, there were large percentage fluctuations in the values in both variables (and particularly outward FDI), and partly because, at the end of the period, there was a marked resurgence in inward FDI in both Korea and Taiwan, and a cutback in outward FDI in the case of Korea.

The data set out in Table 4.4 suggest that H2b is only modestly supported. The correlation coefficient between the share of above-average or average FDI-intensive inward FDI and outward FDI flows and GNP per capita is positive for both countries, but only significant in the case of inward FDI for Taiwan and outward FDI for Korea.

The FDI data disaggregated into three degrees of created asset intensity deliver more detailed information on H2b. As Table 4.5 shows, throughout the period, for each of these types, there were relatively large percentage fluctuations for both inward FDI and outward FDI for Korea and Taiwan. Nonetheless, taking the A and O types together, the data modestly support our predictions, and the expected minus coefficients for the least FDI-intensive products (*B/T*) ratio, though not significant, provide consistent support for the idea that, as development proceeds, the structure of inward FDI and outward FDI undergoes systematic change. The conclusive remarks for H2b, however, should be reserved at this point. The classification of FDI into A, O and B types is conducted at the 2-digit SITC level, which is less detailed and hence less reliable in examining sectoral compositions and their patterns of change.

We now turn to examining the relationship between the pattern of the IDPs and TDPs. What might this relationship be? Our hypothesis (H3), following the discussion of the two paths set out earlier in the chapter and in Figure 4.1, is that *both inward FDI and outward FDI flows in above-average and average FDI-intensive sectors will be positively correlated with their counterparts in trade; but that (A+O) inward FDI will lag (A+O) imports but lead (A+O) exports while (A+O) outward FDI will lag (A+O) exports.*

As set out in Table 4.6, both inward FDI and outward FDI flows in FDI-intensive sectors are positively related to the trade flows in FDI-intensive sectors, with surges in the FDI intensity of inward FDI and outward FDI broadly corresponding to those of exports and imports. Moreover, the positive coefficients of all the equations support the proposition that imports lead inward FDI, that inward FDI leads exports, and also that exports lead outward FDI, though only two out of the six coefficients were statistically significant.[17]

We checked the proposition on a sequence separately for trade and FDI. As shown in Table 4.7, the A+O imports ratio led the A+O exports ratio. When it comes to the FDI data, however, these did not support the leading and lagging sequence between the inward and outward FDI A+O ratios. This may be explained by the fact that an industrial upgrading of both economies has been directed intentionally by government policy which, in the early stages of the IDP, made a conscious attempt to attract FDI towards more capital-intensive sectors and, in the later stages, towards more technology-intensive sectors. These complexities might have prevented us from obtaining a more robust result in practice with respect to the sequencing of imports, inward FDI, exports and outward FDI in Table 4.6.

Our fourth hypothesis (H4) is based on the idea that, as countries develop, the determinants of trade and FDI become less closely related to the comparative advantages of their natural resource endowments, and more to those of their created assets, and also the presence or absence of firm-specific scale economies, including those which result in inward FDI

*Table 4.2   Proportion of A, O and B-type imports and exports as a
percentage of total imports and exports*   .

	GNP per head ($)		Type A			
			Korea		Taiwan	
	Korea	Taiwan	Imports	Exports	Imports	Exports
S1 1968	54	304	26.9	0.0	15.0	8.3
1969	68	345	30.1	0.0	14.3	17.6
S2 1970	85	389	33.4	0.0	16.6	5.8
1971	103	443	35.4	0.0	12.4	5.8
1972	124	522	42.4	28.8	10.4	6.2
1973	158	695	49.7	30.1	8.5	5.7
1974	216	920	36.0	26.0	10.9	9.5
1975	285	964	43.6	22.4	12.0	8.8
1976	385	1132	43.7	20.3	11.6	5.9
1977	489	1301	31.7	10.4	12.3	6.4
1978	649	1577	33.2	9.2	28.9	13.8
1979	821	1920	34.6	10.7	28.6	14.0
1980	964	2344	31.8	8.7	26.2	15.4
1981	1176	2669	33.4	7.9	27.2	15.3
1982	1327	2635	34.7	8.0	28.2	15.2
1983	1556	2823	35.0	10.4	29.1	16.4
1984	1758	3167	33.9	12.5	32.0	19.0
1985	1943	3297	33.5	13.7	31.5	19.8
S3 1986	2255	3993	44.8	20.7	32.8	21.0
1987	2636	5275	43.9	25.1	34.4	23.3
1988	3126	6333	47.6	27.1	35.7	26.4
1989	3485	7512	45.6	25.9	36.8	27.1
1990	4158	7954	43.7	25.9	37.5	29.9
1991	4948	8815	43.1	27.9	36.7	31.2
S4 1992	5457	10470	45.4	30.5	39.9	33.2
1993	6009	10852	46.7	33.8	39.4	35.2
1994	6805	11597	46.1	38.6	40.7	36.7
1995	7740	12396	46.2	45.7	41.8	40.8
1996	8486	12872	54.6	49.1	42.6	42.9
1997	9046	13198	57.4	52.0	44.4	47.1
Coefficients			0.002^{***}	0.004^{***}	0.0021^{**}	0.0027^{***}
R^2			0.5894	0.6597	0.5412	0.9410

| Type O | | | | Type B | | | |
| Korea | | Taiwan | | Korea | | Taiwan | |
Imports	Exports	Imports	Exports	Imports	Exports	Imports	Exports
28.9	10.1	18.3	5.3	44.2	89.9	66.8	86.4
26.9	10.6	17.7	5.0	43.0	89.4	68.0	77.4
17.7	5.2	16.4	5.3	48.9	94.8	67.0	88.9
19.2	7.3	17.0	4.9	45.4	92.7	70.7	89.3
21.5	8.3	16.7	4.3	36.1	62.9	72.9	89.5
12.5	8.8	16.7	4.5	37.8	61.1	74.8	89.8
29.3	10.3	16.9	6.3	34.7	63.7	72.1	84.3
21.0	16.0	20.8	7.0	35.4	61.7	67.2	84.1
25.5	12.2	21.3	7.6	30.9	67.6	67.2	86.5
25.2	8.0	22.2	9.2	43.1	81.7	65.6	84.4
27.3	8.9	23.8	8.4	39.6	81.9	47.3	77.8
27.3	10.3	24.0	8.8	38.2	79.0	47.4	77.2
22.7	10.6	25.1	9.7	45.6	80.7	48.7	74.9
25.8	10.0	24.8	9.9	40.9	82.1	48.1	74.8
27.4	7.6	22.7	9.6	37.9	84.4	49.1	75.2
29.7	7.3	23.9	10.2	35.3	82.2	47.0	73.3
31.6	8.3	25.4	10.2	34.6	79.3	42.6	70.7
35.2	7.9	25.2	10.6	31.3	78.4	43.3	69.5
21.3	8.9	27.2	10.8	33.9	70.4	40.0	68.2
20.1	9.0	27.1	11.1	36.0	65.9	38.5	65.7
17.5	9.0	25.8	12.5	34.9	63.9	38.5	61.2
17.7	9.5	25.6	13.1	36.7	64.6	37.6	59.8
18.0	10.4	25.2	13.9	38.3	63.6	37.2	56.2
17.3	10.0	26.2	14.6	39.6	62.1	37.1	54.2
20.5	9.6	23.6	15.4	34.1	59.8	36.5	51.4
19.3	8.7	22.4	16.2	34.0	57.6	38.2	48.6
19.3	8.2	23.5	16.6	34.6	53.2	35.9	46.7
17.7	7.4	24.1	17.1	36.1	46.8	34.1	42.1
20.2	7.2	26.2	16.4	25.1	43.7	31.1	40.7
17.3	6.2	23.5	13.9	25.3	41.8	32.1	39.1
-0.0009^*	-0.0001	0.0005	0.0008^{***}	-0.0012^{**}	-0.0039^{**}	-0.0026^{**}	-0.0035^{***}
0.2477	0.0352	0.2303	0.7829	0.4306	0.5982	0.4685	0.9207

Note: * significant at 0.1 level, ** 0.05 level, *** 0.01 level; *Im* (or *Ex*) $= a + b^* GNP$ for each type of A, O and B.

MNEs and industrial development

Table 4.3   Inward and outward direct investment and GNP per capita

| | GNP per capita ($) | | Inward FDI ($ mil.) | | | |
| | Korea | Taiwan | Korea | | Taiwan | |
			Total	Man.	Total	Man.
S1 1968	54	304		13	90	66
1969	68	345		12	109	86
S2 1970	85	389		58	139	107
1971	103	443		29	163	132
1972	124	522		58	127	80
1973	158	695		175	249	221
1974	216	920		128	189	160
1975	285	964		52	118	83
1976	385	1 132		53	142	124
1977	489	1 301	<800>*	80	164	94
1978	649	1 577	101	68	213	138
1979	821	1 920	195	111	329	232
1980	964	2 344	131	97	466	435
1981	1 176	2 669	152	115	396	263
1982	1 327	2 635	128	112	380	233
1983	1 556	2 823	122	72	404	341
1984	1 758	3 167	193	29	559	502
1985	1 943	3 297	236	168	702	541
S3 1986	2 255	3 993	477	242	770	584
1987	2 636	5 275	626	375	1 419	984
1988	3 126	6 333	894	559	1 183	742
1989	3 485	7 512	812	504	2 418	1 628
1990	4 158	7 954	895	596	2 302	1 445
1991	4 948	8 815	1 177	941	1 778	1 242
S4 1992	5 457	10 470	803	605	1 461	742
1993	6 009	10 852	1 044	527	1 213	599
1994	6 805	11 597	1 317	402	1 630	781
1995	7 740	12 396	1 941	883	2 925	1 813
1996	8 486	12 872	3 203	1 930	2 460	817
1997	9 046	13 198	6 971	2 348	4 266	2 245
Coefficients				0.156***		0.0718***
R^2				0.7231		0.6317

Outward FDI ($ mil.)				Outward FDI / Inward FDI ($ mil.)			
Korea		Taiwan		Korea		Taiwan	
Total	Man.	Total	Man.	Total	Man.	Total	Man.
		1.8	1.8			0.02	0.03
		0.1	0.0			0.00	0.00
		0.5	0.4			0.00	0.00
		1.2	1.0			0.01	0.01
		4.1	3.7			0.03	0.05
		3.2	3.4			0.01	0.02
		7.3	7.0			0.04	0.04
		2.4	1.4			0.02	0.02
		4.4	3.9			0.03	0.03
<94>		13.8	12.3			0.08	0.13
38		5.2	3.0			0.02	0.02
98		9.3	6.3			0.03	0.03
21	<36>	42.0	37.2			0.09	0.09
109	34	11.0	7.4	0.72	0.30	0.03	0.03
121	2	12.0	9.6	0.98	0.02	0.03	0.04
83	36	11.0	9.9	0.68	0.50	0.03	0.03
67	9	39.0	33.7	0.37	0.31	0.07	0.07
219	8	42.0	35.1	0.93	0.05	0.06	0.06
364	184	57.0	35.9	0.76	0.76	0.07	0.06
367	109	103.0	71.6	0.59	0.29	0.07	0.07
478	212	219.0	86.0	0.53	0.38	0.19	0.12
943	454	931.0	649.8	1.16	0.90	0.39	0.40
1 611	969	1 552.0	915.3	1.80	1.63	0.67	0.63
1 511	677	1 656.0	885.8	1.28	0.72	0.93	0.71
1 206	693	887.0	378.5	1.50	1.15	0.61	0.51
1 876	1 137	1 661.0	703.1	1.80	2.16	1.37	1.17
3 581	2 179	1 617.0	542.4	2.72	5.42	0.99	0.69
4 949	2 939	1 357.0	553.8	1.51	3.32	0.46	0.31
6 220	3 562	2 165.0	622.4	1.94	1.85	0.88	0.76
5 845	2 737	2 894.0	978.1	0.84	1.17	0.68	0.44
0.4666***		0.0553***		0.0004*		0.00006***	
0.8811		0.678		0.4598		0.8807	

Notes:
1. *significant at 0.1 level, ** 0.05 level, *** 0.01 level.
2. The relevant equations for FDI were as follows: *IDI* (or *ODI* and *ODI/IDI*) = $a+b^*GNP$.
3. < > is cumulated value.

Table 4.4 *Proportion of IDI and ODI accounted for by FDI-intensive sectors*

	GNP per capita ($)		IDI $((A_i+O_i)/T_i)$		ODI $((A_o+O_o)/T_o)$	
	Korea	Taiwan	Korea	Taiwan	Korea	Taiwan
S1 1968	54	304	53.8	75.1		65.6
1969	68	345	75.0	88.9		n.a.
S2 1970	85	389	84.5	83.7		24.2
1971	103	443	55.2	40.8		56.7
1972	124	522	84.8	87.1		42.8
1973	158	695	47.4	71.0		54.9
1974	216	920	59.7	60.6		56.5
1975	285	964	60.4	77.9		32.7
1976	385	1 132	85.2	78.9		41.4
1977	489	1 301	91.0	83.4		88.6
1978	649	1 577	94.1	86.0		69.3
1979	821	1 920	89.1	67.6		71.8
1980	964	2 344	92.7	47.0	<59.5>	96.1
1981	1 176	2 669	82.8	77.1	6.8	44.3
1982	1 327	2 635	89.3	70.2	56.2	0.0
1983	1 556	2 823	93.1	90.6	89.9	36.6
1984	1 758	3 167	93.0	94.5	79.8	82.1
1985	1 943	3 297	94.6	86.6	80.1	86.7
S3 1986	2 255	3 993	93.4	87.9	31.0	81.5
1987	2 636	5 275	93.9	78.7	30.5	87.3
1988	3 126	6 333	92.2	79.8	35.6	87.9
1989	3 485	7 512	91.3	80.8	34.5	89.9
1990	4 158	7 954	94.3	80.0	66.6	74.5
1991	4 948	8 815	95.3	80.8	53.6	38.5
S4 1992	5 457	10 470	84.4	87.9	55.5	63.3
1993	6 009	10 852	90.2	75.0	64.4	62.3
1994	6 805	11 597	88.0	81.6	67.4	71.9
1995	7 740	12 396	80.1	94.8	71.2	57.5
1996	8 486	12 872	91.2	83.6	75.6	59.5
1997	9 046	13 198	85.2	56.3	65.6	65.2
Coefficients			0.0017	0.0009*	0.0033*	0.0019
R^2			0.1226	0.2346	0.5415	0.2031

Note: * significant at 0.1 level, ** 0.05 level, *** 0.01 level; *IDI* (or, *ODI*) = $a+b^*$GNP

or outward FDI. Figure 4.1 has already suggested that, in their early stages of development, countries will primarily engage in inter-industry trade. This is followed by inter-industry FDI. Later, and partly as the result of inward FDI, *intra*-industry trade will start to rise, and then eventually, usually much later, intra-industry FDI will also take place.

The fourth hypothesis, like the first two, can be broken into two parts. The first (H4a) is that *the proportion of intra-industry trade*[18] *for A- and O-type products will be positively related to GNP per capita.* The second (H4b) is that *the growth of intra-industry FDI for A- and O-type products will also be positively correlated to GNP per capita, but will lag the growth of intra-industry trade.*

As the data in Table 4.8 and respective correlation coefficients and R^2s show, there is some support for H4a, that is, that the significance of intra-industry trade is positively related to economic development. In respect of H4b, there is also some suggestion that the growth of intra-industry FDI lags that of intra-industry trade. However, there is no real evidence that intra-industry FDI for A and O-type products grows as the economy develops. Again FDI sectoral classification at a two-digit level hampers any definitive analysis of these issues.

CONCLUSIONS

The main conclusion of this chapter is that the understanding of the contents and determinants of the IDP is considerably enriched when trade levels and patterns are encompassed within its ambit. Statistical data from the Korean and Taiwanese economies generally support the idea of an integrated TDP and IDP, and that the growth of each tends to be positively correlated to GNP per capita, and to the created asset intensity of the manufacturing sector. As development proceeds, the composition of both trade and FDI becomes more FDI-intensive, with intra-industry trade and intra-industry FDI assuming an increasing proportion of all trade and FDI, but with intra-industry FDI lagging that of trade. These results are consistent for both Korea and Taiwan. Indeed, little country variance exists, which supports the idea that the two economies have followed similar industrial development paths. There is also a strong suggestion that changes in the sectoral composition of exports lag those of imports. However, there is no evidence that the FDI intensity of outward FDI follows that of inward FDI. Interestingly, for both Korea and Taiwan, the A+O/T ratio of FDI was consistently higher than that of trade. This may imply that both Korea and Taiwan are special cases of truncated, FDI-centred economic

MNEs and industrial development

Table 4.5   Proportion of A, O and B-type FDI as a percentage of total FDI

| | GNP per capita ($) | | Type A | | | |
| | | | Korea | | Taiwan | |
	Korea	Taiwan	IDI	ODI	IDI	ODI
1968	54	304	53.85		71.82	40.81
1969	68	345	75.00		86.72	n.a.
1970	85	389	81.03		83.49	24.15
1971	103	443	48.28		40.69	35.47
1972	124	522	77.97		86.21	2.68
1973	158	695	30.29		70.24	28.91
1974	216	920	56.59		58.18	10.45
1975	285	964	58.49		75.77	29.02
1976	385	1 132	79.63		76.26	41.37
1977	489	1 301	89.74		81.68	88.59
1978	649	1 577	92.65		85.55	68.21
1979	821	1 920	78.18		63.89	71.83
1980	964	2 344	91.67	22.25	43.76	95.47
1981	1 176	2 669	72.41	5.19	70.08	44.34
1982	1 327	2 635	82.14	10.96	61.43	0.00
1983	1 556	2 823	81.94	84.65	87.48	36.64
1984	1 758	3 167	82.03	9.43	92.61	82.09
1985	1 943	3 297	89.88	46.53	82.66	80.24
1986	2 255	3 993	83.82	29.05	86.23	81.51
1987	2 636	5 275	80.80	29.27	70.86	80.35
1988	3 126	6 333	84.31	25.16	72.10	85.66
1989	3 485	7 512	82.18	21.94	67.38	89.92
1990	4 158	7 954	88.55	49.10	72.35	56.59
1991	4 948	8 815	92.78	36.01	77.68	36.93
1992	5 457	10 470	66.17	41.38	80.47	62.20
1993	6 009	10 852	80.41	51.31	65.76	60.28
1994	6 805	11 597	82.45	59.47	69.70	59.98
1995	7 740	12 396	77.70	59.27	57.26	21.02
1996	8 486	12 872	77.09	64.07	23.33	15.91
1997	9 046	13 198	48.25	54.37	28.50	20.09
Coefficients			−0.0002	0.0044***	−0.002**	0.0001
Adj. R^2			0.0005	0.5738	0.1711	0.0002

| | Type O | | | | Type B | | | |
| | Korea | | Taiwan | | Korea | | Taiwan | |
IDI	ODI	IDI	ODI	IDI	ODI	IDI	ODI
0.00		3.27	24.82	46.15		24.91	34.37
0.00		2.22	n.a.	25.00		11.06	n.a.
3.45		0.21	0.00	15.52		16.30	75.85
6.90		0.11	18.18	44.83		59.20	46.34
6.78		0.91	40.13	15.25		12.88	57.2
17.14		0.75	25.94	52.57		29.02	45.15
3.10		2.37	46.10	40.31		39.44	43.46
1.89		2.12	3.70	39.02		22.12	67.28
5.56		2.63	0.00	14.81		21.11	58.63
1.28		1.76	0.00	8.97		16.56	11.41
1.47		0.49	1.10	5.88		13.96	30.69
10.91		3.75	0.00	10.91		32.36	28.17
1.04	37.23	3.22	0.65	7.29	40.52	53.02	3.88
10.34	1.61	6.99	0.00	17.24	93.20	22.92	55.56
7.14	45.24	8.76	0.00	10.71	43.80	29.81	100
11.11	5.30	3.16	0.00	6.94	10.05	9.36	63.36
10.94	70.38	1.85	0.00	7.03	20.19	5.54	17.91
4.76	33.54	3.89	6.40	5.36	19.93	13.45	13.35
9.54	1.95	1.62	0.00	6.64	69.01	12.15	18.49
13.07	1.24	7.83	6.98	6.13	69.48	21.31	12.67
7.84	10.41	7.67	2.22	7.84	64.44	20.23	12.12
9.11	12.61	13.46	0.01	8.71	65.45	19.15	10.07
5.72	17.50	7.63	17.88	5.72	33.40	10.03	25.53
2.55	17.61	3.09	1.56	4.67	46.38	19.23	61.51
18.24	14.09	7.41	1.06	15.59	44.53	12.13	36.74
9.79	13.04	9.24	2.05	9.79	35.65	25.00	37.68
5.50	7.89	11.93	11.92	12.05	32.63	18.37	28.1
3.15	11.95	1.48	2.45	19.15	28.78	5.21	42.48
14.15	11.50	4.40	1.20	8.76	24.43	16.45	40.5
36.90	11.27	1.12	1.93	14.85	34.36	43.72	34.85
0.0011***	−0.0014	0.0003*	−0.001	−0.0016	−0.0022	−0.0003	−0.012
0.2853	0.0451	0.1445	0.0682	0.0391	0.0713	0.0175	0.0209

Note: * significant at 0.1 level, ** 0.05 level, *** 0.01 level; (*IDI* or *ODI*) = $a+b^*GNP$ for each type of A, O and B.

Table 4.6 The FDI-intensity of Korean and Taiwanese trade and FDI (I)

	Imports $((A_m+O_m)/T_m)$ Korea	Taiwan	IDI $((A_i+O_i)/T_i)$ Korea	Taiwan	Exports $((A_x+O_x)/T_x)$ Korea	Taiwan	ODI $((A_o+O_o)/T_o)$ Korea	Taiwan
S1 1968	55.8	33.2	53.8	75.1	10.1	13.6		65.6
1969	57.0	32.0	75.0	88.9	10.6	22.6		n.a.
S2 1970	51.1	33.0	84.5	83.7	5.2	11.1		24.2
1971	54.6	29.3	55.2	40.8	7.3	10.7		56.7
1972	63.9	27.1	84.8	87.1	37.1	10.5		42.8
1973	62.2	25.2	47.4	71.0	38.9	10.2		54.9
1974	65.3	27.9	59.7	60.6	36.3	15.7		56.5
1975	64.6	32.8	60.4	77.9	38.3	15.9		32.7
1976	69.1	32.9	85.2	78.9	32.4	13.6		41.4
1977	56.7	34.4	91.0	83.4	18.3	15.6		88.6
1978	60.4	52.7	94.1	86.0	18.1	22.2		69.3
1979	61.8	52.6	89.1	67.6	21.0	22.8		71.8
1980	54.4	51.3	92.7	47.0	19.3	25.1	<59.5>	96.1
1981	59.2	51.9	82.8	77.1	17.9	25.2	6.8	44.3
1982	62.1	50.9	89.3	70.2	15.0	24.8	56.2	0.0
1983	64.7	53.0	93.1	90.6	17.7	26.7	89.9	36.6
1984	65.5	57.4	93.0	94.5	20.7	29.3	79.8	82.1
1985	68.7	56.7	94.6	86.6	21.6	30.5	80.1	86.7
S3 1986	66.1	60.0	93.4	87.9	25.6	31.8	31.0	81.5
1987	64.0	61.5	93.9	78.7	34.1	34.3	30.5	87.3
1988	65.1	61.5	92.2	79.8	36.1	38.8	35.6	87.9
1989	63.3	62.4	91.3	80.8	35.4	40.2	34.5	89.9
1990	61.7	62.8	94.3	80.0	36.4	43.8	66.6	74.5
1991	60.4	62.9	95.3	80.8	37.9	45.8	53.6	38.5
S4 1992	60.4	63.5	84.4	87.9	40.2	48.6	55.5	63.3
1993	66.0	61.8	90.2	75.0	42.4	51.4	64.4	62.3
1994	65.4	64.1	88.0	81.6	46.8	53.3	67.4	71.9
1995	63.9	65.9	80.1	94.8	53.2	57.9	71.2	57.5
1996	74.8	68.8	91.2	83.6	56.3	59.3	75.6	59.5
1997	74.7	67.9	85.2	56.3	58.2	60.9	65.6	65.2
Coefficients			0.1623	0.2345*	0.1866**	0.0157	0.6904	0.3425
R^2			0.0047	0.1054	0.2066	0.0048	0.0201	0.0339

Note: * significant at 0.1 level, ** 0.05 level, *** 0.01 level; $IDI = a+b*Im$, $Ex = a+b*IDI$, $ODI = a+b*Ex$.

Table 4.7 The FDI-intensity of Korean and Taiwanese trade and FDI (II)

	Imports $((A_m+O_m)/T_m)$		Exports $((A_x+O_x)/T_x)$		IDI $((A_i+O_i)/T_i)$		ODI $((A_o+O_o)/T_o)$	
	Korea	Taiwan	Korea	Taiwan	Korea	Taiwan	Korea	Taiwan
S1 1968	55.8	33.2	10.1	13.6	53.8	75.1		65.6
1969	57.0	32.0	10.6	22.6	75.0	88.9		n.a.
S2 1970	51.1	33.0	5.2	11.1	84.5	83.7		24.2
1971	54.6	29.3	7.3	10.7	55.2	40.8		56.7
1972	63.9	27.1	37.1	10.5	84.8	87.1		42.8
1973	62.2	25.2	38.9	10.2	47.4	71.0		54.9
1974	65.3	27.9	36.3	15.7	59.7	60.6		56.5
1975	64.6	32.8	38.3	15.9	60.4	77.9		32.7
1976	69.1	32.9	32.4	13.6	85.2	78.9		41.4
1977	56.7	34.4	18.3	15.6	91.0	83.4		88.6
1978	60.4	52.7	18.1	22.2	94.1	86.0		69.3
1979	61.8	52.6	21.0	22.8	89.1	67.6		71.8
1980	54.4	51.3	19.3	25.1	92.7	47.0	<59.5>	96.1
1981	59.2	51.9	17.9	25.2	82.8	77.1	6.8	44.3
1982	62.1	50.9	15.0	24.8	89.3	70.2	56.2	0.0
1983	64.7	53.0	17.7	26.7	93.1	90.6	89.9	36.6
1984	65.5	57.4	20.7	29.3	93.0	94.5	79.8	82.1
1985	68.7	56.7	21.6	30.5	94.6	86.6	80.1	86.7
S3 1986	66.1	60.0	25.6	31.8	93.4	87.9	31.0	81.5
1987	64.0	61.5	34.1	34.3	93.9	78.7	30.5	87.3
1988	65.1	61.5	36.1	38.8	92.2	79.8	35.6	87.9
1989	63.3	62.4	35.4	40.2	91.3	80.8	34.5	89.9
1990	61.7	62.8	36.4	43.8	94.3	80.0	66.6	74.5
1991	60.4	62.9	37.9	45.8	95.3	80.8	53.6	38.5
S4 1992	60.4	63.5	40.2	48.6	84.4	87.9	55.5	63.3
1993	66.0	61.8	42.4	51.4	90.2	75.0	64.4	62.3
1994	65.4	64.1	46.8	53.3	88.0	81.6	67.4	71.9
1995	63.9	65.9	53.2	57.9	80.1	94.8	71.2	57.5
1996	74.8	68.8	56.3	59.3	91.2	83.6	75.6	59.5
1997	74.7	67.9	58.2	60.9	85.2	56.3	65.6	65.2
Coefficients			0.7301***	0.3993**			0.0847	−0.3413
R^2			0.2565	0.1711			0.0006	0.0658

Note: * significant at 0.1 level, ** 0.05 level, *** 0.01 level; $Ex = a+b*Im$, $ODI = a+b*IDI$.

89

Table 4.8   Intra-industry trade and FDI

| | GNP per capita ($) | | Intra-industry trade | | | |
| | | | Type A | | Type O | |
	Korea	Taiwan	Korea	Taiwan	Korea	Taiwan
S1 1968	54	304	0.0	65.6	8.0	48.1
1969	68	345	0.0	68.4	11.3	49.3
S2 1970	85	389	0.0	56.2	10.0	52.6
1971	103	443	0.0	75.5	18.5	54.6
1972	124	522	63.2	93.0	41.5	54.9
1973	158	695	68.0	97.3	74.7	54.6
1974	216	920	69.4	94.7	41.0	55.4
1975	285	964	56.4	92.6	73.8	56.7
1976	385	1 132	63.8	85.4	65.1	68.9
1977	489	1 301	56.6	90.1	55.1	78.6
1978	649	1 577	46.9	85.5	52.9	70.8
1979	821	1 920	47.5	85.9	55.1	71.5
1980	964	2 344	52.6	95.1	75.5	74.6
1981	1 176	2 669	50.3	94.8	71.6	78.1
1982	1 327	2 635	55.3	96.7	63.4	84.7
1983	1 556	2 823	64.1	98.2	56.1	87.5
1984	1 758	3 167	71.2	91.5	56.3	88.8
1985	1 943	3 297	75.8	84.5	50.4	95.6
S3 1986	2 255	3 993	84.6	85.8	79.9	90.4
1987	2 636	5 275	97.2	86.3	85.2	88.6
1988	3 126	6 333	95.1	91.5	90.0	87.4
1989	3 485	7 512	89.8	92.3	86.8	89.6
1990	4 158	7 954	88.7	89.5	87.4	92.1
1991	4 948	8 815	88.7	88.2	83.6	90.9
S4 1992	5 457	10 470	95.8	93.5	78.3	94.0
1993	6 009	10 852	97.8	92.4	78.8	97.1
1994	6 805	11 597	97.5	92.8	69.7	95.1
1995	7 740	12 396	92.4	91.2	66.1	93.6
1996	8 486	12 872	96.0	84.3	60.2	91.4
1997	9 046	13 198	89.8	84.8	65.2	86.2
Coefficients			0.0082**	0.000	0.0022**	0.0028***
R^2			0.5719	0.0009	0.5791	0.7846

| | | Intra-industry FDI | | | | | |
| Type B | | Type A | | Type O | | Type B | |
Korea	Taiwan	Korea	Taiwan	Korea	Taiwan	Korea	Taiwan
39.0	82.7		3.02		33.99		7.18
48.1	86.2		0.00		0.00		0.00
51.8	80.7		0.22		0.00		3.53
70.8	75.3		1.32		88.15		1.19
91.4	71.7		0.29		65.23		34.51
84.2	73.9		1.26		69.66		4.68
85.2	90.3		1.57		92.22		9.26
85.7	81.1		1.28		5.73		9.77
62.3	69.4		3.32		0.00		15.89
61.0	66.3		24.77		0.00		16.47
60.9	56.1		3.40		39.35		9.10
64.9	58.8		5.96		0.00		4.64
60.6	59.4		31.41		3.37		1.24
51.6	57.2	4.14	3.51	8.76	0.00	77.12	12.81
42.4	54.7	0.60	0.00	24.85	0.00	16.78	24.33
42.8	52.3	67.84	2.41	38.32	0.00	83.67	32.97
45.1	46.5	1.64	11.21	63.15	0.00	34.15	35.58
42.1	44.6	4.53	11.87	47.95	19.31	28.56	12.12
46.5	44.1	41.84	10.99	26.94	0.00	22.38	17.11
49.7	46.3	19.02	15.24	5.41	12.18	46.65	8.29
51.1	56.3	20.27	24.18	66.81	6.50	48.71	12.97
56.8	56.6	38.70	69.51	89.14	0.05	25.80	34.69
62.0	60.0	95.01	66.27	33.39	80.47	19.00	89.36
68.2	62.8	43.59	50.66	33.53	52.94	24.59	60.94
58.8	68.4	83.54	56.54	93.97	13.56	46.77	78.60
58.0	75.2	84.14	96.33	51.65	41.24	22.59	72.22
68.3	75.0	40.70	74.83	22.77	81.94	12.74	96.97
79.1	78.8	56.54	29.10	14.67	87.09	33.35	57.27
64.7	72.4	77.59	74.99	78.66	38.60	31.76	69.54
61.8	78.2	86.44	64.69	52.51	92.03	54.14	51.54
0.0032**	0.0029***	−0.0009	−0.0002	0.0002	0.0007	−0.0012**	−0.0026***
0.4492	0.9263	0.1288	0.1494	0.0146	0.4433	0.4714	0.7272

Notes:
1. * significant at 0.1 level, ** 0.05 level, *** 0.01 level.
2. *Intra-trade* (or *Intra-FDI*) = $a + b^* GNP$.
3. *Intra-industry trade* = $[1 - abs(X_i - M_i)/(X_i + M_i)]^* 100$, where X = exports and M = imports, *Intra-industry FDI* = $[1 - abs(O_i - I_i)/(O_i + I_i)]^* 100$, where O = outward FDI, I = inward FDI and '*abs*' means the absolute value.

development, the explanation of which is somewhat different from what our general theorizing would suggest.

NOTES

1. We are most grateful for some helpful comments on an earlier draft of this chapter made by H. Peter Gray.
2. The most recent exposition of the IDP is set out in Narula (1996), Dunning and Narula (1996).
3. See Dunning (1992) for a fuller discussion of the difference between natural assets – the fruits of the earth and unskilled labour and created assets, for example, technological and organizational capacity, skilled and professional labor, the fund of individual and corporate experience. Created assets may be tangible or intangible; they represent the intellectual and institutional capital of firms and countries, be they embodied in goods or in services.
4. What in Dunning and Narula (1996) we have referred to as strategic asset-seeking FDI.
5. We have elsewhere (Dunning and Narula, 1996) referred to this as stages 4 or 5.
6. As, for example, shown in the case of the USA and the UK. See United Nations (1999) and earlier editions of the *World Investment Report.*
7. The significance of these variables is discussed at some length in Dunning (1981), Narula (1996), Dunning and Narula (1996) and in Chapter 3, this volume. Here we would simply observe that we include unskilled labour as a natural resource.
8. For a full examination of the different types of FDI, see Dunning (1993, ch. 3).
9. Schumpeterian (S) products are those which have a relatively high content of such assets as technology, skilled labour, managerial and organizational expertise. These are to be distinguished from those dependent on national resources: for example, land and unskilled labour. For a detailed examination of S-type goods and services, sometimes called 'dynamic' or 'advanced' goods and services, see Gray (1998, 1999). Our nomenclature for S-type products throughout this chapter will be created-asset intensive products.
10. Of course, in part, the extent of this switch depends on the fineness of the SITC classification of the products traded. Generally, the degree of inter-industry trade will decrease, as the SITC classification becomes more detailed.
11. See, for example, Balassa (1980), Chenery (1979), Chenery *et al.* (1986) and Helleiner (1989).
12. As, for example, shown by the increase in the R&D/sales ratio and by the number of patents annually registered.
13. See, too, our later discussion of FDI-intensity.
14. Even though we propose that, in general, the creative-asset intensity of FDI follows that of trade, more specifically, by dissecting trade and FDI into imports, exports, inward FDI and outward FDI, we propose the sequence of imports, inward FDI, exports and outward FDI.
15. The FDI-intensity is defined as *the proportion of sales of US foreign affiliates to the sales of their US parent companies.* The rationale for this measure (and we recognize there are several others, but these mainly relate to the technological content of goods) is that the MNE is, first and foremost, an exporter of proprietary created assets (which include not only technology but trade-marks, managerial and marketing knowhow, organizational capabilities and so on) in the markets for which it internalizes through FDI. Since the relative significance of these exports is, in part at least, industry-specific, FDI-intensity, as measured at the sectoral level, may be taken as a useful proxy for created-asset intensity. The higher this ratio, which reflects the extent to which the MNE perceives it can best exploit its O-specific advantages from a foreign location, the more we assume the created asset intensity will be. See Appendix 4.1 for further details.

16. That is, with outward FDI sometimes rising faster than inward FDI and vice versa (for example, as occurred in the case of the US international direct investment patterns over the last two decades or so).
17. We tried with lag structures ranging from 1 to 10 years to find the best statistical fit. The autocorrelation problem arising from equations with lagged variables, however, prevented us from obtaining any consistent patterns.
18. That is, the ratio between the exports and imports of a particular product or group of products: $1-(X_i-M_i)/(X_i+M_i)$, where ($_i$ = a particular product, or group of products).

REFERENCES

Balassa, B. (1980), 'The process of industrial development and alternative development strategies', *Essays in International Finance*, **141**, December, Princeton Department of Economics.

Chenery, H. (1979), *Structural Change and Development Policy*, Oxford: Oxford University Press.

Chenery, H., S. Robinson and M. Syrquin (1986), *Industrialization and Growth: a Comparative Study*, Oxford: Oxford University Press.

Dunning, J.H. (1981), 'Explaining the international position of countries towards a dynamic or developmental approach', *Weltwirtschaftliches Archiv*, **117**, 30–64.

Dunning, J.H. (1992), 'The global economy, domestic governance strategies and transnational corporations: interactions and policy implications', *Transnational Corporations*, **1** (3), 7–46.

Dunning, J.H. (1995), 'What's wrong – and right – with trade theory?', *International Trade Journal*, **2** (9), 153–202.

Dunning, J.H., and R. Narula (eds) (1996), *Foreign Investment and Governments*, London and New York: Routledge.

Dunning, J.H., and G. Norman (1986), 'Intra-industry investment', in H.P. Gray (ed.), *Uncle Sam as Host*, Greenwich, CT: JAI Press.

Gray, H.P. (1998), 'Free international economic policy in a world of Schumpeter goods', *International Trade Journal*, **3** (12), 323–44.

Gray, H.P. (1999), *Global Economic Involvement*, Copenhagen: Copenhagen Business Press.

Helleiner, G. (1989), 'Transnational corporations, direct foreign investment and economic development', in H. Chenery and T.N. Srinivasan (eds), *Handbook of Development Economics*, Amsterdam: Elsevier.

Narula, R. (1996), *Multinational Investment and Economic Structure*, London: Routledge.

United Nations (1999), *World Investment Report*, Geneva and New York: United Nations.

APPENDIX 4.1   THE DATA

Trade

Data for manufacturing exports and imports are available at a three- or four-digit level for each year from 1966 to 1997 in the case of Korea and 1968 to 1997 in the case of Taiwan. The source for Korea is the Bank of Korea and the source for Taiwan is the Ministry of Finance of Taiwan.

FDI

FDI flow data are less comprehensive. For total inward FDI and outward FDI, there are data for each year from 1968 to 1997 in the case of Taiwan, and for 1978 to 1997 in the case of Korea. For manufacturing inward FDI and outward FDI, there are data for 1968 to 1997 in the case of Taiwan, and 1981 to 1997 in the case of Korea. Sectoral data are limited to a two- or three-digit level in the case of both Korea and Taiwan. The source for FDI data for Korea is the Bank of Korea for 'outward' FDI and the Ministry of Finance of Korea for 'inward' FDI; the source for FDI data for Taiwan is the Ministry of Economic Affairs of Taiwan. Both sets of data are for 'approved' investments and exclude reinvested profits.

FDI-Intensity

We use FDI intensity as a proxy for created-asset intensity of particular products or sectors. It is measured by the proportion of the foreign sales of US MNEs to their domestic sales in 1994 as revealed in the US Department of Commerce Benchmark Survey 1998. We checked similar data for the 1982 and 1989 benchmark surveys, and the industrial composition of FDI intensity was broadly the same. We acknowledge that this ratio reflects both the locational (L) advantages (or disadvantages) of host countries and the ownership (O) advantages of US MNEs, but we think it gives a better indication of created assets than those which are purely innovation-based, for example R&D, patents and so on. For example, it incorporates such O-specific advantages as trade-marks and also proxies those advantages resulting from multinationality per se. We first calculated the ratio between the sales of overseas affiliates and the domestic (US) sales of US MNEs in all manufacturing industry. We then did the same for each sector (classified by two-, three-, and four-digit SIC). Sectors up to five percentage points above or below the average for manufacturing industry in 1994, we classified as O – average FDI-intensity. Those above five percentage points we classified as

A – above FDI-intensity. Those below five percentage points we classified as B – below FDI-intensity. We then applied these gradings to the Korean and Taiwanese classifications of exports and imports, and inward FDI and outward FDI flows as best we could.

APPENDIX 4.2   AUTOREGRESSION OF GNP PER CAPITA, TRADE AND FDI

Equations	Variables	Korea Coefficient	R^2	Taiwan Coefficient	R^2
Table 4.1					
$Im = a+b*GNP$	Imports $((A_m+O_m)/T_m)$	0.0012**	0.4254	0.0026**	0.4687
$Ex = a+b*GNP$	Exports $((A_x+O_x)/T_x)$	0.0038**	0.5967	0.0035***	0.9213
$Im = a+b*GNP^2$	Imports $((A_m+O_m)/T_m)$	0.0015**	0.2287	0.0011*	0.1107
Table 4.2					
Im (or Ex) $= a+b*GNP$	Imports (type A)	0.0020***	0.5894	0.0021**	0.5412
	Imports (type O)	−0.0009*	0.2477	0.0005	0.2303
	Imports (type B)	−0.0012**	0.4306	−0.0026**	0.4685
	Exports (type A)	0.0040***	0.6597	0.0027***	0.9410
	Exports (type O)	−0.0001	0.0352	0.0008***	0.7829
	Exports (type B)	−0.0039**	0.5982	−0.0035***	0.9207
Table 4.3					
IDI (or, ODI and ODI/IDI) $= a+b*GNP$	IDI (Manufacturing)	0.1560***	0.7231	0.0718***	0.6317
	ODI (Manufacturing)	0.4666***	0.8811	0.0553***	0.6780
	ODI/IDI (Manufacturing)	0.0004*	0.4598	0.00006***	0.8807
Table 4.4					
IDI (or, ODI) $= a+b*GNP$	IDI $((A_i+O_i)/T_i)$	0.0017	0.1226	0.0009*	0.2346
	ODI $((A_o+O_o)/T_o)$	0.0033*	0.5415	0.0019	0.2031
Table 4.5					
IDI (or, ODI) $= a+b*GNP$	IDI (type A)	−0.0002	0.0005	−0.0020**	0.1711
	IDI (type O)	0.0011***	0.2853	0.0003*	0.1445
	IDI (type B)	−0.0016	0.0391	−0.0003	0.0175
	ODI (type A)	0.0044***	0.5738	0.0001	0.0002
	ODI (type O)	−0.0014	0.0451	−0.0010	0.0682
	ODI (type B)	−0.0022	0.0713	−0.0120	0.0209

Table 4.6

$IDI = a+b*Im$				
$Ex = a+b*IDI$				
$ODI = a+b*Ex$				
$IDI ((A_i+O_i)/T_i)$	0.1623	0.0047	0.2345*	0.1054
$Exports ((A_x+O_x)/T_x)$	0.1866**	0.2066	0.0157	0.0048
$ODI ((A_o+O_o)/T_o)$	0.6904	0.0201	0.3425	0.0339

Table 4.7

$Ex = a+b*Im$				
$ODI = a+b*IDI$				
$Exports ((A_x+O_x)/T_x)$	0.7301***	0.2565	0.3993**	0.1711
$ODI ((A_o+O_o)/T_o)$	0.0847	0.0006	−0.3413	0.0658

Table 4.8

$Intra\ Trade\ (or\ intra\ FDI) = a+b*GNP$				
Intra-industry Trade (A)	0.0082**	0.5719	0.000	0.0009
Intra-industry Trade (O)	0.0022**	0.5791	0.0028***	0.7846
Intra-industry Trade (B)	0.0032**	0.4492	0.0029***	0.9263
Intra-industry FDI (A)	−0.0009	0.1288	−0.0002	0.1494
Intra-industry FDI (O)	0.0002	0.0146	0.0007	0.4433
Intra-industry FDI (B)	−0.0012**	0.4714	−0.0026***	0.7272

Note: * significant at 0.1 level, ** 0.05 level, *** 0.01.

5. Multinational firms, regional integration and globalizing markets

INTRODUCTION

Policy makers in the developing world are once again enthralled by the concept of regional integration (RI) and its potential benefits. This has led to a revival of previously unsuccessful or dormant schemes and the establishment of a clutch of new agreements. Part of this renewed enthusiasm has to do with the benefits that have accrued to members associated with various European RI schemes and NAFTA, and in particular, the experience of Mexico in NAFTA.

It is not a coincidence that this renewed interest in RI has occurred while the concept of globalization pervades our understanding of the world economy. The two are not unrelated, and some have argued that RI projects appear to represent an opportunity to redress the inequities of multilateral agreements (Baldwin, 1997) and to increase their autonomy from outside forces (Vernon, 1996). In other words, RI schemes are seen as a response to globalization. There are several similarities between globalization and RI. Both are processes closely associated with cross-border economic activity, although globalization is more a consequence of increased cross-border activity, while RI is intended to cause it. The proliferation of cross-border activity is regarded as a primary symptom of globalization. Both globalization and RI are believed to provide opportunities for more rapid economic growth, associated in large part with increased FDI and trade that are the consequence of increased opportunities to exploit economies of scale.

Much of the work on RI focuses on trade effects. This chapter seeks to examine the effect of RI on FDI flows and MNE strategies. However, other developments have also significantly affected MNE strategies, and these need to be taken into account. Three powerful influences are highlighted. First, globalization has changed the capacity and the means of MNEs to organize and coordinate their spatially distributed affiliates. Second, a broad policy shift has occurred in most developing countries from import-substituting towards export- and FDI-driven outward orientation.

Third, most countries are involved in multilateral liberalization within the framework of multilateral institutions.

MNE strategies in developing countries are examined in four separate situations: (1) in a non-RI, pre-liberalized environment, (2) with RI in a pre-liberalized environment, (3) in a non-RI, post-liberalization scenario, (4) with RI in a post-liberalization scenario. Furthermore, it is a mistake to assume that all developing countries are homogeneous. This chapter distinguishes between two groups of developing countries. Group I consists of least developed countries (LDCs) with little or no domestic industrial capacity. Group II countries possess an intermediate level of domestic capacity. These are contrasted here with industrialized countries, which are referred to as Group III.

This chapter will argue the following points. First, successful regional integration (*à la* EU, NAFTA) has been a consequence of globalization, a reinforcement of de facto integration (by globalization) with de jure integration (regional integration). Second, successful RI schemes and countries that have participated in globalization share a number of similarities. Both RI and globalization are continuing processes rather than events. Successful RI projects have been marked by considerable efforts in the development of institutions in the participating economies through structural adjustment, and the creation of appropriate cross-border institutions over a long period of time. Third, FDI does not drive economic growth, although it may help enhance it. FDI is not a sine qua non for development. Fourth, the response of MNEs to RI schemes is profit driven, and the net effect of RI schemes on the quality of their investments may well be negative, particularly for Group I countries. RI does not necessarily replace or overcome the inequities of globalization, at least as far as the activities of MNEs are concerned. However, the structural adjustment necessary for de facto RI helps to position countries to participate more effectively in globalization.

THE CHALLENGES OF GLOBALIZATION AND REGIONAL INTEGRATION

Globalization as an Institution-building Process

Although the term 'globalization' is a much-abused one, it is generally accepted that it is a continuing process rather than an event. 'Economic globalization' as used here implies the growing interdependence of locations and economic units across countries and regions. While a large literature has mushroomed describing the increasingly interwoven nature and cross-border dependence of locations and firms, this is by no means the case for all locations, firms or industrial sectors.

Perspectives on globalization vary quite considerably and depend on the unit of analysis. Nonetheless, it is manifest that cross-border interdependence between firms, institutions and locations has increased dramatically over the last 50 years and is likely to continue in this vein. It is not simply the presence of MNEs and their level of trade that defines a country's involvement in globalization, but the extent to which the economy at large is inextricably linked to the rest of the world. It should be emphasized that dependency on non-national actors is not the same thing as interdependence. Through much of modern history, economies have been dependent on others as customers or suppliers, but this has largely been an arm's-length relationship. Termination of a relationship might have had adverse effects, but not disastrous ones. In an interdependent relationship, important components of production are colocated, so that the failure of one prevents the other from functioning. Interdependence includes both firm and non-firm actors. Non-firm actors are privately and publicly controlled organizations that determine the knowledge infrastructure that supplements and supports firm-specific economic activity. 'Knowledge infrastructure' is used in the sense proposed by Smith (1997) as being 'generic, multi-user and indivisible' and consisting of public research institutes, universities, organizations for standards, intellectual property protection and so on, that enable and promote science and technology development. These non-firm actors are also increasingly interwoven across borders and rely on non-domestic actors for crucial inputs, unlike the situation in the past when every country's non-firm sector was sovereign and independent.

Globalization cannot be credited as a primarily MNE-driven process. MNEs are simply the most visible manifestation of these processes. True, MNEs have sought to overcome cross-border market failures in their search for efficiencies, but there are numerous other concurrent and interrelated events, including technological developments (new technologies), political events (such as the Cold War), economic liberalization and the associated development of supranational institutions and regulations.

It is not our intention to delve into the complexities of cause and effect of globalization. What we wish to highlight is that globalization is very much associated (*inter alia*) with changes in the political economy and changes in the frame of reference. At the risk of oversimplification, the last half-century represents a volte-face in terms of policy perspectives. Prior to the Second World War, nation states were *de facto* inviolable, individual and sovereign entities with clearly defined borders in both a political and an economic sense. Well before import-substituting arguments were formalized, the centrepiece of economic growth was the concept of national self-sufficiency.

Dating at least as far back as the first industrial revolution, every nation state has considered it essential to possess national capacity in so-called 'essential' industries. Inward FDI was largely controlled and limited in its scope, unless it met stringent conditions that promoted the self-sufficiency view by enhancing the host country's domestic sector.

Today, whether voluntarily or through World Bank-sanctioned structural adjustment programmes, the view is largely the opposite. Policies are oriented towards export-led growth and increased cross-border specialization and competition, and most countries are now trying to promote economic growth through FDI and international trade: what has been referred to as the 'new economic model' (NEM) (Reinhardt and Peres, 2000). This wave of liberalization is part of the new, received wisdom that is focused on tackling the deep-rooted causes that underlie market distortions. Unfortunately, countries prefer to view their task as 'getting the prices right' because this allows them to avoid root-and-branch restructuring.

Liberalization has happened gradually through the Triad countries over the post-Second World War era, but much more suddenly within the developing countries. Policies among European countries, for instance, have gradually evolved over 50 years, while almost all of the developing world has attempted to restructure since the late 1980s and, along with the formerly centrally planned economies, only seriously during the 1990s.

The point here is that developing countries find themselves in a new multilateral milieu, but one in which they have little experience. They have hitherto operated their economies on a national basis, and by looking inward they have been able to minimize exposure to external shocks. Institutions continue to remain largely independent and national. By 'institutions' is meant the 'sets of common habits, routines, established practices, rules, or laws that regulate the interaction between individuals and groups' (Edquist and Johnson, 1997). Institutions create the milieu within which economic activity is undertaken and establish the ground rules for interaction between the various economic actors, representing a sort of a 'culture'. Institutions are both formal and informal, and will probably have taken years – if not decades – to create and sustain. To modify and develop institutions is a complex and slow process, particularly since they cannot be created simply by government fiat. Such change is even more complex where the new institutions require synchronization between countries. The Triad countries have taken 50 years to adjust and reform institutions, but even here there is inertia. The EU, for instance, has failed to reform its agricultural sector. Norway remains largely mired in an import-substituting world, with a strong tendency towards central planning and state-owned economic actors (Narula, 2002).

Liberalization is an important force in economic globalization since it requires a multilateral view on hitherto domestic issues and promotes interdependence of economies. It is implicit within this view that FDI and MNE activity can be undertaken with much greater ease than before. This view is enforced because countries have explicitly sought to encourage MNE activity as a source of much-needed capital and technology. In addition to financial crises, the general warming of the attitudes towards FDI emanates from an accelerating pace of technical change and the emergence of integrated production networks of MNEs (Lall, 2000).

Comparing Globalization and Regional Integration

Despite being the object of numerous studies, there is no clear consensus on the universality of the welfare effects of regional integration (see, for example, Baldwin and Venables, 1995). Much of the empirical work has been undertaken for various European integration schemes and NAFTA, which point to a positive impact for participants, but rather few studies have been undertaken on almost a hundred other 'lesser' integration schemes. The continued proliferation of South–South integration schemes is a matter of some consternation (see Baldwin, 1997). Indeed, Venables (2000) argues that, in certain situations, regionalism promotes divergence. It should be noted, however, that much of this (more economics-focused) work has concentrated on trade effects, with the effects on FDI being rather neglected, despite the anticipated benefits from RI being associated with trade and investment.

From an economics perspective, the static and dynamic gains from regional integration schemes result in both long- and short-run economic gains. This is due, inter alia, to improved economies of scale and scope, increased efficiency through the rationalization and reallocation of activities of firms, and improved interregional linkages (Eden, 2001). The improved economic conditions are also expected to influence inflows of FDI positively. These positive externalities will, of course, vary by types of RI. At one extreme, there are *shallow integration schemes*, which essentially involve the reduction of tariff and non-tariff barriers between member countries. A vast majority of regional integration schemes in developing countries fall into this category. Other agreements relax restrictions on government procurement and cross-border FDI, as is the case with NAFTA.

At the other extreme, *deep integration schemes* may include common industrial policies, elimination of all intraregional tariff and non-tariff barriers and the adoption of common external barriers, and may progress as far as monetary and political union. Most prominent of these is the European Union initiative, which has itself evolved over time from a rather limited free trade agreement to a political and economic union. The net benefits of accession to regional integration schemes vary by the depth of integration. It is axiomatic that the benefits from membership in shallow agreements that have been in place for a short period are unlikely to prove as substantial as with deep integration agreements that have been implemented for a long period.

There are a number of inescapable parallels and similarities between regional integration and globalization which deserve attention, especially since the current RI schemes are being undertaken with globalization as a backdrop. The big difference is this: RI schemes are attempts at social and economic engineering, while globalization has been almost a virtuous intertwining of a variety of social, political and technological developments and events. However, the most significant similarity is that both create larger de facto markets from several de jure smaller ones (see Chapter 7). In addition to creating larger markets, RI, like liberalization, is expected to generate benefits from rationalization of economic activity across borders by exploiting differences in comparative advantage.

Regional integration, like globalization, is a continuing process. Countries cannot simply 'jump' from non-integration to deep integration. RI also requires the modification of existing institutions and the establishment of new ones. Despite its being primarily a North–North scheme, the experience of European integration is instructive for several reasons. First, the European political economy mirrors the policy shift typical of developing countries today, except that it has occurred gradually rather than suddenly. Second, it illustrates the effects of moving from a shallow agreement to an increasing level of intensity of integration, a professed aim of several developing-country RI schemes. In addition, there exists a series of concentric agreements within European regional integration. Apart from the EU, there are associated agreements within the framework of the European Economic Area linking the European Free Trade Area (EFTA) with the EU, as well as numerous associate members amongst the Central and Eastern European countries. That is, there are (or have been) considerable differences in development levels between participants. Third, it allows us to observe developments over a longer-term perspective, unlike NAFTA (arguably the only other RI scheme that has experienced some level of success) which has a much shorter history. Nonetheless, we should note two important distinctions. First, these schemes have been primarily North–North or North–South and, second, much of RI was initiated prior to the advent of global liberalized markets. Regional integration in the case of the EU can be regarded as a preliminary experiment in multilateralism, a kind of mini-globalization.

Particular emphasis needs to be placed on the European experience of building institutions. Even the most shallow RI scheme requires a considerable transition period. Institutions need to adjust, if they are not to experience adverse shock. There needs to be an alignment of institutions and economic structures amongst members, and this is primarily the reason for there having been multi-track membership trajectories for various applicant countries to join the EU. Countries such as Sweden and Finland did not require a long transition period for full membership, while Poland and the Czech Republic seem to need considerably longer, and Bulgaria longer still. Not all sectors can evolve towards the common standard at the same rate, and various transition periods and exceptions are marked out for particular sectors.

In other words, it seems that a certain congruence of economic systems and relevant institutions must exist as a precondition for successful RI. It is for this reason that considerable investment has been made (through the structural and framework programmes) to achieve such a convergence between member countries of the EU. The level of convergence required for shallow agreements may be much less, but the point is very much the same.

In a sense, RI acts as a catalyst for convergence, and hence globalization. Certainly, in the case of EU integration, this has been an explicit objective. At its heart there has been a belief that cooperation by (both firm and non-firm) economic actors across the various European countries represents a means by which the technological and economic gap between the various participants (as well as relative to the USA) might be narrowed.

MULTINATIONALS AND ECONOMIC DEVELOPMENT

FDI is regarded as a primary (and explicit) means by which growth can be promoted. Further, it is axiomatic that the availability of foreign capital and technology is an important means of achieving economic catch-up. However, although inward FDI does not represent the only option available to developing countries, given their urgency and limited resources it may represent the most efficient option (see Chapter 3). This is for at least four reasons. First, acquiring technological and organizational knowhow through arm's-length means is an expensive undertaking and, given the shortage of capital, this option is not open to many developing country governments with limited resources. Second, liberalized markets mean that firms, *ceteris paribus*, are likely to be more eager to maintain control of their assets and internalize the market for themselves, either through wholly owned subsidiaries or in joint ventures. Third, infant industry protection is *de rigueur* in creating a domestic sector from scratch, and protected markets are a limited option within the framework of WTO. Fourth, the resources, complementary clusters and assets necessary to support a viable and strong domestic sector are also capital and knowledge-intensive. The role of competition in fostering viable domestic industry is an especially important point. This is best illustrated by the failure of the import-substituting programme in a large number of countries to achieve just this objective.

FDI, however, is not a *sine qua non* for economic development. There are three other conditions that need to be satisfied.

1. Does the kind of FDI being attracted generate significant spillovers?
2. Does the domestic sector have the capacity to absorb these spillovers? It is perhaps worth adding (in the case of LDCs particularly) that there needs to be a domestic sector.
3. Is the FDI that is being attracted a substitute or complementary to domestic industry?

It is true that the determinants of economic development are similar to the determinants of FDI, but this does not mean that there is a simple cause and effect between them. Particular types of FDI tend to be attracted to countries with certain levels of economic development and appropriate economic structures (see Chapter 3). But simply to 'pump' a country full of FDI will not lead to its catapulting to a higher stage of development.

Indeed, the presence and condition of the domestic sector is crucial. If no domestic sector were to exist (say, in an LDC) there could be no opportunity to absorb spillovers from FDI. In a perfectly liberalized world, MNEs have no incentive to encourage the development of domestic firms to meet their needs because other MNEs would be able to do so, either through imports or through FDI. In an extreme case, there may actually be no FDI inflow, because MNEs will prefer to locate production in a regionally optimal location and simply import. Thus FDI in a completely liberalized milieu does not necessarily lead to growth in the domestic sector. The benefits of FDI only occur when there is domestic investment, and where the domestic investment has the ability to internalize the externalities from FDI.

Nonetheless, such an idealized world does not exist, and the point is that FDI is not a guarantee of growth. FDI and economic development are highly correlated phenomena, both being strongly dependent on the specific resources, institutions, economic structure, political ideologies and social and cultural fabric of countries. The kind of FDI activity a country might attract (or wish to attract) at different stages of development are different (Dunning and Narula, 1996; Narula, 1996). Indeed, these two issues are closely related. Although every individual investment is a unique event, both the type of investment and the stage of economic development of the host country allow us to generalize that the situation currently faced by the least developed countries is fundamentally different from that of the catching-up and converging countries (see Chapter 3).

We wish to emphasize that the availability of foreign-owned capital (either portfolio or direct) for developing countries is not at issue here. There have been capital flows of both kinds to viable projects in the LDCs, particularly in extractive industries, and through privatization programmes. Nonetheless, in general, these activities do not provide much opportunity for technological spillovers and beneficial externalities. In other words, it is not FDI activities that are hard to attract, but *certain kinds* of FDI. There are two (interrelated) perspectives from a micro level that need to be considered: first, there is considerable variation in the motivation for the investment; second, from an MNE perspective, there is considerable variation in the types of subsidiaries. The following subsections discuss this assertion in some detail.

Motives for Multinational Investment and Developing Countries

It is generally acknowledged that there are four main motives for investment: to seek natural resources, to seek new markets, to restructure existing foreign production through rationalization and to seek strategically related created assets. These in turn can be broadly divided into two types. The first three represent motives which are primarily *asset-exploiting* in nature: that is, the investing company's primary purpose is to generate economic rent through the use of its existing firm-specific assets. The last is a case of *asset-augmenting activity*, whereby the firm wishes to acquire additional assets which protect or augment their existing created assets in some way.

In general, LDCs are unlikely to attract much asset-augmenting FDI. Such investment is primarily an activity undertaken in intermediate industrializing economies and industrialized economies. While there has been an increase in the location of asset-augmentation activity in some developing countries during the last decade, this continues to be the exception rather than the rule. This is simply because the human resources, technological capabilities and organizational skills that these countries (or their firms) possess tend to be in relatively low-technology and natural resource-intensive sectors which have become 'generic' over time (Dunning *et al.*, 1998).

Resource-seeking FDI
Resource-seeking FDI is a case where existing national technological assets and knowledge infrastructure do not play a significant role in determining FDI inflows. Where a region or country possesses an absolute advantage

in a given scarce resource, it is in a strong position to extract rent from the MNE, despite the absence of infrastructure or a domestic sector. Where the resource sought is a natural one, the marginal cost of its extraction to both parties is close to zero. The location is thus able to generate economic rent according to the resource's rarity and accessibility in other locations.

Resource-seeking investment generally (but not always) implies low value-adding activity and low capital expenditure on plant and equipment (extractive industries being the exception). Such FDI is more footloose. A purely resource-seeking investment is not normally tightly integrated into the investing firm's organizational structure: indeed, MNEs rarely engage in complete internalization of raw material markets, preferring instead to conclude non-equity agreements with foreign firms or to purchase their inputs at arm's-length prices.

In general, FDI in LDCs is often almost entirely resource seeking. Since there are few other L advantages to offer MNEs, this is often the only kind of FDI present. Where vertical forward integration and further value adding do occur, either to exploit markets or to exploit other L advantages, the 'stickiness' of the investment increases.

Market-seeking FDI
Market-seeking FDI only gains prominence in situations where the local or adjacent markets provide access to significant opportunities to achieve production economies of scale. This requires not only a sizeable population, but also the ability of the market to support (within a reasonable time frame) the expected demand on which the investment is based. In addition, though, there is often a 'follow-my-leader' strategic response by other firms, whereby a market that might have supported two or three competitors is inundated by a larger number of new entrants than the market can efficiently support. The case of both the Chinese and the Indian car market represents examples of such a scenario where, despite the potential for high demand levels, few participants are actually able to make a profit. This is not the case with all sectors: investments in food and personal products, for instance, are much more likely to achieve economies of scale, since these products have a relatively low income elasticity of demand. Indeed, the car industry may represent a special case in these countries, for what is now described as aggressive market-seeking investments in developing countries, in many cases began life as defensive import-substituting investments. These were only permitted under certain stringent conditions, but the MNE normally expected to have access to a captive protected market in return.

Market-seeking FDI is largely based on a single central locational advantage. Its presence or absence is stage-dependent, but is essentially an exogenous event, with one exception. Membership of a free trade area allows countries that have small domestic markets to expand their de facto market size. In such situations, however, several formerly sovereign markets become integrated, and the choice of location then rests on other L advantages. This may have detrimental effects too: once sanctions against South Africa were lifted, a certain hollowing out of market-seeking FDI in neighbouring countries was observed as a result of their free trade agreements with South Africa.

Efficiency-seeking and strategic asset-seeking FDI
These two types of investment are similar in that they both normally require a certain threshold level of created assets and are generally regarded as being associated with the process of globalization. It is no surprise that they are generally associated with middle-income and industrializing countries, and in the case of asset-seeking FDI, with the industrialized countries.

Efficiency-seeking investment in the least developed countries is an ambiguous concept, although, for many years, MNEs have engaged in export-oriented resource-seeking investment, which is de facto efficiency-seeking FDI. Moreover, efficiency investment, in the sense that different aspects of manufacturing activity are located in particular places to exploit the economies of cross-border specialization and the uneven distribution of immobile created assets, is a relatively new phenomenon.

In both of these types of investments, the role of subnational clusters and the agglomeration of related activities is significant. The externalities available to countries that are home to centres of agglomeration, or possess the science and technology infrastructure necessary to attract asset-augmenting FDI, are considerably different from countries which primarily attract asset-exploiting FDI. It should be noted that, even where centres of excellence or agglomeration exist in a given industry, this does not imply that further knowledge-intensive investments will be attracted to the same location by virtue of a single cluster existing, unless clear spillovers or externalities exist. Nonetheless, countries that have (the basis for) agglomerative economies are the ones likely to receive such FDI.

Typology of MNE Subsidiaries

Although there are several typologies of affiliates, they serve different purposes. In particular, attention has primarily been focused on first-world MNEs located in first-world locations. Some of these typologies have tended to examine particular aspects of value-adding activity, or particular industries. We will utilize a typology based on previous work by Pearce (1989, 1999), but modified for our purposes.

The nature of the activities undertaken by a subsidiary and its potential level of embeddedness in the host economy vary according to the level of competence of the subsidiary, and to the scope of its activities (Benito *et al.*, 2003).

Figure 5.1 illustrates our typology of subsidiaries according to these two scales. A typical value-added chain can be viewed from a 'level of competence' perspective consisting of 'strategic' and 'operational' elements. Activities such as sales and manufacturing are operational in nature, while R&D centres and headquarters functions are strategic in nature. In general, strategic elements tend to be located close to locations which are regarded as important to the MNE. Following Bartlett and Ghoshal (1989), there is a close link between the influence of the subsidiary and the strategic importance of its local environment. Strategic elements perform a critical role in a network of units, adding value through contributing their own expertise as well as by coordinating the flow of knowledge within the network. Second, there is considerable variation between subsidiaries in the scope of their activities, with certain subsidiaries performing single and

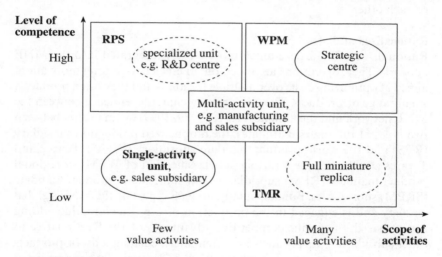

Source: Based on Benito *et al.* (2003).

Figure 5.1 Typology of MNE subsidiaries

specialized activities, and others performing a larger variety and being of greater value (Figure 5.1).

Truncated miniature replicas (TMRs)
As their name implies, truncated miniature replicas are essentially a duplication of the parent firm, although perhaps not with the same scale of

production and not all of the various components of value-adding activity. Typically, they do not undertake basic research but may modify and adapt products originally developed by the parent. Although TMRs vary in the extent to which they are truncated, generally speaking they tend to have a low or medium level of competence (Figure 5.1). TMRs tend to have an extensive market scope, in the sense that they have a large product range, but supply a limited and isolated market (Pearce, 1999). TMRs tend to have a considerable degree of autonomy in their activities, although the parent company exerts overall strategic control. This means, for instance, that the parent decides new additions to the product range. They are nationally responsive and, apart from a few advantages derived from being part of an MNE network, such as lower cost of capital and technology, they are similar to other indigenous firms. Their primary motive is market-seeking, most often associated with import-substituting programmes. The parent–affiliate relationship is weakly developed and the two are essentially independent of each other.

Rationalized affiliates
Rationalized affiliates are much more closely integrated into the MNE network. Their operations are based on an efficiency-seeking motivation, aimed at optimizing costs over multiple locations and they often produce a small range of products. There is a strategic interdependence between the MNE network and the affiliate. Pearce (1989, 1999) distinguishes between two types of rationalized affiliates: the rationalized production subsidiary (RPS) and the world product mandate subsidiary (WPM). Pearce and Tavares (1998) propose a further subclassification of WPMs in regional product mandate (RPM) subsidiaries and subregional product mandate (SRPM) subsidiaries. Fundamentally, an RPS is part of the MNE's global strategy and is engaged in the production of a particular value-adding aspect based on specific competitive advantages of the RPS relative to other subsidiaries. Its products are often intermediate goods, or products or services complementary to other RPS. R&D is typically not associated with an RPS and control over its operations is exerted from headquarters. Its activities are confined to operating activities, but not strategic ones.

WPM subsidiaries, on the other hand, have a greater strategic role, more decision-making power, and are often engaged in higher value-adding activity. They are based on a strategic asset-seeking motivation, as well as an efficiency-seeking one. WPMs maintain global or regional control over a particular product line or functional area, and are designated 'centres of excellence'. That is, 'strategic' activities such as R&D and headquarters functions are included in the affiliate's responsibilities and it exerts control over other affiliates in the same region or worldwide.

RPMs and SRPMs are truncated versions of WPMs, in that they have a broader mandate towards a region (such as participants in an RI scheme) or a subregion (say, the Nordic countries or South Asia). They are designed to be responsive in particular to a smaller catchment area. RPMs and SRPMs aim to meet particular market needs that may be unique to a given group of countries, because the region or subregion requires services and products that need to be differentiated from other RPMs and SRPMs, or because local conditions require a greater responsiveness (Pearce and Tavares, 1998).

Single-activity affiliates
Single-activity affiliates are a cross between TMRs and RPSs. On the one hand, they represent an extreme version of a TMR, in that they undertake a single aspect of value-adding activity. In other words, they are severely truncated. On the other hand, such affiliates may in fact be part of a company's rationalized strategy: the comparative advantage of the location is best suited for such activities. Nonetheless, a differentiation needs to be made, particularly in the developing country scenario, as such affiliates are often marginal to the firm, in terms of strategic importance, unlike RPS subsidiaries which may also be specialized in one form of activity. They are 'generic' in the sense that there are often numerous such affiliates in various developing country locations, and while there may be a dependence, they contribute nothing unique to the assets of the firm and are easily replaced. These affiliates are not involved in decision making or strategic planning, and are virtually at arm's-length to the MNE.

Such affiliates typically tend to be engaged at the extremes of the value-adding chain. The first type is *trading affiliates*, engaged in trading activities and, to a limit, in marketing and after-sales service. The second subcategory is *resource-extractive affiliates*, which are at the other end of the value chain, engaged solely in acquiring (primarily through extractive activity) scarce or otherwise valuable crude resources, for the express purposes of exporting these raw materials for use in other locations, whether by another affiliate or by an unrelated firm.

It bears repeating that there is considerable variation between industrial sectors, individual MNEs as well as host and home country factors. For instance, in the food and beverages sectors, subsidiaries are organized primarily as TMRs. MNEs with greater international exposure and dependence on foreign markets are more inclined towards RPSs or WPMs.

It is axiomatic that subsidiary roles evolve over time, owing both to internal, MNE-specific factors and to changing non-firm exogenous developments, including liberalization of markets and regional integration (Mariotti and Piscitello, 2001; Birkinshaw and Hood, 2000). The changing external environment will inevitably induce some changes in subsidiary roles. Once an MNE rationalizes the number of subsidiaries or reorganizes the activities across borders, the remaining and/or new units will likely experience changes in scope and areas of responsibility. Increases in scope can typically be found when the number of subsidiaries is rationalized or local conditions encourage localization of activities (Birkinshaw, 1996). Similarly, the scope may be narrowed to focus on specific activities and build expertise within the selected area (Surlemont, 1998). Hence changes in scope are often related to both organizational and spatial considerations.

MNE STRATEGIES, LIBERALIZATION AND REGIONAL INTEGRATION

In this section we will examine MNE strategies in response to liberalization and regional integration in four scenarios: (1) in a pre-liberalized environment, (2) participation in an RI scheme in a pre-liberalized environment, (3) in a post-liberalization scenario, (4) participation in an RI scheme in a post-liberalization scenario. We consider three groups of countries. Group I countries are least developed, with little or no domestic capability. Group II are developing countries which possess an intermediate domestic capability, while Group III are industrialized countries which have a high domestic capability and are home countries of MNEs. There are a finite number of RI schemes possible between these three groups, as illustrated by Figure 5.2. We will examine each of our scenarios from every practical option for developing countries.

	Group I	Group II	Group III
Group III	Group I–III integration (e.g. Costa Rica–Canada FTA)	Group II–Group III RI (Mexico in NAFTA, Spain, Portugal and Greece in the EU)	Intra–Group III RI (e.g. EFTA, Canada–US FTA)
Group II	Group I–Group II RI (Uruguay and Paraguay in *Mercosur*)	Group II–Group II RI (e.g. Brazil and Argentina in *Mercosur*)	
Group I	Intra-Group I RI (e.g. Andean community, Caricom CACM)		

Figure 5.2   Different combinations of regional integrations

MNE Strategies in a Non-RI, Non-liberalized World

Let us take the situation of countries prior to liberalization, that is, where import-substituting policies are in force. Group I countries tend to be host to single-activity subsidiaries. In Groups II and III, MNEs respond to investment opportunities primarily by establishing miniature replicas, although the extent to which they are truncated varies considerably between countries. The extent of truncation is determined by the following:

1. the size of the local market in terms of potential and actual demand;
2. the extent to which the MNE is afforded a monopoly;
3. the stringency of the import-substituting regime. Different countries apply different local content requirements and barriers on the imports of intermediate goods;
4. the capacity of domestic industry to supply local content;
5. the stringency of foreign ownership restrictions and the risk of expropriation. Ownership is significant to the MNE because it determines its ability to control the activities of the subsidiary, and the use of its technological assets. Where domestic industry is weak or non-existent, ownership restrictions also influence whether foreign-based suppliers might also be able to engage in FDI to manufacture local content;
6. the cost of capital relative to that available on international markets (or at home) and restrictions on where capital must be borrowed;
7. the potential to generate rent; and restrictions on repatriation of dividends and interest payments to the rest of the MNE in hard currency.

This list is partial, and these factors are interrelated. Numerous trade-offs exist between these factors. For instance, where local demand is large and rent-generation opportunities are high (such as in China), MNEs are willing to accept greater restrictions on ownership (than, say, in Peru). IBM's decision to divest from India in the mid-1970s was triggered by increased local content requirements, and a potential loss of majority ownership. The issue in this case was *control*, rather than ownership: during the same period, IBM's Indonesia subsidiary was a shell company, while its operations locally were undertaken by a domestically owned company. However, IBM had full operational and strategic control of the Indonesian firm.

But by far the most important determinant of truncation, and thereby the scope of activities and competence level of the subsidiary (since broadly speaking most countries maintained similar import-substituting regulations prior to the mid-1980s), is associated with market size, and the capacity and capability of domestic industry. Group I countries without a domestic sector and with low demand were host to the most truncated subsidiaries, often to the point of their being single-activity subsidiaries. Activities were primarily in sales and marketing, and natural resource extraction. Larger Group II and Group III countries (for much of Europe still maintained some form of import substitution into the 1970s, and non-EU countries such as Norway well into the 1980s) with domestic technological capacity (such as Brazil and India) were host to the least truncated subsidiaries, often with R&D departments. Nonetheless, products manufactured by these TMRs were either obsolete in the home country or designed domestically strictly for local competition, or for a limited export market (Mortimore, 1998). In Group II, competition was considerably limited, domestic productivity low and, in many cases, economies of scale were not achieved. Production costs are therefore higher than equivalent imports, and tariff and non-tariff barriers induced market imperfections, allowing for rent generation.

Shallow Regional Integration with Non-liberalization

Assume an RI scheme that proposes a common internal tariff and a (higher) common external tariff, such that this *de facto* enlarges the market, while maintaining an import-substituting (pre-liberalization) stance.

Group I–Group II and Group II–Group III RI schemes
First, take the case of RI between countries A and B at different levels of domestic capability. Assume that Country B is at a lower level (whether Group I or II) than Country A (Group II or III). Country A's existing TMRs might see an increase in the scope of their activities. Country B might see an upgrading of its single-activity subsidiaries to TMRs, as market size increases. In addition, there may be a redistribution effect to take advantage of differences in comparative advantage. Broadly speaking, however, this will be relatively small, with shallow integration, depending upon the extent and sectors for which intraregional barriers decline. It will also be lower with a Group I–Group II RI scheme than with a Group II–III RI scheme. In either case there will be a net increase in FDI to both countries, and an increase in competence and scope of subsidiary activity. There will be no crowding out of domestic investment, and possibly a 'crowding in' in the case of Country A that has the technological capability to nurture a domestic sector. Intraregional FDI will occur, primarily from A to B, depending on the industry, but this is relatively minor, particularly where Country A is a Group II country, in the form of single-activity subsidiaries to exploit resources in Country A, or as sales affiliates. With a Group II–III RI scheme, intraregional FDI will be greater, but primarily downwards, and intended to exploit differences in comparative advantage (as with the maquiladoras in Mexico).

Broadly speaking, however, investments in shallow agreements will tend to be 'local', with the objective of gaining access to individual local markets separately, rather than combined markets. This is borne out by investments in the earlier stages of NAFTA and the EU. Much of the earlier FDI in European RI in the 1970s was of a defensive local market-exploiting nature (Dunning, 1997). Investments in each country were primarily associated with its domestic market, and with overcoming barriers to imports.

The evidence points to a *potential* for a greater scope of MNE activities in a non-liberalization RI scenario for Group I and Group II countries, regardless of whether the RI was South–South or North–South. In the case of Group I countries, certainly, MNEs invested in response to RI where, otherwise, little or no FDI might be attracted. However, owing to import substitution and alternative possibilities in Country A, opportunities are limited for sequential FDI and upgrading. Potential for a higher quality and quantity of FDI does not however mean that spillovers and externalities are internalized. Where domestic firms are able to internalize spillovers and improve their capabilities, for instance by becoming efficient suppliers to MNEs, this acts as a reinforcing mechanism for the upgrading of the MNEs' competence levels. If the efficiency of the TMR approaches international levels, it is possible that the subsidiary in Country A will be upgraded to a SRPM or RPM.

Intra-Group I RI schemes

Second, take the case of a regional integration between Group I countries with similar comparative advantages. Neither A nor B, on its own, possesses sufficient location advantages to attract TMRs, but together their combined market size may justify TMRs in some sectors. This will be in basic sectors such as resource processing and food sectors: in other words, Heckcsher–Ohlin industries. There is little likelihood, however, that affiliates will improve domestic capacity, mainly because the domestic sector is non-existent.

MNE Strategies after Liberalization

Most South–South agreements established prior to the liberalization of the 1990s were de facto inoperational, as were most North–South agreements, with the exception of the Mexico–US FTA. Therefore, in a sense, liberalization was undertaken in a de facto unintegrated environment. Liberalization as undertaken by most developing countries has had the following consequences for MNE activity.

1. Floating currencies, removal of exchange restrictions and subsequent devaluation.

2. Reduction of tariff and non-tariff barriers to manufactured imports.
3. Reduction of local content requirements for incumbent MNEs.
4. Removal of export requirements from MNEs.
5. Reduction of direct and indirect subsidies to domestic industry.
6. Privatization of some state-owned assets.

However, as discussed earlier, liberalization is one facet of globalization. Globalization has affected the ownership assets of MNEs in that it has changed the way in which they organize and undertake cross-border activities. This is not just a result of the global wave of economic liberalization and regional integration (particularly NAFTA and EU) but also a result, inter alia, of the increasing enforceability of transactions across borders, increased competition, the growing need for competences in multiple technologies and improved information and communications technologies.

Although the amount of total FDI stock directed towards developing countries may have increased, an increasing proportion of new investment is of a kind that requires the use of specialized created assets, and therefore tends to be directed to the developed and wealthier developing countries with the necessary level of technological assets. On the one hand, MNEs seek more specialized inputs, and, on the other, more countries offer generic inputs. Liberalization has meant that a much larger pool of countries (possibly twice as large as two decades previously) offer 'generic' location advantages such as access to natural assets and basic infrastructure. The problem of too many countries chasing a limited amount of FDI is exacerbated by the competition between provinces and regions within countries, which offer their own set of incentive schemes to funnel scarce investments to their locations (Mytelka, 1996). Countries and provinces are therefore under pressure to 'give away' bigger investment incentives in order to attract the FDI that is often central to their development strategies. There is a danger that due to the increased competition, countries may give away more than the potential benefits that accrue from the MNE activity (Mytelka, 1996; McIntyre et al., 1996).

It is important to realize that the process of liberalization has increasingly become an exogenous event with a pervasive influence beyond any single country's control (see Chapter 3). Although the opening up or liberalization of any particular country is a country-specific (and therefore endogenous) event, the benefit that accrues to the country from this event is a function of how many other countries have also liberalized. Furthermore, membership of multilateral institutions such as the WTO (as well as free trade areas and other forms of economic integration) obliges the participating countries to conform their liberalization policies to a common standard. Membership of multilateral blocs can affect an involuntary change in policy since, with increasingly few countries still operating within a command economy or an import-substituting regime, there are few opportunities for such countries to engage in economically sound non-market arrangements.

To sum up, globalization has affected the spatial distribution of MNE activity on a multi-country, international level as well as on an individual country basis. This is due, not just to liberalization in an individual country, but also to liberalization as a multi-country phenomenon. Combined with the changing nature of MNEs' ownership-specific assets, this has led to a reorganization of MNE activities within countries and across countries.

The strategies of MNEs in any given developing country can be affected vis-à-vis their operations in three possible ways.

1. New and/or upgraded affiliates: there are opportunities for new FDI inflows, firstly through new initial investment, resulting in subsidiaries that did not exist previously, and secondly through sequential investment as firms upgrade the scope and competence of existing subsidiaries. In a static and simplistic view, this leads to an increase in total capital (that is, domestic investment plus foreign investment).
2. Downgrading of subsidiaries: MNEs may divest their operations in response to better location advantages elsewhere, or reduce the intensity of operations by lowering the level of competence and/or scope of their subsidiary. Total capital in this scenario may decrease.
3. Redistribution effect: there is the possibility of a redistribution effect, with total capital staying constant. That is, sectors that were dominated by domestic capital may be transferred to foreign ownership.

Of course, in reality it is hard to separate these three effects, since these developments are hard to measure, not least because individual countries and MNEs are idiosyncratic and path dependent. Firms may take particular strategic decisions because of long-term and non-economic considerations, and policies of countries may vary between sectors and subsectors.

Nonetheless, there are certain broad trends which can be observed. It is clear, for instance, that the erosion of the kind of location advantages associated with protected trade and investment regimes has had far-reaching consequences. Although the benefits of liberalization in terms of encouraging inward FDI are notable, some MNEs have divested in response to liberalization where the initial MNE activity was to overcome tariff and non-tariff barriers. Since the conclusion of NAFTA, for example, defensive import substitution FDI in Canada has fallen sharply. Although information on divestment in developing countries has not been systematically collected, it is likely that, since proportionally more FDI prior to liberalization was defensive market seeking, this phenomenon might be a significant one. It is important to note that, although data suggest that there was a drastic decline in FDI stocks in Group I countries in the late 1980s, this reflects in part the devaluation of domestic currencies relative to the dollar. Thus, while the property, plant and equipment, and the scope and competence of an affiliate in, say, Argentina or Chile may have remained identical pre- and post-liberalization, its value on the books of the MNE may have declined in hard currency terms. Nonetheless, a wide variety of Group I countries have seen a decline in the quality of TMR subsidiaries, particularly in sectors where the low productivity of affiliates' production was supported through trade barriers-induced market distortions. MNEs have taken advantage of liberalization to exploit production capacity in fewer locations, to exploit economies of scale, especially where local consumption patterns are not radically different to justify local capacity and where transport costs are not prohibitive. This has meant that some TMRs have been downgraded to sales and marketing affiliates. Except for sectors where policy-induced distortions persist, FDI now largely reflects comparative advantages. Group I countries with abundant natural resources now receive much more resource-seeking FDI, and less upstream FDI in manufacturing (ECLAC, 2001).

Countries with superior 'non-generic' locational assets (in other words, Group II) tend to receive such higher value-adding, knowledge-intensive FDI. Countries without the capacity, in terms both of infrastructure and necessary skilled human capital, are unlikely to be hosts to RPSs, RPMs or WPMs. Deepening of affiliate activity is increasingly associated with the location's ability to be integrated with the rest of the MNE and its ability to provide unique knowledge-intensive inputs not available elsewhere. Data published by ECLAC (2001) suggest that FDI activity in Latin America, with the exception of Mexico and the Caribbean, continues to focus on serving local markets and traditional resource-seeking activities.

In other words, domestic capacity – whether in the form of knowledge infrastructure or of an efficient domestic industrial sector – is a primary determinant of high-competence foreign affiliates. Some countries, notably Mexico and the Caribbean Basin, have succeeded in attracting such FDI (ECLAC, 2000, 2001; Mortimore, 2000). In addition to providing domestic capabilities and a threshold level of infrastructure, these countries have invested in developing knowledge infrastructure (although to a lesser extent in the case of Mexico). More importantly, these countries have had long-term bilateral agreements with the USA. Like incentives, bilateral ties are not on their own sufficient conditions to attract FDI, but studies have shown that, the longer they persist, the greater their effect (Mudambi, 1998; Blonigen and Davies, 2000).

An important avenue through which redistribution effects of FDI can be seen is privatization. Between 1988 and 1999, $107.3 billion worth of privatized firms had been acquired through cross-border mergers and acquisitions (M&A). The share of Latin America and the Caribbean was roughly 79.8 per cent (UNCTAD, 2000). In other words, during this period, about 20 per cent of the total inflows to this region were associated with privatization. Overall, liberalization has been very beneficial to MNEs. Privatization, in particular, has allowed foreign investors to acquire fully operational (albeit often inefficient) firms in countries at relatively low cost, owing, inter alia, to depreciation of exchange rates of the recipient economies. From a national perspective, inflows from privatization represent a single, one-off phenomenon: MNE acquisitions through privatization schemes may initially generate a large initial infusion of capital, but subsequent inflows are by no means guaranteed. Indeed, in many cases, state-owned companies that have been most attractive to FDI have often been the more efficient ones, requiring relatively little in the way of upgrading. It should be noted that a majority of privatizations are in the services sector. Furthermore, because MNEs intend to generate some rents from these investments, the net inflows can be expected to be significantly smaller in subsequent years. Consequently, the net effect on the economy is possibly neutral, and FDI represents simply a redistribution of assets from domestic to foreign capitalists or from the state to foreign firms.[1]

Regional Integration after Liberalization

Intra-Group I RI
Take the case of two Group I countries undertaking shallow integration after liberalization. Let us assume that this implies common external barriers, but relatively free (or at least lower) intraregional trade barriers. This gives MNEs (and domestic firms) an opportunity to exploit scale economies in market-seeking investment. Thus an MNE may consider a TMR where two single-activity affiliates might previously have existed. But such an operation can be either in country A or in country B. Assuming similar factor endowments and de facto freedom of movement of goods and services, the decision is often based on incentives and subsidies. Such contests can only erode the net benefits of FDI. In general, RI will have no influence on the spatial distribution of resource-seeking investments, since these are already based on comparative advantage.

Group I–Group II RI
Here a clearer variation in endowments and location advantages exist. An RI-driven reorganization of MNE activity is certainly possible with the higher competence activities in the Group II country ('A') and lower factor-endowment type activities in the Group I country ('B'). However,

liberalization in neighbouring countries means that, unless external barriers are very high, the MNE may yet prefer to locate higher competence in country C located outside the boundaries of the RI. However, the determining factor on whether Country A becomes host to an RPM subsidiary is the efficiency of its existing operations relative to other countries, and only secondarily its participation in an RI scheme.

North–South RI

Although redistribution of MNE activity follows along similar lines to Group I–Group II integration, there are two obvious advantages of participation in a North–South scheme that are not evident in a Group I–II RI. First, the Group III country ('A') is home to a large group of MNEs who are more likely to invest in Country B. The technological gap is much larger, and the pool of potential spillovers greater. Furthermore, such intraregional FDI is more likely to be efficiency-seeking. Second, Country A provides a much larger market. Thus in terms of linkages, and simply in terms of FDI, there is a greater order of magnitude in terms of benefits. As an example, Mexico with NAFTA has enjoyed increased FDI flows, both from within NAFTA and from its agreement with the EU. This has two advantages that (say) MERCOSUR does not have. First, NAFTA provides it with access to the USA. Certainly, many EU firms would not have invested in Mexico if it provided ease of access to, say, Honduras, or Brazil. Second, the EU, the USA and Canada are home countries of a majority of the largest MNEs. South–South RI schemes do not always have the managerial, technological or capital capacity within the region to lead to an increase in intraregional FDI of the same order of magnitude. In addition, MNEs from the South are themselves interested in improving their global competitiveness since they too must survive in global markets. *Ceteris paribus*, improved or cheaper access to another developing country is not in itself sufficient incentive, unless that location enjoys some considerable advantage over other developing countries.

We have taken the example of a two-country RI for illustrative purposes. It is self-evident that a larger group of participants obviously acts as a more powerful magnet for investment, although coordinating policy across a larger group is fraught with complications. We have also had to assume that RI schemes have been implemented uniformly. Unfortunately, this is rarely the case. There are certain limitations that are associated with achieving even the most modest gains from RI. First, there is the lack of common institutions, and the lack of political consensus in creating these. Take for instance the various and overlapping Latin American RI schemes, some of whose members have been in the throes of regional integration on a sporadic basis for over two decades. A recent study by the Inter-American

Development Bank (2000) highlights the various problems in regulatory and institutional frameworks between Latin American countries. For instance, a truck carrying goods from Brazil to Chile requires 200 hours for a 3500km journey, of which 50 per cent is spent in the two border crossings. As we have highlighted before, the development of common institutions is a slow and gradual process. It is here that the benefit of a history of regional integration attempts and a similarity of cultures helps the most. Previous cooperative institution building allows countries to continue in that vein, but political differences and a lack of congruity in goals means that RI schemes remained largely incomplete.

A second limitation of actual RI schemes compared to the stylized one is that there is rarely conformity to a common external barrier that is higher than the (common) internal barriers. A third related limitation is the reluctance to agree amongst members about structural adjustment. Each country wishes to maintain its national champions and 'status' projects, so that considerable duplication exists. Achieving consensus as to how to rationalize this is avoided by excluding such sensitive sectors from agreements. For instance, one industry in Latin America which might benefit from intra-RI rationalization of production is the car sector. However, in the case of the MERCOSUR countries, which are hosts to a sizeable presence of MNEs producing cars for each domestic market dating back to the import-substituting era, there is some reluctance to allow intraregional free access (Mortimore, 1998). This was also the case initially with European integration. Until the early 1980s, much of the FDI was defensive market-seeking, and intra-European FDI was very low, as each country maintained its national champions. European firms are significant home countries for MNEs (indeed, many European countries are net outward investors, but not to other European countries). European MNEs possess significant ownership-specific assets, whether technological, managerial or through privileged access to complementary assets, not available to developing country firms. This means that prior to RI there was already a large untapped potential for intra-European activity. Secondly, the presence of such large and competitive firms implies location-specific advantages in the form of institutions, infrastructure and other economic actors that can act as a 'magnet' to foreign (whether intra-or extraregional) MNEs, quite apart from the attractions of a large market. However, intra-EU FDI and rationalization of production within the EU only took place after considerable efforts were made by the European Commission to 'push' EU firms to rationalize and create trans-European efficiency of their activities (see Chapter 7). Member countries provided EU firms with a grace period of protection within which to improve their competitiveness, after which market forces would decide which players survived (in theory) regardless of national origin.

CONCLUSIONS

This chapter has tried to illustrate how the strategies of MNEs have responded to globalization and attempted to evaluate MNEs' response to regional integration separately in both a pre- and a post-liberalization environment.

From the MNEs' perspective, liberalization has had a greater effect on their strategies than regional integration. Globalization of MNE activity and liberalization of countries has led to a downgrading of MNE activity in most LDCs and some more advanced developing countries. Only a handful of countries have seen an improvement in the *quality* of FDI. These countries have a threshold level of domestic capability and infrastructure, as well as institutions that are more efficient. In general, RI schemes have reinforced these trends, benefiting those countries that have developed their domestic sector and worked towards creating the appropriate multilateral institutions to exploit cross-border efficiencies. Furthermore, these countries have been involved in North–South RI schemes.

The objective of development strategies in both pre- and post-liberalization phases has been to develop and sustain the competitiveness of domestic industry. Liberalization has brought with it more MNE-friendly policies, with the objective of leveraging FDI for capacity building. However, the quality of FDI and the potential for spillovers varies considerably, depending on the motivation for FDI and the kind of subsidiary. In general, there has been a downgrading of MNE activity in most Group I countries and some Group II countries. Many of the gains in FDI flows have been a result of redistribution, associated with the transfer of state and privately owned domestic firms to foreign ownership, and the gains therefrom are dubious from a developmental perspective. The only countries that have attracted 'the right kind' of FDI have been those that have the appropriate knowledge infrastructure, sound, stable economic policies and the potential for a competitive domestic sector. MNE subsidiaries do not develop in isolation from the domestic sector. In other words, participants of South–South agreements are unlikely to receive much FDI over and above that which they might have received in the first place in a post-liberalized world, on the basis of their comparative advantage, and indeed, may suffer from negative redistribution effects. It is important to emphasize that the analysis here has focused solely on MNE strategies: there can be (and are) considerable other benefits from participation in RI schemes through other mechanisms.

For most developing countries, RI on the heels of liberalization has not improved matters, except possibly for Group II countries in South–South RI schemes, and within North–South RI schemes. In other words, the situation has improved for the 'haves' and not the 'have-nots'. Regional integration improves only one type of location advantage: RI is associated with increases in de facto market size and thus, logically, the largest benefits from increased FDI are those that are motivated by efforts to acquire access to these markets. This is no different from the advantages that liberalization is purported to offer. From the MNEs' perspective, liberalization is a bigger 'pull' than a smaller, closed club of regional integration, unless that club offers some unique advantage not available elsewhere. Besides, increases in market size are rarely achieved in most South–South RI schemes, because the multilateral institutions necessary to promote de facto cross-border efficiencies are simply not present. RI schemes have a completely different outcome post- and pre-liberalization vis-à-vis MNE strategies, and RI simply reinforces changes in MNE strategies in response to liberalization, rather than counteracting them. Our reading of the secondary evidence on RI is broadly in line with the findings of Blomstrom and Kokko (1997), who concluded that the greater the liberalization associated with RI, and the stronger the location advantages, the more likely it is that RI will lead to increased FDI inflows.

The sudden change from import-substituting to multilateral liberalization has taken most countries by surprise (Mortimore, 2000). They need to respond to globalization, but this requires time and new institutions that are responsive to multilateral issues and an interdependent world. However, institution building is a slow and gradual process. This is where RI provides long-term benefits, because it potentially allows countries to respond gradually to globalization in a controlled (and stepwise) manner. Adjusting institutions and improving intraregional efficiencies with a small group of similar countries should logically be easier to respond to immediately than with the entire membership of the WTO. RI should be regarded as a stepping-stone to globalization. To elucidate, RI offers developing countries a window of opportunity to dampen the shock of entry into a fully multilateral and globalizing world, by 'practising' on a smaller version. Mexico is illustrative of the slow and gradual process of structural adjustment. Mexico has undertaken increasing RI within NAFTA while also deepening its integration with other partners such as the EU. This is acknowledged as part of a broader integration into the world economy (ECLAC, 2000). The danger, of course, is that RI schemes may act as an excuse to return to a pre-liberalization world of excessive protection.

Additionally, development policies need to integrate a more sophisticated view of FDI. As Mortimore (2000) illustrates well, although Latin American countries have succeeded in attracting a large quantity of FDI, the issue of quality of FDI has thus far been ignored. Additionally, Mortimore points out that there is a failure fully to integrate and coordinate domestic capacity improvement goals with FDI policies.

RI can be seen to be a useful policy tool in promoting competitiveness if exploited carefully, and within an integrated development policy agenda. Although RI per se may not have any great benefit for Group I countries in terms of quality of FDI, or in terms of direct spillovers to their domestic sectors, there are other reasons to participate. First, RI does increase FDI flow (albeit of limited quality) and helps the least developed countries escape the vicious cycle of poverty. Increased resource-seeking investment and market-seeking investment is better than no investment at all. Second, RI does allow them to prepare for greater liberalization, allowing for a gradual widening and deepening of cross-border interdependence. The reasons for countries not enjoying greater welfare benefits from RI are the same as those that limit the benefits from liberalization in general: firstly, the lack of a threshold level of domestic capabilities (Borenszstein *et al.*, 1998); secondly, the lack of long-term political stability (Freeman and Lindauer, 1999); thirdly, the absence of efficient institutions, both domestic and multilateral. Participation in an RI scheme creates an imperative to improve at least some of these and in many cases acts as a catalyst to escape structural inertia and lock-in (Hannan and Freeman, 1984). Fourthly, like liberalization, the costs of non-participation in a *genuinely integrated* RI scheme are high, particularly when most other countries are participating.

NOTE

1. Many of the state-owned assets acquired by MNEs are in services and infrastructure. It needs to be acknowledged that such investments have an important welfare effect.

REFERENCES

Baldwin, R.E. (1997), 'The causes of regionalism', *The World Economy*, **20** (7), 865–88.
Baldwin, R.E. and A.J. Venables (1995), 'Regional economic integration', in G.M. Grossman and K. Rogoff (eds), *Handbook of International Economics*, Amsterdam: Elsevier.
Bartlett, C.A. and S. Ghoshal (1989), *Managing Across Borders: The Transnational Solution*, Boston: Harvard Business School Press.
Benito, G., B. Grogaard and R. Narula (2003), 'Environmental influences on MNE subsidiary roles: economic integration and the Nordic countries', *Journal of International Business Studies*, **34**, 443–56.

Birkinshaw, J. (1996), 'How multinational subsidiary mandates are gained and lost', *Journal of International Business Studies*, **27** (3), 467–95.

Birkinshaw, J. and N. Hood (2000), 'Characteristics of foreign subsidiaries in industry clusters', *Journal of International Business Studies*, **31** (1), 141–54.

Blomstrom, M. and A. Kokko (1997), 'Regional integration and foreign direct investment', NBER working paper 6019.

Blonigen, B. and R. Davies (2000), 'The effects of bilateral tax treaties on U.S. FDI activity', NBER working paper 7929.

Borenszstein, E., J. De Gregorio and J.W. Lee (1998), 'How does foreign direct investment affect economic growth?', *Journal of International Economics*, **45**, 115–35.

Dunning, J.H. (1997), 'The European internal market programme and inbound foreign direct investment (Part 2)', *Journal of Common Market Studies*, **35**, 190–223.

Dunning, J.H., and R. Narula (1996), 'The investment development path revisited: some emerging issues', in J.H. Dunning and R. Narula (eds), *Foreign Direct Investment and Governments: Catalysts for Economic Restructuring*, London: Routledge.

Dunning, J.H., R. van Hoesel and R. Narula (1998), 'Third world multinationals revisited: new developments and theoretical implications', in J.H. Dunning (ed.), *Globalization, Trade and Foreign Direct Investment*, Oxford: Pergamon.

ECLAC (2000), *Foreign Investment in the Latin America and the Caribbean 1999*, Santiago: United Nations.

ECLAC (2001), *Foreign Investment in the Latin America and the Caribbean 2000*, Santiago: United Nations.

Eden, L. (2001), 'Regional integration and foreign direct investment: theory and lessons from NAFTA', in M. Kotabe, P. Aulakh and A. Phatak (eds), *The Challenge of International Business Research*, Cheltenham, UK and Northampton, MA, USA: Edward Elgar.

Edquist, C., and B. Johnson (1997), 'Institutions and organisations in systems of innovation', in C. Edquist (ed.), *Systems of Innovation: Technologies, Institutions and Organisations*, London and Washington, DC: Pinter.

Freeman, Richard, and David L. Lindauer (1999), 'Why not Africa?', NBER working paper no. 6942.

Hannan, M. and J. Freeman (1984), 'Structural inertia and organisational change', *American Sociological Review*, **49**, 149–64.

IDB (2000), 'Periodic note on integration and trade in the Americas', mimeo, Washington, DC.

Lall, S. (2000), 'Foreign direct investment and development: policy and research issues in the emerging context', QEH working paper series 43.

Mariotti, S., and L. Piscitello (2001), 'Localized capabilities and the internationalization of manufacturing activities by SMEs', *Entrepreneurship & Regional Development*, **13**, 65–80.

McIntyre, J., R. Narula and L. Trevino (1996), 'The role of export processing zones for host countries and multinationals: a mutually beneficial relationship?', *International Trade Journal*, **10**, 435–66.

Mortimore, M. (1998), 'Getting a lift: modernizing industry by way of Latin American integration schemes, the example of automobiles', *Transnational Corporations*, **7** (2).

Mortimore, M. (2000), 'Corporate strategies for FDI in the context of Latin America's new economic model', *World Development*, **28** (9), 1611–26.

Mudambi, Ram (1998), 'The role of duration in MNE investment attraction strategies', *Journal of International Business Studies,* **29** (2), 239–62.

Mytelka, L. (1996), 'Locational tournaments, strategic partnerships and the state', mimeo, Carleton University, Ottawa.

Narula, R. (1996), *Multinational Investment and Economic Structure*, London: Routledge.

Narula, R. (2002), 'Innovation systems and 'inertia' in R&D location: Norwegian firms and the role of systemic lock-in', *Research Policy*, **31**, 795–816.

Pearce, R. (1989), *The Internationalisation of Research and Development by Multinational Enterprises*, London: Macmillan.

Pearce, R. (1999), 'Multinationals and industrialisation: the bases of "inward investment" policy', University of Reading discussion papers no. 279.

Pearce, R., and A. Tavares (1998), 'Strategies of multinational subsidiaries in a context of regional trading blocs', University of Reading discussion papers no. 257.

Reinhardt, N., and W. Peres (2000), 'Latin America's new economic model: micro responses and economic restructuring', *World Development*, **28** (9), 1543–66.

Smith, K. (1997), 'Economic infrastructures and innovation systems', in C. Edquist (ed.), *Systems of Innovation: Technologies, Institutions and Organisations*, London and Washington: Pinter.

Surlemont, B. (1998), 'A typology of centres within multinational corporations: an empirical investigation', in J. Birkinshaw and N. Hood (eds), *Multinational Corporate Evolution and Subsidiary Development*, Basingstoke: Macmillan.

UNCTAD (2000), *World Investment Report 2000*, Geneva and New York: United Nations.

Venables, A. (2000), 'Winners and losers from regional integration agreements', mimeo, LSE.

Vernon, R. (1996), 'Passing through regionalism: the transition to global markets', *Journal of World Trade*, **19** (6), 621–33.

PART II

R&D, alliances and developed countries

6. Explaining international R&D alliances and the role of governments

INTRODUCTION

One of the distinctive features of the process of globalization has been the growth of cross-border value-adding activities by firms, and the subsequent increasing interdependence of economies. However, the growth of globalization has led to a chain reaction, in that there has been an increasing trend for the activities of firms (both domestically and internationally) to be undertaken not just through internalization of intermediate product markets by hierarchies (referred to as 'hierarchical capitalism'), but through what has been coined 'alliance capitalism' (Gerlach, 1992; Dunning, 1995a). Specifically, alliance capitalism refers to the growing use of non-market, quasi-hierarchical modes of corporate activity, whereby firms do not completely (or formally) internalize their value-added activities, but utilize a variety of cooperative and collaborative agreements with other firms as a means to augment their own competitive advantage.

This growth in the use of cooperative agreements is particularly pervasive amongst firms from industrialized economies (Hagedoorn, 1996). It is generally the case that these firms are engaged in value added activity that is capital- and knowledge-intensive. National governments are thus frequently involved in promoting the human and physical resource competitiveness within their jurisdiction. They are also involved, directly or indirectly, in the generation and diffusion of knowledge, in the sense both of technology and of acquiring access to foreign markets. This is of particular interest to governments, since these assets are crucial in determining the competitiveness of firms from these countries as well as the competitiveness of these countries as locations for economic activity (see, for example, Porter 1990). One of the critical aspects of created assets concerns the generation and subsequent diffusion of intellectual capital, particularly that arising from investment in research and development (R&D) activities and human resource development. The growth of alliance capitalism and the need to improve competitiveness in response to globalization has naturally resulted in the growing use of cooperative agreements as a means to enhance competitiveness, particularly knowledge generation activities such as R&D (for example, Ohmae, 1985; Mowery, 1988; Hagedoorn, 1993).

These developments are relatively axiomatic and uncontroversial. However, although most national governments agree on the need to intervene to improve and sustain created assets, not all agree on the optimal method to do so. It should be noted that the extent of government intervention through industrial policy varies considerably between countries, from a sporadic intervention in the case of the USA, to a more systematic view taken by, say, France. Nonetheless, the differences between the views taken by individual industrialized countries would seem to be a matter of degree.

This disagreement about the extent to which intervention should be undertaken extends to the case of R&D alliance activity, although it is by now accepted that cooperative R&D can have net positive effects on the economy (see, for example, D'Aspremont and Jacquemin, 1988; Katz, 1986; Vonortas, 1994, 1997). It should be noted that a distinction needs to be made regarding the difference between three elements of R&D: basic research, applied research and development. While there is relatively little controversy regarding the role of government in basic R&D, this is not the case with government involvement in applied R&D activities, and particularly R&D alliances. The roots of this controversy derive from the nature of knowledge capital and the problems of fully appropriating its benefits, due to its two contradictory aspects. On the one hand, knowledge is partly of a public good nature, but, on the other hand, in high-technology sectors, it is also highly tacit and context-specific in nature. As such, because of its inherent uncertainty, there tends to be suboptimal R&D investment (including training programmes) by firms (for example, Arrow, 1962). Therefore one of the primary roles of governments is universally acknowledged as reducing the risks and costs and increasing the social benefits of the generation and diffusion of intellectual capital.

More controversially, however, there has been an increasing tendency among a number of industrialized country governments towards direct intervention favouring particular domestic firms, in what has been described as 'techno-nationalism' (Ostry and Nelson, 1995); that is, the decision of governments to 'target' certain firms in industries as primary recipients of government incentives to generate innovation. This chapter is primarily focused on evaluating techno-nationalism and the welfare implications on competitiveness, when applied to R&D alliances. The purpose of this chapter is thus threefold:

- to explain the increasing propensity to undertake R&D alliances in an age of globalization, with particular focus on international alliances;
- to understand the role of governments in promoting and engaging in generation and diffusion of intellectual capital in general, and in facilitating inter-firm technological alliances in particular;
- to evaluate the efficacy of techno-nationalism, in light of the welfare and social responsibilities of governments.

Our analysis attempts to draw together several strands of scholarly research in order to develop the basis for an interdisciplinary explanation of the phenomenon of international R&D alliances. This is based on aspects of economics of technology pioneered by, inter alia, Arrow (1962) and developed by Nelson and Winter (1982) and the knowledge-based theory of the firm (see Madhok, 1997, for a review), within the framework of the eclectic paradigm (for example, Dunning, 1993). The second area of theory building that is undertaken here is relating welfare economics issues to the strategic management issues of alliance stability (for example, Inkpen and Beamish, 1997).

The remainder of this chapter is organized as follows. First we will discuss the growth of alliance capitalism. We will then concentrate on understanding the growth of R&D alliances by firms, and then theorize on its nature. Thirdly we will specifically address the development of cross-border alliance activity. The next section presents arguments on why governments are interested in the R&D activities of firms, while the fifth section discusses the interaction between governments and international R&D alliances. We will then evaluate the various modalities (both direct and indirect) by which governments are involved in strategic alliance activity. Finally we will present the conclusions of the chapter and discuss some policy implications.

UNDERSTANDING THE GROWTH OF ALLIANCE CAPITALISM

Although the use of cooperative and collaborative agreements as a means of protecting or advancing the competitiveness of the participating firms is not new, the propensity of firms to engage in such activities has increased dramatically since the beginning of the 1980s (see, for example, Ohmae, 1985; Mytelka, 1991; Contractor and Lorange, 1988; Tallman and Shenkar, 1994; Hagedoorn, 1996; Hagedoorn and Narula, 1996). We make the distinction here that strategic alliances differ from networks in that, while strategic alliances are both value-enhancing (that is, are aimed at improving the long-term product-market positioning of at least one of the partnering firms) and cost-economizing, networks are primarily cost-economizing in nature (Madhok, 1997; Narula and Hagedoorn, 1999). This has prompted suggestions that economic activity through inter-firm alliances is no longer an inferior option to the use of hierarchies, and that in many cases it is regarded as the 'first-best' option (Ciborra, 1991). Moreover, where firms do engage in hierarchies, it is increasingly through the use of mergers and acquisitions (M&A) which, like strategic alliances, are undertaken not so much as a means of reducing transaction costs but as a means of protecting and augmenting the competitiveness of the participating firms, and can also be regarded as an extreme form of collaboration. Indeed, there is a strong link between M&A and strategic alliances, in that firms often establish a strategic alliance with a prospective M&A target (Hagedoorn and Sadowski, 1999).

Globalization, as discussed here (see Figure 6.1) signifies, inter alia, (1) an increasing interdependence and convergence in consumption patterns and technologies across countries; (2) the increasing internationalization of production through networks of MNE affiliates, and (3) the increasing overlapping and merging of industrial sectors, increasing capital and knowledge intensity as well as a concurrent shortening of technology life cycles (Narula and Dunning, 1999). This has resulted in global supply and demand pressures that have affected the competitiveness of firms as they increasingly compete, not just with firms in the home country, but also with those firms in the same industry in different countries (Cantwell and Sanna Randaccio, 1990).

The relationship between globalization and the growth of alliances has been sketched by several authors, including Hagedoorn (1993), Glaister and Buckley (1996), Ohmae (1985), Mowery (1988) and Mytelka (1991) and suggests there are five interrelated phenomena at work here. First, there has been an increase in such activity across all of the advanced industrialized economies, as opposed to being a phenomenon peculiar to certain economies, such as Japan. Second, there is an increasingly strategic aspect to this activity, as alliances are no longer simply undertaken as a means of avoiding transaction and coordination costs of markets (a second-best, 'exit' response), but rather as a first-best 'voice' strategy to reduce market failure due inter alia, to barriers to entry (Dunning, 1995a), where this was thought preferable to the complete internalization of these markets, where such internalization was not possible (see Hood and Young, 1979). Third, one of the original motives for alliance formation was to acquire market access and/or to overcome supply bottlenecks, that is, to achieve vertical integration where such integration was not possible through hierarchies. Firms engaged in very little alliance formation on a horizontal basis as they

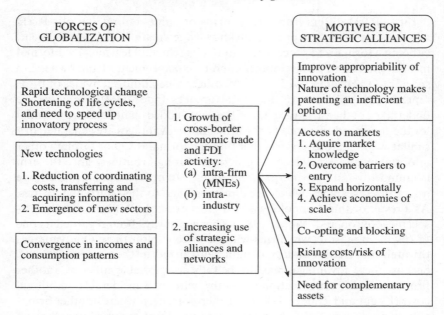

Figure 6.1   Relating globalization to the motives for strategic alliances

do today. Fourth, inter-firm alliances are increasingly being undertaken, through various modes, as a direct response to pressures brought about by contemporary technological developments and globalization. Fifth, whereas alliances were primarily undertaken for the purpose of achieving or improving market entry and presence, an increasing number of alliances are being undertaken to protect or enhance the created assets of the participating firms.

WHY FIRMS UNDERTAKE R&D ALLIANCES

The previous section outlined the exogenous issues defining the growth of strategic alliances. In this section we propose to understand the firm-specific reasons for the growth of R&D alliances sometimes referred to as 'strategic technology partnering' (STP). It is important to understand that STP represents a special case of alliances, given the unique nature of innovating and creating especially through R&D activities. In order to understand the growth of alliances we refer to aspects from evolutionary theory and the nature of technology (see, for example, Teece, 1977; Nelson and Winter, 1982; Cantwell, 1989; Kogut and Zander, 1993).

First, R&D differs from other forms of value-adding activity. R&D activities represent the process of knowledge creation and development, either in a formalized process or through incremental learning by informal means, and from the development and/or enhancement of the ownership specific ('O') advantages of firms. All other value-adding activities of firms represent the utilization of these O advantages. Indeed, R&D activities are undertaken at the various stages of the value-added chain, and are essential for the continued existence of the firm. All O advantages are generated in a similar way, regardless of whether through formal R&D or through other informal means. Knowledge is generated through routines, since the firm is boundedly rational and path-dependent. In other words, firms engage in 'localized searches' which are directly related to their current activities. As a result of this, technology is to a great extent both firm- and context-specific (Nelson and Winter, 1982). This has always been regarded as one of the main reasons why firms will prefer to exploit these O advantages through hierarchies and/or remain centralized in their home country, because these advantages may not be fully appropriable either by another firm or at a different location (or both), without considerable additional costs (Kogut and Zander, 1993). Furthermore, even where another firm is able to do so efficiently, the public good nature of technology will mean that the innovating firm will not receive compensation for its R&D output commensurate to its value. This tendency would be greater the higher the tacit and non-codifiable aspect of the technology (Cantwell, 1989).

In addition, the benefits of innovations are only partly appropriable through markets, given the public good nature of technology.[1] The seller cannot get a buyer for his innovation without revealing it, and thus losing some of its value. On the other hand, the buyer cannot make a rational decision regarding the value of the innovation without full disclosure, thus making a suboptimal offer for it. This implies that the innovator can only generate maximum rents from the technology through internalizing its use, since he alone is aware of its actual value.

In summary, since the level of tacitness of knowledge generated through routines is higher, it is logical to expect newly generated O advantages to be more firm- and context-specific than current O advantages of the firm. It may then be reasonably argued that firms, *ceteris paribus*, will have a higher propensity to internalize the market for R&D-related output than for intermediate products generated through production activities at other parts of the value added chain. Likewise, it can be argued that firms will prefer to centralize their R&D activities to a greater extent than production.

The evidence on internalization of R&D activities, however, remains ambivalent: not only are firms engaging in a growing number of STP agreements that explicitly involve joint technology development, but a large percentage of these are in knowledge-intensive sectors (Hagedoorn and Narula, 1996). Furthermore, it would also be reasonable to expect that in the event that full internalization were impossible, for whatever reason, firms might prefer to use organizational modes that provided the maximum amount of control over the innovatory process. This, however, does not appear to be the case: recent evidence indicates that there is an increasing propensity to utilize non-equity types of agreements, and this trend cuts across sectors and countries (Narula and Hagedoorn, 1999).

Recent evidence on decision taking loci by firms continues to indicate a preference for centralization of formalized R&D activities (see, for instance, Patel, 1996; Pearce and Singh, 1992). Moreover, the extent of internationalization of R&D of firms continues to be considerably less than production, there has nonetheless been a distinct shift towards internationalization of R&D activities, one reason for which has been the sharp growth of strategic asset-seeking FDI activity (Dunning and Narula, 1994, 1996; see also Chapter 3).

In other words, the economic imperative to internalize the markets for knowledge-based activities and to locate these activities in the home country of the innovating firm is being challenged by changes in the way firms view the global market place. What we are trying to emphasize here is that the forces underlying globalization have considerably influenced the way in which firms locate their R&D activities and the organizational modes used. There have been several attempts to develop a taxonomy of reasons why firms are gradually challenging the conventional wisdom about the modality and geography of R&D alliances; these were summarized in Figure 6.1.

WHY ALLIANCES OCCUR ACROSS BORDERS

In recent years a growing body of literature (see Osborn and Hagedoorn, 1997, for a review) has examined the phenomenon of cross-border alliances. We now direct our attention to explaining international alliance formation, that is, what are the additional factors to be taken into account in cross-border activity. The transaction costs approach has been extensively studied (for example, by Kogut, 1988, and Hennart, 1993, among others) and suggests that pure hierarchies are sometimes a more costly strategy than alliances, because of the associated higher financial risks and barriers to entry. However, there is another aspect to this, from FDI theory. The eclectic paradigm (for example, Dunning, 1993) suggests firms engage in foreign-based value added activity if they possess O advantages that they wish to utilize in conjunction with the location advantages of the host region or country. In the case of technology development, however, these advantages are often of a non-codifiable nature and, given the firm-specific nature of such assets, it may be that the location advantages cannot be completely captured by the foreign investor because they are specific to domestic firms rather than the country where they are located. Therefore firms are obliged to engage in STP rather than subsidiary (that is, majority-owned) FDI activity.

In short, firms from one country with O advantages may seek to utilize them in a foreign country either in conjunction with immobile but generally available assets of the host region, or with the ownership advantages of firms in that location, when the advantages it seeks are firm-specific. Such a firm may be a competitor, supplier or customer to the foreign firm.

However, it is pertinent to point out that what we have described here could very well also apply to a network, or some other transaction cost-economizing agreement. The difference between a cost-economizing agreement (like networks) and a strategic alliance is the presence of a 'strategic' element, which is described as 'an agreement which affects the long term product-marketing positioning of the firm' (Hagedoorn and Narula, 1996) or, in other words, does not simply minimize the net costs, but also improves the future value of the firm.[2] Focusing our sights once again on the special case of STP, 'strategic' implies the transfer of some extent of knowledge, on at least a unilateral basis, by at least one of the partners as part of the agreement. In other words, an R&D alliance may be undertaken in a *location with a complete absence of 'traditional' location advantages*, when the objective is primarily to acquire firm-specific O advantages through the process of partnering. While the presence of this firm may signify a concentration or agglomeration of firms in a given location (an L advantage), this is not necessarily always the case. That is, while L advantages may have determined the nature of the O advantages of the domestic firms, their transfer to a foreign partner within the framework of an alliance constitutes the utilization of the domestic partner's O advantages and not the L advantages from which they may have originally derived. It is pertinent to note that STP does not necessarily imply that it is not simply technology that is being shared or created, but generally also includes market-related knowledge, be it intra-firm, intra-industry or country-specific. That is, STP may also include the transfer of knowledge which is normally associated with transaction cost-minimizing activities, that are referred to as O_t advantages in the FDI literature.

Nonetheless, there is a caveat to be noted here, as the preceding discussion might suggest that both partners should not have a particular preference for the location at which their partnership might be consummated. As we explained earlier, the knowledge base of any given firm is context-specific, since the O advantages, being path-dependent, are a direct result of the comparative and competitive advantage of the home location (Cantwell, 1989; Archibugi and Pianta, 1992; Narula, 1996b). Therefore, where the foreign partner wishes to internalize these O advantages through STP, it can more efficiently do so in the location where they were generated. This is equally valid for market-oriented STP and R&D-oriented STP.

So far we have sought to explain why firms prefer to engage in non-market mechanisms to develop technology, because of the nature of technology creation vis-à-vis technology exploitation. Although there is a distinct tendency for MNEs to prefer to conduct much of their R&D activities in their home country, there are suggestions that firms are developing multiple home bases for these activities and engaging in foreign-based R&D activities to augment as well as to exploit their competitive advantages (Keummerle, 1996). It is therefore logical to expect that, where the firm finds it necessary to engage in alliances to develop technology (R&D), (rather than gaining market knowledge), it will prefer to engage in alliances with 'local' partners, given the costs of adapting the context-specific nature of their ownership advantages. Duysters (1996) demonstrates that R&D-related STP tends to be less international than market-oriented STP.

THE ROLE OF GOVERNMENTS: A WELFARE PERSPECTIVE

It should by now be patently obvious that national governments have a strong interest in the ability of firms in a given location to conduct competitiveness-enhancing activities, and particularly those associated with the creation and deployment of knowledge capital. These reasons can be qualified under two main headings, namely, the promotion of wealth-creating assets of its firms (O advantages), and maintaining and improving indigenous resources and capabilities (L advantages). By doing so, it can help maintain and improve its own locational attractiveness to mobile and footloose investors (of whatever nationality) to conduct high value-adding activity. These two issues are strongly related, since the presence of highly competitive firms at a given location act as an L advantage, often prompting a virtuous circle. Conversely, strong L advantages, such as the presence of support institutions and firms, infrastructure and skilled manpower (that is, the national systems of innovation) will enhance the O advantages of firms located there.

In other words, the reduction of market imperfections in the creation and utilization of knowledge capital has considerable welfare benefits, which stem both from a direct result of these activities and from externalities generated by them. It is also to be noted that governments may intervene for at least three other reasons which are only indirectly related to advancing competitiveness. Among these we might mention first protection or advancement of economic or political sovereignty. The second is for strategic reasons, such as in defence-related issues. The third is where investment in R&D is primarily undertaken to promote social goals, such as in the health and environment sectors. It is to be noted that, in all of these cases, even though R&D may be undertaken by private firms for commercial application elsewhere, the interest of government is to limit diffusion (for example, in the defence sector) of the technology to non-national firms, or to maximize diffusion (such as the health and environment sectors) of innovations, by, for example, acquiring the property rights and providing it at marginal cost to all firms. However, in our current exposition we are interested in the role of governments in affecting commercial R&D activity, and therefore we shall not explore other issues in greater detail. We identify three main reasons for governments having an interest in fostering R&D activities.

1. *Level of investment in R&D*: countries with low expenditures in R&D tend not to be as competitive (for examples, see Archibugi and Pianta, 1992). Consequently, governments have an incentive to encourage R&D activities. Without government intervention, firms may tend to underinvest, given their bounded rationality and the path-dependent nature of their activities. Since firms prefer to engage in new activities closely linked to their current activities, this may result in too little R&D investment, relative to other kinds of investment (Hall, 1986). Further, greater uncertainty may arise from competition: another firm may be doing similar research. Neither the time that the research will be completed nor the identity of the winner of the race to innovate is known. The risk from these and other problems is often reflected in the cost of capital to the firm intent on undertaking R&D, and, the higher the risk, the more difficult it may be to acquire capital to undertake it. In the limit, financial capital may be unavailable for risky research projects. On the other hand, it is possible that too many, rather than too few, resources may be applied to R&D (Barzel, 1968). This might occur, for example, where several firms are in a 'race' to solve a given technological problem, and this may lead to overinvestment in R&D. In other words, there is (a) the danger of firms underinvesting in new technologies with which they are unfamiliar or which are too risky; and (b) the risk of overinvestment in a given project due to duplication of investment by several firms.

2. *Problems from appropriability*: society is faced with the difficulty of sustaining economic growth through encouraging innovative activity

by, on the one hand, providing monopoly power to the inventor so that he may continue to innovate at a socially optimal level, but, on the other, maximizing diffusion and availability of products at the lowest possible costs, generally by encouraging competition. However, firms will underinvest in R&D when they are uncertain of appropriating sufficient returns. This occurs for three reasons: first, because the value of an innovation is not always apparent to the market ex ante; second, even where the value of the innovation is known to the inventor, he cannot convince others without revealing the details of the innovation, thereby losing some its value because of its public good nature; third, even where the firm overcomes these two hurdles, it cannot charge the market the actual value of the innovation, but the opportunity cost, or the value of the next best option available on the market (Barzel, 1968). As such, it will remain uncertain as to whether it can recuperate the costs of its investment, unless the government is able to act as a broker in this process. The traditional route taken by governments is to administer and issue patents, but these are highly imperfect tools to assign property rights, and are also inefficient. It is to be stressed that, while government intervention is a possible solution, it is not the *only* solution, and indeed, there are several instances and situations where the market is able partially to rectify itself. Firms that are unable to patent utilize secrecy and lead times as methods to protect their property rights (Levin *et al.*, 1987), but are also unlikely to spread the risks and costs of R&D among the potential users of the innovation.

3. *Industry structure and concentration*: the third concern is the prevention of oligopolistic and/or monopolistic behaviour in asset creation and utilization. It is axiomatic that demand is necessary as a catalyst to innovation, and the competition to survive among firms in a given industry drives the generation and diffusion of technology. However, it remains unclear what the optimal level of competition is. Dasgupta and Stiglitz (1980), among others, have shown that there is a positive relationship between competition in R&D and the level of innovation, but it is as yet unclear what the appropriate level of innovatory activity is. On the one hand, there is evidence to indicate that, when there are a larger number of firms engaged in R&D in a given industry, the average level of R&D investment per firm falls, but the total investment in the industry rises. On the other hand, there is also evidence that would conform to the Schumpeterian idea that innovative activity may be encouraged by industry structures in which firms are few and concentration is substantial. This is a complex issue that remains unresolved, and is very much a question of country-specific policy. Certainly, it would appear that, given the cost and risk of R&D in the age of globalization, a few

large firms are more likely to be successful than a large number of small ones. How the implementation of R&D alliances affects the optimum industry structure is unclear, but, in general, governments have preferred to limit strategic alliances of firms in a given industry to pre-competitive research (for example, SEMATECH, ESPRIT).

GOVERNMENTS AND INTERNATIONAL R&D ALLIANCES

The chapter thus far illustrates the importance attached by national governments to the creation and diffusion of knowledge capital, which is regarded as the bedrock upon which the economic prosperity (that is, the competitiveness) of the advanced industrial countries is built. However, the influence of governments on the competitiveness of their economies has been somewhat diluted with the advent of globalization and, in its wake, alliance capitalism. To take a couple of examples. First, governments find it much more difficult to enforce the appropriability of technology when intellectual property rights are violated in countries where such protection is limited, thereby perhaps raising the cost of products to domestic consumers, and further affecting the willingness of these firms to invest in R&D.

Second, there is increasing difficulty in identifying and determining where R&D investment is made, and who reaps the benefits therefrom, especially when the innovation is done in, say, Philips' R&D facility in the USA, or, even more complex, when the innovation is from the UK laboratory of, say, the Anglo–Dutch conglomerate, Unilever.

Ostry and Nelson (1995) suggest that, because of the difficulties of enforcing and monitoring international compliance with property rights as well as the declining efficacy of patents, government support of R&D is the best way to induce industrial innovation, rather than relying on the market to provide an adequate return. This line of reasoning has a considerable following, not least among economists who advocate 'strategic trade theory', as well as most neo-Schumpeterian economists. Essentially, the argument made is that, since technology defines competitiveness, and as the cost of R&D activity is rising, an oligopolistic market structure would be optimal. A small number of firms would reap higher profits, which would support higher wages. However, since every country would like its firms (or one of them) in each high-tech, capital-intensive sector to be among the surviving firms, this has led to a sort of 'techno-nationalism' where every country supports its national champions through various means in the bid to maintain its technological competitiveness.

However, this techno-nationalism has resulted in a sort of prisoner's dilemma, as globalization makes it much more difficult to identify what constitutes a national champion, as has proved to be the case with ICI or Rover. Indeed, Ostry and Nelson (1995) argue that policies that have sought to create national champions have actually furthered the process of transnationalization, since barriers to imports have encouraged foreign MNEs to establish local value-adding activities and undertake alliances in order to receive national treatment.

It should be noted that it is by no means necessary that national governments regard STP as a first-best option, or even a second-best one: it is debatable, for example, whether R&D investment through alliances is quite at the same level as that achieved through internalized R&D activity by national firms. Certainly, it would seem obvious that government financial support being given to a collaboration between a national champion with a firm of another nationality may represent a subsidy to the foreign firm. Likewise, a firm may see R&D subsidies given to it by the government as a substitute for its own R&D efforts rather than an additional source of investment, leading to a net reduction in R&D expenditures on a national level. However, the question is not whether R&D investment through STP is a better solution than R&D investment by domestic firms, but whether it represents a better solution than that offered by the free market; and there is good reason to suspect that the market will be unable to achieve a welfare optimum. The argument against intervention suggests that governments may not be able to do better than markets and that, since innovation occurs in response to market demand, it cannot be seriously suboptimal (this line of reasoning is succinctly summarized in Hall, 1986, pp. 9–14). Moreover, it is important to realize that it is not simply a question of maintaining the *level* of R&D investment, but also the *efficiency* of this investment.

Our chapter heretofore underlines the unresolved question of the prudence of government intervention in R&D activity. Indeed, there remains considerable variation between countries in the extent to which they intervene. For instance, although public sources in the USA account for over 40 per cent of R&D expenditures, US intervention is by and large sporadic at the applied R&D level. On the other hand, France and Japan are much more systematically involved in subsidizing and coordinating applied research. Since R&D activity is highly uncertain by nature, especially when such R&D activity is close to or at the technology frontier, and where the R&D is basic and conceptual, the efficacy of government intervention is unclear. This is for two reasons. First, governments need to concentrate on industries and sectors which offer promise in the medium and long term, and are not sunset industries. Besides, there may be several different, competing technologies, but only limited funds. In such cases, choices have to be made, and firms do not have an incentive to reveal their true opinions, especially where the most 'deserving' firm is a rival one. As Farell (1987) has emphasized, a central authority is bound to have less complete information than the firms in a given sector. When firms are engaged in R&D some distance away from the technological frontier, the direction in which investment is to be made is obvious since firms at the frontier (that is, the technology leaders) have already done this. (However, it is necessary to emphasize the difference between firms that are some distance from the technology frontier, and those that are simply experiencing X-inefficiency. The latter group are simply using an inferior technology, while the former are operating at an earlier stage of the product life cycle.) The astounding success of Japan's Ministry of International Trade and Industry (MITI) in picking winners in the 1950s and 1960s, and their less successful interventions in the 1980s and 1990s, illustrate this point well. However, non-intervention is not the answer either, since firms that are risk-averse will avoid investments in highly risky, economically less viable, 'blue sky' projects.

Secondly, where a 'worthy' project is defined, there are clear difficulties in identifying whether the government subsidies are being utilized for the purpose for which they were provided, or simply as a mechanism for cross-subsidization of other R&D projects. This arises from the tacit nature of basic R&D in high technology industries, since the output may not be patentable or have an identifiable tangible form.

It is not our aim here to evaluate the wisdom of government involvement in promoting R&D activity, or to criticize techno-nationalism.[3] Our position is based on the assumption that these are the implicit goals of national governments of the advanced industrial countries (for a review, see Ostry and Nelson, 1995). However, the evidence reviewed so far indicates that firms must necessarily engage in asset exploitation on a global (or at least regional) basis if they are to remain competitive, and, albeit to a lesser degree (but to a growing extent), to develop and acquire new assets globally. The evidence reviewed would also indicate that, in general, firms are more willing to engage in collaborative R&D activities in overseas locations than in wholly owned R&D activities, and this has much to do with techno-globalism (Archibugi and Michie, 1994).

Having said this, however, there is no consensus on the optimal way to boost the competitive advantage of firms through strategic alliances. On the one hand, countries such as the USA have hitherto attempted to deal with the root causes of market failure by trying to make markets more efficient, but only directly intervening on a reactive, case-by case basis (for instance, in sectors in which defence applications may exist). Countries such as France and Japan, on the other hand, have taken a more active or direct role (see Nelson, 1993).

OPPORTUNITIES FOR GOVERNMENTS: DIRECT VERSUS INDIRECT INTERVENTION

We have thus far illustrated that, as far as governments are concerned, their primary interests lie in strengthening the competitiveness of their national firms. The evidence would suggest that the role of governments, at least in the case of the industrialized countries, is most effective as a facilitator of competitive advantage, in terms of providing the complementary assets needed by firms, rather than as a direct intervention. These assets are best described as the national systems of innovation (NSI), and are defined as the network of institutions in the public and private sector in a given country that support the generation and diffusion of innovations (Freeman, 1987). In the parlance of the eclectic paradigm, the NSI represent the location-bound resources and capabilities that sustain, complement and enhance the O advantages of firms. In other words, indirect intervention takes the form of improving the O advantages of firms by affecting the L advantages of the country. By direct intervention we refer, inter alia, to attempts by governments to enhance the O advantages of firms by fiat, through restrictions on domestic operations of foreign MNEs (for example, the US airline industry), through the provision of exclusive contracts to develop products for the use of governments (for example, the French TGV, eurofighter project, space shuttle, and so on) or through exclusive (or subsidized) access to public sector research facilities. It must be noted that few countries desist completely from direct intervention. We will briefly discuss the options available to governments in connection to encouraging R&D alliances under these two headings.

Direct Intervention

We identify four primary means by which governments can engage in direct intervention. The first is as a participant. Governments can engage as direct participants in R&D alliances as a partner. This is especially common in basic research projects, as public research institutes and universities have the human and capital resources to undertake fundamental R&D, or what is referred to as 'pre-competitive research' by the EU. This is one of the means used by the EU to improve the competitiveness of European firms; indeed, almost 60 per cent of funding within the second and third framework programmes which covered the period 1987 and 1994, 12 billion ECUs, was directed towards universities and public institutes (Geuna, 1996). An additional advantage of direct participation is that it is better able to monitor the utilization of the resources and act as an honest broker, and prevent the misallocation of funds by commercial (and profit-oriented) partners. NTT, the Japanese telecommunications giant, has played a similar role in enforcing the partnership agreements undertaken by firms in telecommunications and computers, by sponsoring complementary research to that of MITI, and allowing the consolidation of national champions in each of these industries (Levy and Samuels, 1991).

The second is by guaranteeing a market for the output of the alliance. This can be undertaken in at least three ways: first, by providing consortia of firms with project-specific contracts, as is the case with most EU aerospace projects, and US defence-related projects (this substantially reduces the risk associated with R&D, and at the same time improves the appropriability of the innovation); second, by directly affecting the returns to the innovator by creating a market for the product (for example, in the 1970s, the Japanese government established the Japan Robot Company which bought all the output from the robot manufacturers, and then leased the robots to the customers); third, by establishing a particular technology standard, which may be proprietary to a particular firm, and requiring firms to adhere to them. This has the added advantage that it prevents duplication of investment in other, inferior, alternatives. This is achieved through establishing cross-licensing agreements. The most successful of these, the aircraft patent agreement among US firms which remained in force between 1917 and 1968, was established at the behest of the US government during the First World War in order to standardize the use of the 'best-practice' technology in airframes across the various manufacturers (Bitlingmayer, 1988). The difficulty in doing so is that, first, governments may not necessarily select ex ante what is the superior technology, and, second, it requires a suspension of antitrust regulations in most cases. In fact, the aircraft patent agreement was eventually terminated by the US Supreme Court, when it was deemed contrary to antitrust regulations.

The third means is by providing a domestic firm with market access in exchange for technology, excluding foreign firms by insisting that a foreign-based MNE have certain minimum local content, and thereby create linkages, or that it take a domestic partner in exchange for access to the domestic market. The case of both European and US voluntary export restrictions with Japanese firms led to an increase in FDI (and alliance formation) during the 1980s. A similar approach was taken by Korea during the 1960s (Amsden, 1989), where technology transfer was made a condition for market access.

Finally, governments can engage in direct intervention by making participation in alliances a precondition for future government contracts: Both the direction of research and the availability of subsidies can be used as leverage to encourage firms to undertake collaborative research. This is the case with the Japanese computer industry, in which major Japanese firms were asked to collaborate on joint R&D, with the understanding that it affected future subsidies from MITI. Levy and Samuels (1991) note that, when Matsushita left the computer industry in 1964, it was unable to enter MITI-sponsored computer alliances for two decades.

Indirect Intervention

The literature is replete with policy prescriptions to improve the L advantages and the quality of location-bound resources, and there is no reason to revise this literature here. The enhancement of L advantages has received considerable attention in various guises (see Porter, 1990; Dunning and Narula, 1996; Nelson, 1993, Dunning, 1993, among others), and is relatively uncontroversial. There is therefore no need to develop an exhaustive typology of options here. We shall, however, highlight two important issues regarding countries' indirect intervention.

First, although governments are unable to prevent alliances from being unstable or, indeed, from reducing the inherent risk of R&D activity – whether collaborative or otherwise – there is a role for governments in providing information to help identify synergies, complementarities and opportunities, since there are imperfections in the market for partners. Governments can help diffuse the results of basic research output produced either by government research institutes or by private establishments to interested parties by creating a sort of 'market place' where potential partners can meet and exchange information. This is undertaken on a regular basis through trade fairs, but also directly through government institutions (Niosi, 1995). Even where governments do not own the technologies, they can play an important role in match-making of firms.

Second, there is an important and growing role for governments in encouraging and monitoring cross-border R&D alliances, and reducing uncertainty attached to this. First, this can be done by the development of binding multilateral intellectual property rights protection through agencies such as the World Trade Organization, thereby improving appropriability of innovation, both domestically and internationally. There is a very real danger of cross-border duplication of activity, especially in terms of multiple (and not necessarily compatible) standards which can be suboptimal in terms of expenditure on a global basis. Recent initiatives by the G7 members to subsidize space research jointly is such an example. The failure to develop a common standard on high definition TV has largely affected its successful commercial launch. However, intergovernmental initiatives are, in general, the exception rather than the rule.

Areas in which Government Intervention is Futile

Despite the best efforts of governments, there nonetheless remain considerable risks associated with success or failure of an alliance (see Inkpen and Beamish, 1996). Even where complementarities exist, and potential partners are identified, there are several hazards. Das and Teng (1996) suggest that these can be viewed as being of two types. The first, relational risk, occurs as a result of one or more of the partners in an alliance being unwilling to work towards the mutual interest of the partnership, thereby breaching the agreement. Such behaviour may be rational or irrational, and includes asymmetrical learning, or a lack of trust. There is limited scope for government intervention in such an instance, since we would have to assume perfect information ex ante on the failure of a partner to provide inputs in the prescribed manner. Given the nature of R&D alliances, such an assumption is clearly unrealistic and, in the case of basic R&D, the asymmetrical learning may not be evident in the short term. Nor, it must be said, does relationship risk arise only from the failure of partners to maintain the agreement; it may also occur where they interpret the agreement literally. Lastly, relational risk may be unintentional, since partners may have different objectives. The second sort of risk, performance risk, occurs when all partners have cooperated fully, but the partnership has nonetheless not achieved its objective, and represents the opposite problem. The role of government here is also limited, except where such alliances had received government subsidies, since the question is whether in fact the failure of the partnering was due to inefficient and/or inappropriate use of the funds, or whether the research trajectory was 'too far' from commercialization for any tangible output to be generated. Such questions have been raised about the ESPRIT programme of the European Commission (Mytelka, 1991).

CONCLUSIONS

Globalization has led to profound changes in the ways in which business activities are conducted, not least because of the growing use of networks and alliances by firms from the advanced industrial countries. This process, dubbed 'alliance capitalism', represents a new phase in the evolution of the market economies. There has also been a concurrent growth in the use of alliances to acquire and develop knowledge capital. The growth of strategic technology partnering is somewhat strange, in that firms have hitherto preferred to internalize their R&D activities because of the inherent nature of the innovation process. Further, they have tended in the past to concentrate these activities in their home base. We have attempted to develop an explanation for the growth of R&D alliances, and particularly international R&D alliances within existing paradigms of FDI activity and evolutionary theory. Furthermore, we have developed a framework to understand the welfare and social rationale for government involvement in promoting and partaking in R&D activities in general and alliances in particular, paying special attention to the evolution of international strategic technology partnering. We have also demonstrated the possible suboptimal outcome of nation states attempting to 'target' innovatory activity by particular companies. This last point forms the primary focus of the discussion in this chapter.

It would seem that countries are increasingly engaged in promoting the competitiveness of their domestic firms, in what can loosely be described as 'techno-nationalism' (Ostry and Nelson, 1995), with the intention of developing 'national champions'. Most of the major industrial economies practise some sort of government intervention to boost the O advantages of their firms. While some governments do so through indirect means that improve the quality of location-bound resources and capabilities to attract mobile O advantages of domestic and foreign-owned firms, others attempt more direct intervention by directly participating in O advantage-generating activities.

Much of this intervention was originally a response to globalization, with the desire to protect weak domestic firms from international competition. Ironically, this has led to a greater use of alliance and network-forming activity and, therefore, techno-nationalism is doomed to failure, as the question of 'who is us' and 'who is them' makes such policies increasingly redundant (Reich, 1990). National champions are equally willing to act as free agents, and are in some instances receiving national treatment (and support) from several governments, both national and regional. The example of IBM being involved in several research consortia funded by the EU and the US governments best illustrates this point.

As for the underlying motive of improving levels of R&D activity, this too would seem to be in doubt. It should be noted that R&D alliances are even more footloose than traditional majority-owned production or R&D activities; nor, it must be stressed, do R&D alliances provide significant levels of spillovers to the host economies where they might be located. Funds invested in joint research by governments are notoriously hard to track down, in terms of their application, both in a geographic and in a technical (that is, project-specific) sense. Furthermore, firms are more interested in establishing themselves near centres of agglomeration, regardless of where these might be located. This indicates a very real danger of entering an incentive war, with so many countries willing to subsidize R&D (Niosi, 1995) and with so few obvious spillovers therefrom.

Policy Implications

It is important to realize that the extent of government intervention is idiosyncratic and country-specific. Consequently, the motive for supporting R&D alliances, and the nature of the intervention, may vary according to different government policies. We have noted four means which are most favoured by countries for intervening directly, and two by which governments do so indirectly, all of which are utilized to differing extents by policy makers. Our most fundamental advice, based on the preceding analyses, is to avoid picking 'winners', in terms of both specific firms and particular technological trajectories, as this is bound to lead, *ceteris paribus*, to suboptimal outcomes in the long run. In specific terms, our advice to policy makers, based on our analyses, can be succinctly summarized as follows.

1. View strategic technology partnering as complementary to domestic R&D, rather than as a substitute. There is a danger that firms may see R&D subsidies given to it by the government as a substitute for its own R&D efforts rather than an additional source of investment, leading to a net reduction in R&D expenditures on a national level. It is also important to note that, even though the level of investment may have gone up, what is more crucial is whether the efficiency of use of this investment has increased. That is to say, although R&D alliances may lead to greater R&D expenditures, it is by no means certain that such inputs will lead to a proportional increase in output, as the benefits may accrue to other projects and firms, since learning in an alliance is not always symmetrical.
2. Furthermore, a distinction needs to be made regarding the various aspects of R&D: basic research, applied research and development. There is relatively little controversy about basic research and the need for governments to subsidize them, although the ability of governments to pick who to subsidize is another matter. However, strategic technology partnering is also relatively uncontroversial in basic research. The debate primarily revolves around applied research and development. In a roundabout sense, Krugman (1994) is right: countries do not compete, companies do. It is not the role of governments to try and enhance the O advantages of its firms, to the exclusion of foreign-owned establishments; nor can they expect to do so in this age of alliance capitalism. Instead, the onus should be on improving the 'L' advantages of countries and the 'O' advantage-augmenting resources such as education and training, infrastructure, institutions, intellectual property rights protection and other non-specific R&D support. Nonetheless, in many other ways, Krugman was also wrong: competitiveness of countries does matter,

since markets are imperfect, and resources are mobile, thereby making government intervention necessary. Its urgency is further enhanced by the fact that the current extent of involvement by governments represents a sort of prisoner's dilemma, since no country is likely to back down from the current competitiveness-enhancing 'war'. We would be safe in concluding that, in this age of strategic trade policies and selective industrial development, nations that rely only on market forces to determine outcomes are not just not playing on a level playing field, but are playing on a different playing field altogether.

3. The evidence on globalization and alliance capitalism would seem to point towards a role for governments in improving the efficiency of R&D activities on an international basis. It is understandable that countries duplicate R&D investments for strategic and political reasons, especially in basic research, but the failure to create international standards, in many instances, leads to considerable misallocation of resources, particularly in applied R&D. Furthermore, several countries are often, unknowingly, engaged in subsidizing the same projects of transnational firms. There is clearly a growing need to address these and other issues on an international basis, as is currently being undertaken for intellectual property rights within the framework of the WTO.

4. There is a role for governments in providing information to help identify synergies, complementarities and opportunities, since there are market imperfections in the market for partners. Governments can help diffuse the results of basic research output produced either by government research institutes or by private establishments to interested parties by creating a sort of 'market place' where potential partners can meet and exchange information. This is undertaken on a regular basis through trade fairs, but also directly through government institutions (Niosi, 1995).

NOTES

1. It should be noted that, throughout the remainder of this chapter, our arguments apply to the more formalized process of R&D rather than the informal processes of R&D.
2. The important differences between the transaction cost school (which emphasizes cost) and the organizational capability school (which emphasizes value) are succinctly summarized in Madhok (1997).
3. See Krugman (1994) for such a critique. For a counterargument, see Dunning (1995b).

REFERENCES

Amsden, A. (1989), *Asia's Next Giant*, New York: Oxford University Press.
Archibugi, D., and J. Michie (1994), 'The globalisation of technology: a new taxonomy', *Cambridge Journal of Economics*, **19**, 21–140.

Archibuigi, D., and M. Pianta (1992), *The Technological Specialization of Advanced Countries*, Dordrecht: Kluwer Academic Publishers.

Arrow, Kenneth (1962), 'Economic welfare and the allocation of resources for invention', *The Rate and Direction of Inventive Activity*, National Bureau for Economic Research, Princeton, NJ: Princeton University Press, pp. 609–25.

Barzel, Yarom (1968), 'Optimal timing of innovations', *The Review of Economics and Statistics*, **50**, 348–55.

Bitlingmayer, George (1988), 'Property rights, progress, and the aircraft patent agreement', *Journal of Law and Economics*, **31**, 227–48.

Cantwell, J. (1989), *Technological Innovation and Multinational Corporations*, Oxford: Basil Blackwell.

Cantwell, J., and F. Sanna Randaccio (1990), 'The growth of multinationals and the catching up effect', *Economic Notes*, **19**, July, 1–23.

Ciborra, C. (1991), 'Alliances as learning experiments: cooperation, competition and change in high-tech industries', in L. Mytelka (ed.), *Strategic Partnerships and the World Economy,* London: Pinter, pp. 51–77.

Contractor, F., and P. Lorange (1988), *Co-operative Strategies in International Business*, Lexington, MA: D.C. Heath.

Das, T., and B-S. Teng (1996), 'Risk types and inter-firm alliance structures', *Journal of Management Studies*, **33**, 827–43.

Dasgupta, P., and J. Stiglitz (1980), 'Uncertainty, industrial structure and the speed of R&D', *Bell Journal of Economics*, **11**, 1–28.

D'Aspremont, C., and A. Jacquemin (1988), 'Cooperative and noncooperative R&D in duopoly with spillovers', *American Economic Review*, **11**, 33–7.

Dunning, J.H. (1993), *Multinational Enterprises and the Global Economy*, Wokingham: Addison-Wesley.

Dunning, J.H. (1995a), 'Reappraising the eclectic paradigm in the age of alliance capitalism', *Journal of International Business Studies*, **26**, 461–91.

Dunning, J.H. (1995b), 'Think again, Professor Krugman: competitiveness does matter', *The International Executive*, **37**, 315–24.

Dunning, J.H., and R. Narula (1994), 'Transpacific direct investment and the investment development path: the record assessed', *Essays in International Business*, March.

Dunning, J.H., and R. Narula (1996), 'The investment development path revisited: some emerging issues', in J.H. Dunning and R. Narula (eds), *Foreign Direct Investment and Governments: Catalysts for Economic Restructuring*, London: Routledge.

Duysters, Geert (1996), *The Dynamics of Technical Innovation: The Evolution and Development of Information Technology*, Cheltenham, UK and Brookfield, USA: Edward Elgar.

Farell, Joseph (1987), 'Information and the Coase theorem', *Economic Perspectives*, **1**, 113–29.

Freeman, C. (1987), *Technology Policy and Economic Performance*, London: Francis Pinter.

Gerlach, M. (1992), *Alliance Capitalism*, Oxford: Oxford University Press.

Geuna, Aldo (1996), 'The participation of higher education institutions in European Union framework programmes', *Science and Public Policy*, **23**, 287–96.

Glaister, K., and P. Buckley (1996), 'Strategic motives for international alliance formation', *Journal of Management Studies*, **33**, 301–32.

Hagedoorn, J. (1996), 'Trends and patterns in strategic technology partnering since the early seventies', *Review of Industrial Organization*, **11**, 601–16.

Hagedoorn, J., and R. Narula (1996), 'Choosing modes of governance for strategic technology partnering: international and sectoral differences', *Journal of International Business Studies*, **27**, 265–84.

Hagedoorn, J., and Sadowski, B. (1999), 'Exploring the potential transition from strategic technology partnering to mergers and acquisitions', *Journal of Management Studies*, **36**, 87–107.

Hagedoorn, John (1993), 'Understanding the rationale of strategic technology partnering: inter-organizational modes of cooperation and sectoral differences', *Strategic Management Journal*, **14**, 371–85.

Hall, Peter (1986), 'The theory and practice of innovatory policy: an overview', in Peter Hall (ed.), *Technology, Innovation and Economic Policy*, New York: St Martin's Press.

Hennart, J.-F. (1993), 'Explaining the swollen middle; why most transactions are a mix of market and hierarchy', *Organization Science*, **4**, 529–47.

Hood, N., and S. Young (1979), *The Economics of the Multinational Enterprise*, London: Longman.

Inkpen, A., and P. Beamish (1997), 'Knowledge, bargaining power, and the instability of international joint ventures', *Academy of Management Review*, **22**, 177–202.

Katz, M.L. (1986), 'An analysis of cooperative research and development', *Rand Journal of Economics*, **17** (4), 527–43.

Keummerle, W. (1996), 'The drivers of foreign direct investment into research and development: an empirical investigation', Boston, working paper no. 96–002.

Kogut, B. (1988), 'Joint ventures: theoretical and empirical perspectives', *Strategic Management Journal*, **9**, 319–32.

Kogut, B., and U. Zander (1993), 'Knowledge of the firm and the evolutionary theory of the multinational enterprise', *Journal of International Business Studies*, **24**, 625–46.

Krugman, P. (1994), 'Competitiveness: a dangerous obsession', *Foreign Affairs*, **73**, 28–44.

Levin, R., A. Klevorick, R. Nelson and S. Winter (1987), 'Appropriating the returns from industrial research and development', *Brookings Papers on Economics Activity*, **3**, 783–820.

Levy, J., and R. Samuels (1991), 'Institutions and innovation; research and collaboration as technology strategy in Japan', in L. Mytelka (ed.), *Strategic Partnerships and the World Economy*, London: Pinter, pp. 120–48.

Madhok, A. (1997), 'Cost, value and foreign market entry mode: the transaction and the firm', *Strategic Management Journal*, **18**, 39–61.

Mowery, D. (1988), *International Collaborative Ventures in US Manufacturing*, Cambridge, MA: Ballinger.

Mytelka, L. (1991), 'States, strategic alliances and international oligopolies', in L. Mytelka (ed.), *Strategic Partnerships and the World Economy*, London: Pinter, pp. 182–210.

Narula, R. (1996a), 'Forms of international cooperation between corporations', in C. Jepma and A. Rhoen (eds), *International Trade: A Business Perspective*, Harlow: Longman, pp. 98–122.

Narula, R. (1996b), *Multinational Investment and Economic Structure*, London: Routledge.

Narula, R., and Dunning, J.H. (1999) 'Developing countries versus multinationals in a globalising world: the dangers of falling behind', *Forum for Development Studies*, 261–87.

Narula, R., and J. Hagedoorn (1999), 'Innovating through strategic alliances: moving towards international partnerships and contractual agreements', *Technovation*, **19**, 283–94.

Nelson, R., and S. Winter (1982), *An Evolutionary Theory of Economic Change*, Cambridge: Belknap Press.

Nelson, R.R. (ed.) (1993), *National Innovation Systems*, New York: Oxford University Press.

Niosi, J. (1995), *Flexible Innovation: Technological Alliances in Canadian Industry*, Montreal: McGill-Queens University Press.

Ohmae, K. (1985), *Triad Power*, New York: Free Press.

Ostry, S., and R. Nelson (1995), *Techno-Nationalism and Techno-Globalism: Conflict and Cooperation*, Washington, DC: The Brookings Institution.

Patel, Pari (1996), 'Are large firms internationalising the generation of technology? Some new evidence', *IEEE Transactions on Engineering Management*, **43**, 41–7.

Pearce, R., and S. Singh (1992), *Globalising Research and Development*, London: Macmillan.

Porter, M.E. (1990), *The Competitive Advantage of Nations*, New York: The Free Press.

Reich, R. (1990), 'Who is us?', *Harvard Business Review*, January–February, 53–64.

Tallman, S., and O. Shenkar (1994), 'A managerial decision model of international cooperative venture formation', *Journal of International Business Studies*, **25**, 91–113.

Teece, D.J. (1977), 'Technology transfer by multinational firms: the resource cost of transferring technological knowhow', *Economic Journal*, **22**, 242–61.

Vonortas, N.S. (1994), 'Inter-firm cooperation with imperfectly appropriable research', *International Journal of Industrial Organization*, **12** (3), 413–35.

Vonortas, N.S. (1997), *Cooperation in Research and Development*, Dordrecht: Kluwer Academic Publishers.

7 Explaining strategic R&D alliances of European firms

INTRODUCTION

The Single European Market (SEM) initiative, through its various stages of economic cooperation until the establishment of the European Union, can arguably be said to be one of the most important socio-economic developments of the twentieth century. At the heart of much of this activity has been a belief that cooperation by institutions and firms across the various European countries represents a means by which the technological and economic gap between the USA and Europe after the Second World War might be narrowed. As Peterson (1991) has pointed out, although technological collaboration has constantly remained high on the agenda of European policy makers, pan-European R&D activities have only been developed systematically by policy makers since the 1980s. Several initiatives by the European Commission have been implemented over the past two decades in an attempt to bolster the competitiveness of European firms, particularly in high technology sectors.

In addition to these Europe-specific changes, though, there have been several changes in the global economy which are generally described under the rubric of 'globalization'. These developments have also had a significant impact on the growth of cross-border economic activity in general, as well as the increasing popularity of alliance activity in particular.

In this chapter, we first seek to explain the reasons for the increasing importance of alliance activity, and the growth of a special class of alliances, that of strategic technology partnering (STP) or R&D alliances, paying special attention in our discussion to the role of European integration. In addition, we focus on explaining the need to acknowledge the strategic reasons for their growing popularity, in addition to the cost-minimizing ones. Second, we intend to evaluate the extent to which private (that is, non-subsidised) cooperative agreements in R&D by EU firms have evolved, paying particular attention to the extent to which economic integration and globalization may have influenced intra-EU activity relative to extra-EU agreements (that is, EU–USA and EU–Japan) over the period 1980–94.

Given the crucial nature of technology development to the competitiveness of firms, we wish to enquire whether in fact the SEM initiative has had a significant effect on the propensity of EU firms to collaborate in R&D-type activities, with special attention paid to information technology, new materials and biotechnology. Our analysis is somewhat anecdotal and qualitative, and utilizes data from the MERIT-CATI database, which contains records of over 10 000 instances of strategic technology partnering (see Appendix 7.1).

CROSS-BORDER ACTIVITY AND EUROPEAN INTEGRATION

The SEM initiative has been judged to be reasonably successful, in terms of encouraging intra-European economic activity – at least as regards trade and FDI – although there have been some reservations expressed about the qualified nature of these gains, given the interrelation between the two. For instance, there has been an increase in trade in particular sectors that are sensitive to non-tariff barriers that were to be scrapped by 1993, as firms have sought to improve their efficiency through the rationalization of production in order to achieve economies of scale. However, as Hughes (1992) has argued, US and Japanese firms have been as well positioned as EC firms to exploit the SEM initiative. She points out that the only way firms can take advantage of scale economies is by the relocation and readjustment of production activities, something which US and Japanese firms have also undertaken in response to the SEM initiative. Indeed, as numerous studies have shown,[1] there has been a growing amount of FDI inflows during the run-up period to 1993 as non-EU firms have established (or consolidated) their presence within the EU partly in the fear of a 'fortress Europe' as well as to exploit potential benefits of a vibrant single market of 300-odd million consumers.

In terms of FDI, Dunning (1997a, 1997b) in a survey of inward FDI into the EU, concluded that (a) FDI into the EC since the early 1980s has grown faster than in most other parts of the world; (b) the geographical and industrial distribution of inward FDI stocks has changed to reflect a certain level of rationalization, with the more labour-intensive aspects moving to the periphery (Portugal, Spain and Greece) and with the bulk of technology and information sensitive sectors remaining in the 'core' countries of the EU; and (c) intra-EC FDI and Japanese FDI inflows have outpaced US inward FDI. He also observed that, overall, the spatial distribution of production activities has not undergone a major shift.

The present chapter aims to throw some light onto the third area that has been expected to promote the growth of intra-EU economic activity, that of industrial collaborative activity, or strategic alliances. In particular, we focus on understanding the behaviour of a rather important subset of cooperative agreements, that of R&D alliances, or strategic technology partnering (STP). In this chapter we use R&D alliances and STP as synonyms, which refer to strategic alliances where innovative activity is at least part of the agreement. By strategic alliances we mean inter-firm cooperative agreements which are intended to affect the long-term product market positioning of at least one partner (Hagedoorn, 1993).

It is clear that there has been an explosion in the propensity of European firms to undertake strategic alliances, but to what extent can this be attributed to or explained by the SEM initiative? To what extent can changes in the propensity to undertake alliances be attributed to SEM-specific factors, rather than changes that can be ascribed more generally to the phenomenon of globalization? Can we apply our understanding of European integration as applied to trade and FDI to explain collaboration in general and R&D cooperation in particular?

This is an area that has received considerable attention: the European Commission, through its framework programmes, has encouraged R&D collaboration by public and private EU-based institutions, significantly relaxing its prohibition on anti-competitive agreements where they are related to technology development (Urban and Vendemini, 1992). In addition, under the auspices of programmes such as ESPRIT, RACE, BRITE and BRIDGE, it has provided considerable subsidies to collaborative R&D. This chapter focuses on examining the growth in *non-subsidized* EU strategic technology alliances, that is, those R&D alliances that are not established directly through the programmes of the European Commission.

THE GROWTH OF ALLIANCE ACTIVITY

The worldwide growth of alliance activity has been described (Dunning 1995, 1997c, Narula and Dunning 2000, see also Chapters 1, 2 and 3, this volume) as being a distinctive feature of globalization. Globalization as used here refers to the increasing cross-border interdependence and integration of products for goods, service and capital. Dunning (1995, 1997c) goes further to propose that we are moving to a new age where flexible economic arrangements find increasing favour, in what he describes as one of 'alliance capitalism', shifting from the older paradigm of hierarchical capitalism, where economic activity was conducted through hierarchies.

The exact means and nature of this shift, as well as the implications of alliance capitalism and globalization are a matter of some debate, and have been addressed elsewhere. In the context of the present chapter, we are interested in understanding what the implications of these changes are for the growth of EU alliances. European integration, it can be posited, is a sub-process within globalization, one that is driven by economic imperative, simply emphasizing de facto economic integration by globalization through de jure political and economic integration initiatives. In other words, the growth of cooperative agreements by EU firms illustrates the growth of alliance activity worldwide, with the SEM-related developments being somewhat secondary to those due to the forces of globalization.

Nonetheless, simply by invoking globalization one cannot explain the growth of this form of economic activity. As Kay asks: 'if cooperation is such a good thing ... why did firms generally wait until recently before pursuing such activities so enthusiastically?' (Kay, 1997, p. 177)

One of the fundamental reasons for the growth in alliances lies in the reduction of transaction costs. These have occurred as a result of, inter alia, the introduction of new space-shrinking technologies, particularly information and computer technologies, which have reduced cross-border communication, information and organizational costs; and the harmonization of regulations and barriers as a result of growing economic liberalization. These have been further enhanced by the establishment of supranational regional and interregional agreements such as NAFTA and the EU, as well as multilateral protocols and agreements under the auspices of the WTO, WIPO, and so on. These agreements have, *ceteris paribus*, reduced the risks of shirking as the costs of monitoring and enforcing cross-border alliances have fallen. The harmonization of regulations within the SEM initiative, in such a view, represents a more advanced version of this activity, and further lowers transaction costs for firms within the Union. If this were the primary reason determining the growth of alliance activity, and if the European economy were dominated by EU firms, it might be argued that these costs reductions accrue to a greater extent to intra-EU alliances than to extra-EU agreements. However, as implied by Hughes (1992) and Ramsay (1995), many of the major foreign-owned MNEs already present (and in many cases, firmly embedded) in the EU economy would enjoy the same benefits as EU firms. As Narula and Hagedoorn (1999) have shown, there are no significant country-specific differences in the propensity to engage in alliances. As such, it is more likely that the benefits of integration will result in lower costs for all firms regardless of nationality, and regardless of the organizational mode employed. However, there continues to be a considerable bias of MNEs towards the home country: it can thus also be argued that, *ceteris paribus*, greater absolute cost reductions might occur for EU firms since the extent of their European value-added activity is generally higher and the significance of their European operations much larger relative to their total worldwide activity. This reasoning might suggest that, other things being equal, EU firms should derive a larger benefit when engaging in collaboration with other EU firms as a result of European integration relative to collaboration involving non-European firms.

We emphasize that our argument heretofore focuses on comparing the benefits of one organizational mode between nationalities. Kay (1991, 1997) and others have suggested, however, that full internalization will also have fallen proportionally, thereby still making quasi-internalization a second best option. However, while reduced transaction costs might lead firms which otherwise might have considered full internalization to undertake collaborative agreements, this assumes that these firms were already interested in international expansion. Firms that might not have had the resources to engage in overseas activity on their own would now also be able to consider it, since a collaboration would require fewer resources than it might otherwise have done before integration. In other words, this line of reasoning would suggest, *ceteris paribus*, that the number of firms undertaking alliances within the EU would have increased since the 1980s in response to integration.

In addition to this objection, though, transaction costs provide only a partial explanation for the growth in alliances and only suggest why one group may derive greater benefits from collaboration than other groups. They do not explain why firms increasingly prefer quasi-hierarchical arrangements to fully-internalized ones. If transaction cost theory were to provide a complete explanation, the decline in costs due to either globalization or integration should lead to at least a similar extent of benefits for traditional hierarchical arrangements. In answering this, it is important to reflect on the presence of the word 'strategic' in strategic alliances. What differentiates a strategic alliance from a customer–supplier network is the underlying motive of the cooperation (Narula and Hagedoorn, 1999). The primary motivation for a customer–supplier network is that it is primarily cost-economizing in nature, while strategic alliances embody a second motivation, which is strategic in nature. The word 'strategic' suggests that such agreements are aimed at long-term profit optimizing objectives, attempting to enhance the value of the firm's assets.

Several reasons exist for the growth in popularity of cooperative agreements which embody a strategic element. One explanation is based on the increased competition due to liberalization of markets and the globalized nature of the operations of firms. Such increased competition has led to a low-growth scenario over the past two decades or so, and firms need to seek cheaper sources of inputs or divert sales from slow or negative growth markets

(Buckley and Casson, 1998). Such changes often need to be undertaken with rapidity. Declining transaction costs associated with contractual or quasi-internalized relationships in addition to falling profits margins have led to a disintegration of certain firms in particular industries, as they seek flexibility and lower risk, which have hitherto preferred vertical integration. Indeed, some notice has been taken of the process of disinvestment that, coincidentally or not, appears to have become quite commonplace during the last decade (Benito, 1997).

In addition, though, the emergence of new technological sectors (such as biotechnology) and the growing technological convergence between sectors (such as computers and cars, or new materials and transport) have also played an important role. The cross-fertilization of technological areas has meant that firms need to have an increasing range of competencies (Granstrand *et al.*, 1997). This encourages the use of alliances to seek complementary assets. As has been emphasized by others (for example, Kogut, 1988), the use of M&A is not a viable option where the technology being sought is a small part of the total value of the firm. Greenfield investment does not represent a viable option either, in most instances, as the time and costs involved in building new competencies from scratch may be prohibitive. It should be noted that in some instances alliances are used as a precursor to M&A (Hagedoorn and Sadowski, 1996). In connection with this, there has also been a growing cost of development, and of acquiring the resources and skills necessary to bring new products and services to market. Increasing the market size, and the sharing of costs and risks associated with staying on the cutting-edge of technology, create strong motivation to undertake alliances, no matter how much firms may prefer to go it alone.

Last but not least, there are the game-theoretic considerations. As Kay explains, 'it is necessary to engage in networks with certain firms not because they trust their partners, but *in order* to trust their partners' (Kay, 1997, p. 215). In addition, there is the follow-my-leader strategy, as originally highlighted by Knickerbocker (1973). Firms seek partnerships in response to similar moves made by other firms in the same industry, not always because there is a sound economic rationale in doing so, but in imitation of their competitors.

THE SPECIAL CASE OF STRATEGIC ALLIANCES TO CONDUCT R&D

Our focus in this chapter is on strategic technology partnerships or R&D alliances, which concentrate on cooperative arrangements where technological innovation is at least part of the agreement. These alliances are of a different and special nature: this is the one aspect of value-adding activity that continues to be highly centralized and internalized, even in a domestic scenario. In general, while production activities have gradually been increasingly internationalized, there has been relatively little internationalization of R&D (see, for example, Patel and Pavitt, 1991, Dunning and Narula, 1995, Archibugi and Michie, 1995).

Nonetheless, it is worth noting that there has been some growth in the technological development activities of MNEs relative to the level 20 years ago, and these changes indicate two trends worthy of note. First, in addition to overseas R&D activities associated with demand-side factors, there has been a growth of foreign R&D activities by firms in response to supply-side factors (Florida 1997, Kummerle, 1997). Second, there has been a growing use of external or quasi-external technological sources. Tidd and Trewhella (1997) suggest that the most important external sources of technology are universities, consortia, licensing, customers and suppliers, acquisitions, joint ventures and alliances and commercial research organizations. Although there is little systematic and thorough analysis of this process, companies such as Philips and Akzo-Nobel are currently attempting to source 20 per cent of their technology needs externally (van Hoesel and Narula, 1999). Indeed, there is a direct relationship between how much R&D a firm does internally and its external acquisition of technology. Veugelers (1997) demonstrates that there is a positive relationship between external technology sourcing and internal R&D. Indications are that collaborative arrangements to undertake R&D are becoming ever more popular, having tripled in significance since the early 1980s (Gugler and Pasquier, 1996).

There is a fundamental difference in the definition of R&D alliances and non-R&D alliances. Traditionally alliances have been defined as agreements which have a long-term and formal aspect which links areas of their businesses (Porter and Fuller, 1986). Strategic technology partnering, as used here, refers to agreements that are intended to undertake specific tasks and are generally terminated on completion of these tasks, and are by definition short-term (and often fixed-term) in nature.

There are other important considerations due to the special nature of R&D alliances. First, it is important to note that there is a strong causality between size and the propensity to engage in STP, given the need to have sufficient resources to undertake R&D (Hagedoorn and Schakenraad, 1994). Second, trade barriers, as we have noted in the previous section, have not played a major role in inhibiting the relocation of R&D, except where such R&D is associated with production (that is adaptive R&D). Stand-alone R&D facilities, which are common in knowledge-intensive sectors, are often located according to supply-related considerations. Such activities have not necessarily been affected by the decline in transaction costs due to the SEM initiative: skilled human capital and knowledge (in either tacit or non-tacit form), has long enjoyed relative freedom of movement across borders. Although certain improvements such as the common patenting system and the harmonization of regulations may have lowered costs in general, the benefits of lowered communication costs (due inter alia to ICTs) have occurred on a global level.

Although the reduction in trade barriers may affect both exporting and foreign direct investment through wholly owned subsidiaries, R&D alliances are largely unaffected by these. While it is true that firms engaged in asset-exploiting activities such as production or sales have a broader choice of options that include wholly owned subsidiaries and arms-length technology acquisition, some of these options are simply not available to firms that are seeking to undertake R&D, first, because technology is tacit by nature and, as far as technology development is concerned, even more so. Arm's-length transactions are simply not as effective, particularly in technology-intensive sectors or new, 'emerging' sectors, even if markets for these technologies were to exist. The further away these technologies are from the market (that is, research-oriented rather than development-oriented) the less likely that technology can be obtained through market mechanisms. Besides, its partly public-good nature prevents prospective selling firms from making technology available for evaluation and, without their doing so, the prospective buyer is unable to determine its worth. Markets are therefore liable to fail in their ability to function.

The choice of partner in R&D alliances can be international or domestic. Why do firms prefer in certain instances to partner with a foreign firm rather than a domestic firm? This is related to the question of why firms do not undertake all the R&D at their home location in the first place. The literature suggests that this is due to both supply and demand issues. The demand issues are well known, and are generally associated with adaptive R&D in response to specific market conditions. More recently, attention has been drawn to the supply issues. Firms are seeking to utilize immobile assets, which may be either firm-specific or location specific. In the former case, they are often associated with clusters of firms and country-specific characteristics. It is well acknowledged that location advantages are idiosyncratic and path-dependent, and the nature of innovatory activities in a given location is associated with the national systems of innovation (Edquist, 1997; Lundvall, 1992). The nature of the benefits arising from a non-cooperative arrangement requires physical proximity to the firm or cluster in order to seek indirect technology spillovers, which can be a highly costly, uncertain and random procedure that requires a long-term horizon. In the case of basic research, for instance, this might occur through the hiring of researchers that hitherto worked for a competitor. Where such immobile assets are country- but not firm-specific, they may be embodied in aspects of the national systems of innovation. Whether the advantage being sought is firm- or country-specific, the establishment of a greenfield laboratory is a feasible option, but involves high costs of start-up and considerable time. In fields where innovation is rapid, it may not provide a fast enough response. The use of M&A is even less attractive, as Kay acknowledges, where the area where the complementary resources sought only cover a small area of the firm's interests. Even where a firm wishes to acquire an R&D facility, it is generally not possible to do so, except in rare circumstances.

It is true, nonetheless, that there are also strategic limitations to the use of alliances. First, there is a danger that an alliance may represent a precursor to M&A. Indeed, Hagedoorn and Sadowski (1996) show that 2.6 per cent of strategic technology alliances lead to M&A, a figure that is quite significant given the high percentage (estimates vary between 50 and 70 per cent) of alliances that are terminated before completing their stated objective.

Why would a potential partner wish to collaborate with another which has limited or as yet undemonstrated resources to offer? First, because of the nature of innovation, the only way to determine the nature of a potential partner's research efforts is to examine them. One way it can do so is by engaging in some form of mutual hostage exchange, which an alliance provides. Second, even where the partner's resources prove to be of a limited or inappropriate nature, and the alliance is terminated prematurely, information about its former partner's competencies is then available to either firm in future periods, should it require competencies similar to those on offer by its ex-partner. Third, as Hagedoorn and Duysters (1997) have argued, while selecting partners that are well-established players in existing technologies may represent a profit maximizing situation, it is optimal only in a static environment. In a dynamic environment, where there is a possibility of technological change (or even a change in technological trajectories), having ties to a wide group of companies, including companies that have yet to demonstrate their value, represents a higher learning potential.

Strategic technology alliances are not only undertaken by firms seeking complementary resources. As we note in Chapter 6 of this volume, firms may also engage in alliances in order to coopt the competition. Take the situation where two firms in the same industry are pursuing an important new breakthrough. Neither can be certain that they will win the race to innovate. Therefore it may be in their best interest to collaborate, thus ensuring that they are jointly 'first': half a pie may be considered better in conditions of uncertainty while there is a probability that there may be none at all.

Let us put this into the context of the current chapter. The evidence on strategic technology partnering points to the fact that the need for complementary assets and the reduction of risk have become increasingly important as these are global phenomena, while open markets may have aggravated the use of need to coopt and block competitors, since firms are obliged to restructure to strengthen or even maintain their competitive position, through either aggressive or defensive means. Indeed, such a restructuring of EU industry has occurred since the early 1980s in response to the impending single market agreement (Dunning 1997a). Many of the EU-subsidized R&D programmes were aimed at achieving this renewed competitiveness and, indeed, were undertaken in earnest by most firms with a view to being able to compete on equal terms with other EU firms as well as US and Japanese firms by 1993. Indeed, Hagedoorn and Schakenraad (1993) show that there was a concurrent rise in non-subsidized and subsidized R&D during the later half of the 1980s.

It is important to note that the definition of strategic technology alliances as used in the MERIT-CATI database includes both equity and non-equity agreements. Consequently, while we have made general comments about the choice between markets, hierarchies and quasi-hierarchies, there is a significant difference between various organizational modes of STP. Broadly speaking though, it is possible to consider these as being of two major groups: equity-based agreements and contractual, non-equity based agreements. It is significant to note that the choice of alliance mode is determined by the technological characteristics of sectors of industry (Hagedoorn and Narula, 1996). Equity agreements are preferred in relatively mature industries while contractual alliances are more common in so-called 'high-tech' industries.

There is, however, another dimension that is worth noting. There has been a decline in the use of equity agreements on a global basis, whereby the percentage of equity STP has fallen steadily from 46.9 per cent in 1980–84 to 26.1 per cent during the period 1990–1994 (Narula and Hagedoorn, 1999). A similar tendency has been noted for all alliance groupings by region (Narula and Hagedoorn, 1997). This points to an important issue which relates to the process of learning. Given the novelty of R&D alliances, it can be hypothesized that firms prefer to undertake more hierarchical arrangements, but as they have acquired experience with this form of technological innovation, they have gradually switched to more flexible, but inherently riskier agreements. The effect of industry-specific trends is also quite apparent: these changes have occurred across industries, rather than countries; although it is true that there are differences between countries, they are not significant.

European R&D alliances have demonstrated a similar tendency, and indeed, the fact that these patterns demonstrate industry-wide rather than national trends suggests that the same process of learning about the mechanics of alliance formation and management apply to all firms regardless of nationality. It also highlights the need of firms, again regardless of nationality, to partner with the most appropriate firms regardless of national origin.

EXAMINING THE EVIDENCE

What of the trends of European firms in undertaking strategic technology partnering? Figure 7.1 is a plot of the number of newly established STP agreements by regional pairings. For instance, in the case of European–Japanese STP, we count how many alliances contain at least one Japanese and one European partner. The data show that, in the case of intra-EU alliances, between 1980 and 1984, there were a total of 270 alliances, and over the next five years this number almost doubled to 534. Between 1990 and 1994, the volume of intra-EU partnering dropped to its pre-1985 level. In the case of EU–US alliances, the trend is somewhat different. Although there was a sharp increase in transatlantic partnering activity in the mid 1980s, the level of this activity (on an aggregate basis) continued unabated until 1993, with a sharp increase in the last year. In the case of EU–Japanese alliances, the level of activity has remained at more or less the same level over the entire 15-year period for which data are available. Table 7.1 examines the trends for the UK, France and Germany and shows the change over time in their alliance activity with the seven most significant industrial countries of partner firms between 1980 and 1994. These trends tell a similar story.[2]

What do these data imply? First, that European industry began to undertake a much more serious view of alliances in the mid-1980s, with a doubling of activity over a short period. This can in part be attributed to three things. First, the process of economic integration had by this time been seen to be a reality. Second, European firms had begun to realize by the mid-1980s that they were lagging technologically in new core high-technology sectors such as information technology, and leading European firms had begun to cooperate by this period (Mytelka and Delapierre, 1987, Mytelka, 1995). This cooperation in R&D was further enhanced by encouragement from the European Commission around this same period, with the commission establishing a 'Big 12 roundtable' to develop proposals for new collaborative R&D projects (Peterson, 1991). Although our data exclude information from EU-subsidized projects, the availability of funds through the establishment of EU-subsidized R&D programmes (which expanded to include other non-IT national champions which were major consumers of IT products, such as Volvo, Aérospatiale and Volkswagen) further enhanced the intra-EU collaborative efforts of European companies. It is indeed no

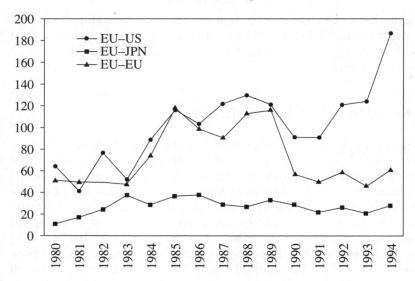

Figure 7.1   Number of new STP per year by EU firms, 1980–94

coincidence that the launch of the EC's framework programme and Eureka occurred around the same time as the surge in alliance activity. In other words, European firms, driven by the need to improve their competitive position in the face of increasing competition on a global basis, sought to improve their technological advantages through collaboration, a process which was further encouraged through financial and legal support from the European Commission. It is worth noting that it is exceedingly difficult for governments to determine, where R&D collaboration is concerned, which projects within a large company's research portfolio actually benefit from the R&D subsidies (see Chapter 6).

Third, given the realities of the SEM initiative, the need to become competitive within the European context required a certain level of restructuring on the part of the various individual EU firms. Although Kay *et al.* (1996) argue that intra-EU collaboration was inhibited because potential partners are also potential competitors, the fact is that this is also one of the primary attractions of partnering: strategic partnering also affords firms a chance (temporarily) to pre-empt competition, in addition to allowing the partners to evaluate the capabilities of the partner firm. Indeed, Hagedoorn and Schakenraad (1993) found that, over the period 1980–89, the subsidized R&D networks and private R&D networks were started almost simultaneously, and that the intensity of private R&D cooperation could be predicted by the intensity of subsidized R&D cooperation.

Table 7.1   Strategic technology partnering by the three largest EU countries

STP by German firms with companies from:	1980–84	85–89	90–94
UK	9	29	21
France	11	26	21
Netherlands	10	25	16
Italy	5	13	7
USA	51	108	163
Japan	22	33	41
STP by UK firms with companies from:	**1980–84**	**85–89**	**90–94**
Germany	9	27	18
France	10	31	24
Netherlands	9	27	8
Italy	5	13	8
Japan	117	159	121
USA	69	139	140
STP by French firms with companies from:	**1980–84**	**85–89**	**90–94**
Germany	9	24	21
UK	10	31	24
Netherlands	5	24	15
Italy	14	17	14
Japan	23	27	27
USA	58	69	100

Source: *MERIT-CATI dataset.*

The subsequent decline of the number of new alliances in the 1990s, as predicted by Kay (1991), is quite dramatic. We postulate that this reflects the result of restructuring of European industry, in part through the series of M&A that occurred in the run-up to the single market (for example, Nixdorf by Siemens, ICL by Fujitsu, Plessey by Siemens-GEC) as well as the repositioning of firms' technological profiles (for example, the exit of Philips from computers and its entry of the telecommunications sector with AT&T) (Mytelka, 1995).

The second reason for the decline in intra-EU alliances may have to do with the growth of extra-EU alliances. As Table 7.1 and Figure 7.1 both show, the propensity for EU firms to engage in alliances with Japanese and US firms also increased in the mid-1980s. This reflects in part the desire for Japanese and US firms to seek strategic positions within European industry prior to 1992 to avoid any question of being excluded from 'fortress Europe'. In addition, there had been some attempt to spur transatlantic R&D cooperation though the strategic defence initiative (SDI) programme of the US government in the mid 1980s (Carton, 1987). Perhaps most significant of all, however, was that EU firms were primarily spurred to partner with US and Japanese firms because of the technological lead that US firms possessed, in information technology and biotechnology and, to a lesser extent, new materials, while Japanese firms had a technological lead in information technology and new materials. In other words, EU firms would be interested in partnering with firms regardless of nationality, depending primarily on their relative competitive positions in the industry, or the presence of significant clusters at given locations.

Figure 7.2 shows trends in STP by the three core technological areas, biotechnology, information technology and new materials, for which data are available, further subdivided by geographic groupings. EU firms prefer to engage in transatlantic STP, particularly in sectors such as biotechnology where there is a considerable technological gap with the USA. Two other reasons can be presented as plausible explanations. First, the decline in the number of new intra-EU agreements may be attributed to the rules regarding the participation of non-EU firms in EU-subsidized consortia being relaxed. Second, as suggested by Mytelka (1995) in relation to the European IT sector, the EU 'big 12' failed to act in an orchestrated way, owing to a lack of consensus on strategy.

This relates to our earlier discussion on the motives for STP since firms are often engaged in partnerships to gain access to resources that they are unable to acquire as easily by going it alone. These resources may be either firm-specific or even location-specific, associated with the national systems of innovation of a region or a country. For instance, centres of agglomeration of economic activity exist, and firms may wish to collaborate with other firms located there in order to benefit from externalities that derive therefrom. More importantly, however, companies will prefer to partner with technology or market leaders, regardless of where they might be located, or what their nationality is. Furthermore, given the increasing tendency for the cross-fertilization of technologies, firms prefer to collaborate rather than develop a simultaneous expertise in several seemingly unrelated technologies. A second aspect of motivation is that firms may simply engage in alliances to coopt a competitor. It is well known, for instance, that firms

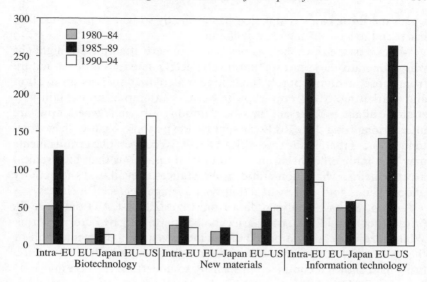

Figure 7.2   STP by EU firms, by core sectors and regional groupings

do not always have recourse to patenting as a means to protect new and rapidly evolving technologies, and must rely on secrecy or co-inventing with a potential competitor (Levin *et al.*, 1987). In other cases, by co-invention, firms are able to determine that they will jointly have 'won' the race to innovate (see Chapter 6). Other less R&D-specific reasons also exist. For instance, Veugelers (1996) notes that European firms are more active in alliances in industries in which they lack a comparative advantage, but are more defensive in sectors where they have a comparative advantage. Furthermore, weak EU firms actively seek strong partners, and strong EU firms ally with weak partners. Given that most of the EU firms in the biotechnology and information technology sectors do not enjoy a significant competitive advantage, it is not surprising that a majority of STP by these companies is with Japanese and US firms.

CONCLUSIONS

The effect of the SEM initiative has been studied from both the FDI and the trade perspective and, as far as these two modalities of undertaking economic activity are concerned, it has been judged a qualified success. Relatively little has been said about strategic technology alliances, an area which the European Commission has explicitly sought to promote. This has been the focus of the present chapter.

We have tackled two main issues. First, we have attempted to highlight why cooperative agreements that involve R&D activities differ in nature from those involving purely 'mainstream' activities such as production and marketing. Most importantly, we have attempted to explain why strategic alliances represent 'first-best' options, especially where firms are internationalizing their R&D for supply-side reasons. What we have tried to illustrate is that, in the case of R&D activity, cooperative arrangements may be a more efficient means to conduct transactions than hierarchical arrangements, where non-static circumstances prevail and the activity undertaken is governed by uncertainty and a high degree of tacitness.

Second, we have analysed data from the MERIT-CATI database on private (non-subsidized) strategic technology partnering by European firms. While intra-EU cooperation did in fact increase during the second half of the 1980s, this level was not sustained through the early 1990s. Instead, EU firms have shown a continued propensity to undertake EU–US and EU–Japanese R&D collaboration, particularly in the information technology, biotechnology and new materials sectors.

In addressing these two issues we have inadvertently also addressed an area of controversy, which relates to the efficacy of the framework programmes. This relates to pioneering work by Neil Kay (1991) and subsequent contributions of Ramsay (1995) and Kay et al. (1996). Kay's original analysis predicted that strategic alliances by European firms would not increase as a consequence of the SEM, despite expectations of the European Commission to the contrary. While our data do indeed confirm his prediction, our analysis and theoretical reasoning suggest a different interpretation.

The basic reasoning of the Kay article is that alliances are in fact a last resort. Although one cannot say with certainty that they are now a first resort in all cases, the evidence on alliances would seem to indicate that, in certain instances, particularly that of technological innovation in emerging and rapidly evolving sectors, they are often a preferred option over wholly owned activities, including greenfield investments or M&A. R&D alliances have two important features which distinguish them from marketing or production-based alliances. First, R&D alliances are designed with a fixed-term (generally short-term) horizon. Second, R&D activities cover only a small part of the value-adding activities of firms.

In addition, we do not believe that transaction costs alone explain R&D alliances. While Kay agrees with the need to consider strategic issues, his work suggests that 'good fences make good neighbours'. However, if firms were to go it alone, they would forgo the opportunity to observe what the other firms in the same industry are up to. This goes for firms that have proven abilities in a given area of specialization, as well as firms that have not. In addition, where new technologies are concerned, there is an increasing need to seek a broad range of competencies in unrelated fields. Firms generally have limited resources and cannot possibly engage in vertical and horizontal integration to internalize all their needs. As we noted earlier, there is a growing tendency to focus on a few selected core technologies, rather than to integrate vertically. By engaging in alliance activity rather than internalization, as Buckley and Casson (1998) have noted, firms are able to be more flexible, and can respond to low growth scenarios and, at the same time, optimizing returns. In addition to the benefits of flexibility, the need for complementary assets, market power and economies of scale, there are other reasons which are peculiar to strategic technology partnering. First, firms have to monitor the activities of their competitors since, at the frontier, it is difficult to determine who might be the winner in the race to innovate. Alliances allow firms to do so, and they allow firms that are engaged in conducting similar research to pre-determine (if they so desire) the winner by agreeing to win jointly the race to innovate. Second, at the technology frontier, it is optimal to partner with all sorts of companies, even those that are without a demonstrated track record (Hagedoorn and Duysters, 1997). This line of research suggests there is some value in the adage, 'hold your friends close, and your enemies even closer'.

Although our chapter does not analyse the framework programmes, in our reading, the evidence both here and elsewhere would suggest that the underlying objective was not to encourage cooperation per se. The underlying objective, rather, was to encourage collaboration in the run-up to the SEM so as to allow EU industry to restructure in order to face better the competitive milieu of the single market in the post-1992 scenario. In that the prediction of the commission that the popularity of intra-EU alliances would continue at the same levels after 1992 was wrong, we agree with the view held by Kay and associates. We also agree that, in a post-1992 scenario, it does indeed make sense to partner, *ceteris paribus*, with non-EU firms rather than other EU firms, particularly since firms from these countries are technologically superior to EU firms in some of the core technologies.

We do, however, also believe that the decline of intra-EU STP in the 1990s is an unforeseen consequence of the rejuvenation of European competitiveness. One of the consequences, perhaps unintended, has been that the major European players have repositioned themselves so as not to compete directly amongst themselves. This, it would seem, is as a direct result of the slimming down and restructuring that firms such as Philips and Siemens have undertaken, as well as the result of the failure of cooperative activities such as the 'big-12 roundtable'. The framework programmes need to be seen in the overall impact, rather than the success or failure, of particular instruments, although it is true that certain aspects (such as cooperative activity) of the framework programmes were more unsuccessful than others.

APPENDIX 7.1   THE COOPERATIVE AGREEMENTS AND TECHNOLOGY INDICATORS (CATI) INFORMATION SYSTEM

The CATI data bank is a relational database which contains separate data files that can be linked to each other and provide (dis)aggregate and combined information from several files. The CATI database contains three major entities. The first entity includes information on over 10 000 cooperative agreements involving some 4 000 different parent companies. The data bank contains information on each agreement and some information on companies participating in these agreements. We define cooperative agreements as common interests between independent (industrial) partners which are not connected through (majority) ownership. In the CATI database only those inter-firm agreements are being collected that contain some arrangements for transferring technology or joint research. Joint research pacts, second-sourcing and licensing agreements are clear-cut examples. We also collect information on joint ventures in which new technology is received from at least one of the partners, or joint ventures having some R&D programme. Mere production or marketing joint ventures are excluded. In other words, our analysis is primarily related to technology cooperation. We are discussing those forms of cooperation and agreements for which a combined innovative activity or an exchange of technology is at least part of the agreement. Consequently, partnerships are omitted that regulate no more than the sharing of production facilities, the setting of standards, collusive behaviour in price setting and raising entry barriers – although all of these may be side-effects of inter-firm cooperation as we define it.

We regard as a relevant input of information for each alliance the number of companies involved, names of companies (or important subsidiaries), year of establishment, time-horizon, duration and year of dissolution, capital investments and involvement of banks and research institutes or universities, field(s) of technology,[3] modes of cooperation,[4] and some comment or available information about progress. Depending on the precise form of cooperation we collect information on the operational context, the name of the agreement or project, equity sharing, the direction of capital or technology flows, the degree of participation in the case of minority holdings, some information about motives underlying the alliance, the character of cooperation, such as basic research, applied research or product development, possibly associated with production and/or marketing arrangements. In some cases we also indicate who has benefited most.

The second major entity is the individual subsidiary or parent company involved in one (registered) alliance at least. In the first place we assess the company's cooperative strategy by adding its alliances and computing its network centrality. Second, we ascertain its nationality and its possible (majority) owner in case this is an industrial firm, too. Changes in (majority) ownership in the 1980s were also registered. Next, we determine the main branch in which it is operating and classify its number of employees. In addition, for three separate subsets of firms, time-series for employment, turnover, net income, R&D expenditures and numbers of assigned US patents have been stored. The first subset is based on the *Business Week* R&D scoreboard, the second on Fortune's International 500, and the third group was retrieved from the US Department of Commerce's patent tapes. From the Business Week R&D Scoreboard we took R&D expenditure, net income, sales and number of employees. In 1980, some 750 companies were filed; in the following years this number gradually increased to 900 companies in 1988, which were spread among 40 industry groups. The *Fortune* International 500 of the largest corporations outside the USA provides, amongst other things, information about sales (upon which the rankings are based), net income and number of employees.

NOTES

1. See Dunning (1997a and 1997b) for a review.
2. The data in Table 7.1, while indicative of similar trends to those in Figure 7.1 and Figure 7.2, cannot be directly compared. This is because of the method of counting: an alliance between, say, a US and a German firm would count as one alliance if we count US–EU alliances or US–German alliances. However, an alliance between a German, a French and a US firm would be counted as a US–French alliance and a US–German alliance although, on an aggregate basis (that is, US–EU alliances), it would represent a single alliance.
3. The most important fields in terms of frequency are information technology (computers, industrial automation, telecommunications, software, microelectronics), biotechnology (with fields such as pharmaceuticals and agro-biotechnology), new materials technology, chemicals, automotive, defence, consumer electronics, heavy electrical equipment, food and beverages, and so on. All fields have important subfields.
4. As principal modes of cooperation we regard equity joint ventures, joint R&D projects, technology exchange agreements, minority and cross-holdings, particular customer-supplier relations, one-directional technology flows. Each mode of cooperation has a number of particular categories.

REFERENCES

Archibugi, D., and J. Michie (1995), 'The globalisation of technology: a new taxonomy', *Cambridge Journal of Economics*, **19**, 121–40.
Benito, Gabriel R.G. (1997), 'Divestment of foreign production operations', *Applied Economics*, **29** (10), 1365–77.
Buckley, P., and M. Casson (1998), 'Models of the multinational enterprise', *Journal of International Business Studies*, **29** (1), 21–44.

Carton, A. (1987), 'Eureka: a western European response to the technological challenge posed by the SDI research programme', in H. Brauch (ed.), *Star Wars and European Defense*, New York: St. Martin's Press, pp. 311–28.

Dunning, J.H. (1995), 'Reappraising the eclectic paradigm in the age of alliance capitalism', *Journal of International Business Studies*, **26**, 461–91.

Dunning, J.H. (1997a), 'The European internal market programme and inbound foreign direct investment (Part 1)', *Journal of Common Market Studies*, **35**, 1–30.

Dunning, J.H. (1997b), 'The European internal market programme and inbound foreign direct investment (Part 2)', *Journal of Common Market Studies*, **35**, 190–223.

Dunning, J.H. (1997c), *Alliance Capitalism and Global Business*, London: Routledge.

Dunning, J.H., and R. Narula (1995), 'The R&D activities of foreign firms in the US', *International Studies in Management and Organisation*, **25**, 39–73.

Edquist, C. (1997), *Systems of Innovation*, London: Pinter.

Florida, Richard (1997), 'The globalisation of R&D: results of a survey of foreign-affiliated R&D laboratories in the USA', *Research Policy*, **26**, 85–103.

Granstrand, O., P. Patel, and K. Pavitt (1997), 'Multi-technology corporations: why they have "distributed" rather than "distinctive core" competencies', *California Management Review*, **39**.

Gugler, P., and M. Pasquier (1996), 'Strategic alliances of Swiss firms: theoretical considerations and empirical findings', Institut für Marketing und Unternehmungsführung working paper No. 27.

Hagedoorn, J. (1993), 'Understanding the rationale of strategic technology partnering: interorganizational modes of cooperation and sectoral differences', *Strategic Management Journal*, **14**, 371–85.

Hagedoorn, J., and G. Duysters (1997), 'Satisficing strategies in dynamic inter-firm networks – the efficacy of quasi-redundant contacts', MERIT working paper series 97-016.

Hagedoorn, J., and R. Narula (1996), 'Choosing modes of governance for strategic technology partnering: international and sectoral differences', *Journal of International Business Studies*, **27**, 265–84.

Hagedoorn, J., and B. Sadowski (1996), 'Exploring the potential transition from strategic technology partnering to mergers and acquisitions', MERIT working paper series 96-010.

Hagedoorn, J., and J. Schakenraad (1993), 'A comparison of private and subsidised R&D partnerships in the European information technology industry', *Journal of Common Market Studies*, **31**, 374–90.

Hagedoorn, J., and J. Schakenraad (1994), 'The effect of strategic technology alliances on company performance', *Strategic Management Journal*, **15**, 291–311.

Hoesel, R. van, and R. Narula, (1999) 'Outward investment from the Netherlands: introduction and overview', in R. van Hoesel, and R. Narula, (eds), *Multinationals from the Netherlands*, London: Routledge, pp. 1–31.

Hughes, K. (1992), 'Trade performance of the main EC economies relative to the USA and Japan in 1992-sensitive sectors', *Journal of Common Market Studies*, **30**, 437–54.

Kay, N. (1991), 'Industrial collaborative activity and the completion of the internal market', *Journal of Common Market Studies*, **29**, 347–62.

Kay, N. (1997), *Pattern in Corporate Evolution*, Oxford: Oxford University Press.

Kay, N., H. Ramsay and J-F. Hennart (1996), 'Industrial collaboration and the European internal market', *Journal of Common Market Studies*, **34**, 465–75.

Knickerbocker, F.T. (1973), *Oligopolistic Reaction and the Multinational Enterprise*, Cambridge, MA: Harvard University Press.

Kogut, B. (1988), 'Joint ventures: theoretical and empirical perspectives', *Strategic Management Journal*, **9**, 319–32.

Kummerle, W. (1997), 'Building effective R&D capabilities abroad', *Harvard Business Review*, March–April, 61–70.

Landes, David (1998), *The Wealth and Poverty of Nations*, London: Little, Brown and Company.

Levin, R., A. Klevorick, R. Nelson and S. Winter (1987), 'Appropriating the returns from industrial research and development', *Brookings Papers on Economics Activity*, **3**, 783–820.

Lundvall, B. (1992), *National Systems of Innovation: Towards a Theory of Innovation and Interactive Learning*, London: Pinter Publishers.

Mytelka, L. (1995), 'Dancing with wolves: global oligopolies and strategic partnerships', in J. Hagedoorn (ed.), *Technical Change and the World Economy*, Aldershot, UK and Brookfield, USA: Edward Elgar, pp. 182–204.

Mytelka, L., and M. Delapierre (1987), 'The alliance strategies of European firms in the information technology industry and the role of ESPRIT', *Journal of Common Market Studies*, **26**, 231–53.

Narula, R., and J.H. Dunning (2000), 'Industrial development, globalisation and multinational enterprises: new realities for developing countries', *Oxford Development Studies*, **28**, pp. 141–67, (see also Chapter 3, this volume).

Narula, R., and J. Hagedoorn (1997), 'Globalisation, organisational modes and the growth of international strategic technology alliances', MERIT research memoranda, 97-017.

Narula, R., and J. Hagedoorn (1999), 'Innovating through strategic alliances: moving towards international partnerships and contractual agreements', *Technovation*, **19**, pp. 283–94.

Patel, P., and K. Pavitt, (1991), 'Large firms in the production of world technology: an important case of non-globalization', *Journal of International Business Studies*, **22**(1), 1–21.

Peterson, John (1991), 'Technology policy in Europe: explaining the framework programme and Eureka in theory and practice', *Journal of Common Market Studies*, **29**, 269–90.

Porter, M., and M. Fuller (1986), 'Coalitions and global strategy', in M. Porter (ed.), *Competition in Global Industries*, Boston, MA: Harvard Business School Press, pp. 315–43.

Ramsay, Harvie (1995), 'Le défi européen. Multinational restructuring, labor and EU policy', in A. Amin and Tomaney (eds), *Behind the Myth of European Union*, London: Routledge, pp. 174–97.

Tidd, J., and M. Trewhella (1997), 'Organizational and technological antecedents for knowledge creation and learning', *R&D Management*, **27**, 359–75.

Urban, S., and S. Vendemini (1992), *European Strategic Alliances*, Oxford: Blackwell.

Veugelers, R. (1996), 'Alliances and the pattern of comparative advantages: a sectoral analysis', *International Business Review*, **4**, 213–31.

Veugelers, R. (1997), 'Internal R&D expenditures and external technology sourcing', *Research Policy*, **26**, 303–15.

8 R&D collaboration by 'stand-alone' SMEs: opportunities and limitations in the ICT sector

INTRODUCTION

The closing decades of the last century have seen fundamental changes in economic realities, often referred to as the process of globalization. In particular, there has been an increasing enforceability of cross-border agreements (due in part to growing *de facto* and *de jure* regional and global economic integration), a convergence in technological trajectories across countries, and an increased cross-border competition. In the context of this chapter these developments have changed the way firms arrange their innovative activity both spatially and organizationally. There is also an increasing international aspect of R&D activity, and a growth in the use of collaborative R&D between firms, both within and across borders (for a comprehensive survey, see Hagedoorn, 2002).

From a technology perspective, there has been a growing knowledge content of products and processes, such that an increasing breadth of technologies and a growing level of competence in each of these technologies is required. Cars have more computing power than most desktop computers. Fridges are nowadays Internet-enabled. And so on. This is associated (*inter alia*) with the pervasive role of information and computing technologies (ICT) in sectors other than purely ICT products, as an enabler of fusion of technology and as a means to coordinate spatially dispersed operations efficiently (Santangelo, 2001).

The need for multiple technological competences is partly responsible for the need for higher R&D resources. One response to the growing breadth of knowledge requirements has been to utilize non-internal means to undertake innovation, and by this we refer specifically to the use of strategic alliances and outsourcing. The developments have led to a prominent use of external resources belonging to non-affiliated firms as a way to reduce, *inter alia*, innovation time spans, costs and risks, and to acquire greater flexibility in their operations (Narula 2001). The improved enforceability of contracts and declining transaction and monitoring costs resulting from developments associated with globalization have made it easier for firms of all sizes to monitor, identify and establish collaborative ventures than previously had been the case (see Chapter 7). In other words, they have increased the flexibility of firms' innovatory activities. At the same time, however, they have also led to an increased level of inter-firm and cross-border competition, and to new risks and threats for the technology-intensive firm.

Although these developments have profoundly affected the small and medium enterprise (SME), there has been very little research focusing on the R&D collaboration of SMEs. These developments have affected SMEs in two ways. On the one hand, SMEs have always sought to specialize in niches, given their limited resources, and their role as specialized suppliers to large firms has increased as larger firms have sought to utilize non-internal means to maintain a sufficient breadth of technological competences. On the other hand, the cross-fertilization of technologies has meant that SMEs also (like their larger counterparts) need to span several competences. This dualistic state of affairs has altered the raison d'être of the SME and has created both new opportunities and threats for the SME. In this chapter we will argue that, inasmuch as the improvements in communication and the ease of enforceability of contracts have helped the SME, these benefits have accrued to at least the same extent for large firms too, and perhaps to a greater extent. Traditionally, large firms have had material (that is, resource) advantages, while SMEs have had the advantages of flexibility and rapid response to change. ICTs and transaction cost reductions due to economic integration have further increased the flexibility of the large firm, thereby narrowing the competitive advantage of flexibility due to smaller size. Indeed, the disadvantages due to SMEs' absolute size limitations may have been enhanced as a result of increased cross-border competition, and their need for multiple technological competences. Nowhere is this more obvious than in collaborative activity with regard to innovation. It puts pressure on SMEs (already resourceful in their use of collaboration) to be even more efficient. Although alliances may overcome barriers to growth due to size (Ahern, 1993), there are cognitive limits to efficiency gains from non-internal R&D, and the extent to which SMEs can afford to use non-internal R&D without weakening their technological advantages (Narula, 2001).

The extent and intensity with which SMEs can use collaboration varies by the maturity of their primary technologies. Some firms may operate in subsectors which are increasingly paradigmatic and mature, while others are pre-paradigmatic and nascent. Furthermore, SMEs have different objectives and operate in differing environments, particularly as regards their relationship to larger firms. The interdependence of large firms and small firms during the evolution of new technologies and industries is best described as one of 'dynamic complementarities' (Rothwell and Dodgson, 1994). Differing motivations and objectives of different types of SMEs influence the nature of their interaction with larger firms, as well as their markets.

We shall concentrate here on evaluating the state of affairs vis-à-vis SMEs by discussing these two important concurrent dynamics, although there are several other important dynamics at play, for instance those related to the extent to which activities are internationalized (see, for example, Lu and Beamish, 2001). The next section evaluates the first dynamic, examining the various types of SMEs and how the industrial structure and external environment influence their collaborative activity. We then examine the second dynamic, which is sector-specific and relates to the evolution of technologies, technological paradigms and trajectories. We explain how different types of SMEs tend to dominate the industry structure at a given stage of the evolution of a given core technology. Next we examine evidence from a survey on the collaborative activities of one particular form of the SME – the 'stand-alone' SME – in the ICT sector. Our analysis is based on in-depth interviews and questionnaire surveys of over 100 European technology firms. We discuss how these SMEs utilize R&D collaboration relative to large firms. We shall attempt to discuss the reasons for the preference of one type of collaboration over another, and the limitations of collaboration as an alternative to in-house R&D. The last section presents some conclusions.

THE FIRST DYNAMIC: EXTERNAL ENVIRONMENT AND THE DIFFERENCES IN SMES

The SME is not a monolithic organizational form. Apart from the obvious differences associated with different size categories,[1] it is important to emphasize that there are different types of SMEs with different motivations and operational objectives. The nature of an SME's value-adding activities varies considerably, and we propose that it can be usefully argued that the variation in the kinds of SMEs is determined by their raison d'être, which in turn influences the extent and nature of innovatory activities, and therefore the kinds of collaborative activities they are prone to undertake. We shall also provide a taxonomy of SMEs in this section.

The first dynamic is associated with the external (and largely exogenous) environment. Although this is a large and imprecise category, we focus particularly on the competitive structure of a given industrial sector in terms of the concentration of competitors and customers in a given market, and the relationship of the SME to the large firms in the sector. The SME–large firm relationship has also been fundamentally affected by the growing trend towards products requiring multiple (and formerly unrelated) technological competences, and the growing knowledge content in manufacturing processes and products. This is a broader, non-sector-specific, development that has occurred in most industries to varying extents, and often linked to the process of globalization. This development has been associated with the breadth of knowledge content in manufacturing. In addition to the declining costs of monitoring and exploiting networks, there has also been a growing need for firms to possess multiple technological competences (Granstrand *et al.*, 1997). This trend has largely been a result of the increased knowledge content of products in general, and the cross-fertilization of previously distinct technological areas. Firms of all sizes have sought to utilize 'non-internal' means more efficiently to undertake innovation. This trend has been noted by Tidd and Trehwalla (1997), Hagedoorn (1996, 2002) and Narula and Hagedoorn (1999), among others. This has affected both the large firm and the SME, since both need a broader range of competences than was previously the case. There has therefore been a consequent increased need for SMEs by large firms, which have sought to use external networks for innovation much more than they have in the past (Narula, 2001).

A Taxonomy of SMEs

Despite the dominant role of the SME in many countries (in terms of number of firms) in ICTs in particular, they have a symbiotic relationship with the large firm. That is to say, their existences are inexorably linked. Indeed, this relationship has been described as one of dynamic complementarities (Rothwell and Dodgson 1994). Generally speaking, their competitive advantages relative each to the other are different: the literature on the innovative activities of SMEs highlights the fact that they have a behavioural advantage over large firms, which have material advantages (ibid.). There is considerable evidence to suggest that SMEs tend to have a higher R&D productivity, and this is largely due to their ability to innovate by exploiting knowledge created outside the firm (Audretsch and Vivarelli, 1996). Of course, there is great variation by industry. SMEs have tended to have an innovation advantage in highly innovative industries where the use of skilled labour is relatively important. Their cognitive limits on resources mean that, most often, SMEs in manufacturing are specialized in niches, but we believe a distinction can be made between two broad types of SMEs. The first are 'specialist supplier SMEs', whose value-adding activity is closely tied to that of larger firms, through formal and informal collaboration. Their existence is primarily in an oligopsonistic environment (that is, one with few buyers, not an atomistic market). They are in the business of value adding in intermediate stages of the production chain of a large firm. Here it is important to make a further distinction between subgroups of specialist supplier firms.

The first subgroup is the *keiretsu* SME. These SMEs are dedicated to a single customer (or a few), with whom there is an exclusive customer–supplier relationship. They often specialize in a single product or process. The proliferation of such customer–supplier relationships (often as a result of disintegration of hitherto vertically integrated large firms) has increased the scope for such SMEs. The SME often undertakes to subsidize fully or partly the R&D for the customer as part of the agreement, and the large firm in turn may provide or subsidize capital and/or technology, as well as long-term contracts. A subcategory of a *keiretsu* SME that is particularly relevant to the ICT sector is those involved in global production networks (GPN) (see Ernst, 2000). Although these also specialize in the production of subassemblies or intermediate products coordinated by a large firm, there is an important difference. First, there is a co-dependent relationship between all the firms in the GPN, since each partner in the network provides and receives inputs (both technologically and through products). Second, they tend to be associated with locations with significant clusters of activity in their industry.

The second group is the knowledge-based SME, which also acts as a supplier to larger firms, but is primarily engaged in R&D and not production. It bases its existence on supplying specialized knowledge-based assets for sale to small and large firms alike. This group is not new, but its use has now proliferated as a result of the number of radically new technologies that have, as yet, undefined dominant technological paradigms, and because larger firms cannot afford to undertake in-house developments of all possible technologies and technological trajectories. The knowledge-based MNE has proliferated in the last two decades in particular, as larger firms have systematically sought to use non-internal innovation sources. Indeed, many large MNEs require that 20 per cent or more of their R&D budget be spent on external sourcing of R&D (Narula, 2001). This is associated with the growing need for multiple technological competences, since large firms could not hope to maintain in-house expertise at the technological frontier in all technological areas, even if the costs of doing so were not prohibitive. We will expand on this in the next section.

The second broad type of SME is the 'stand-alone' SME. These are SMEs that produce final goods directly for atomistic markets (or industrial markets) and undertake most of the value-adding aspects internally, or coordinate with other SMEs who act as specialist suppliers to them. In other words, they operate much as larger firms in the same industry might, and are often in competition with them. Stand alone SMEs tend, however, to be in industries where economies of scale are not a dominant issue. The limits due to resources place them at a disadvantage, so that they must place limits (as do all SMEs) on the aspects of the value chain they can undertake in-house. This may mean, for instance, that they seek to outsource aspects of their production to other SMEs, or seek alliances with other firms in sales and marketing. Nonetheless, the focus of their activities is still on specialization. Their focus may be on one product or process (or a few), in which they are familiar and in which they have a technological advantage. That is, disadvantages due to lack of economies of scale must be offset by technological assets, and SMEs must concentrate where smaller size is an attribute, such as in batch or custom production. The SME's existence is predicated on the presence of an efficiency (often technological) not available to the larger firm, or the presence of some other niche advantage (including exclusive access to markets). Vertical integration, and the cost savings therefrom, provide larger vertically integrated firms with an advantage over SMEs, who must rely on their greater flexibility to compete effectively against the larger firms. But their most important advantage derives from utilizing their more extensive external networks of partners to achieve flexibility, cost savings and market share and doing so more intensively than large firms.

Stand-alone SMEs may sell under their own brands (own brand manufacturing, OBM), rather than as original equipment manufacturer (OEM) suppliers, as is typically the case for specialist supplier SMEs. Such firms are more likely to be in direct competition with larger firms, and exploit the most important competitive advantage of SMEs, that of flexibility and rapid response to change. Although they are often in competition with the large firm, their 'point of reference' in terms of (inter alia) products, pricing and technology is the large firm, and thus there remains a dependence. The growing need for multiple technological competences puts pressure on the 'stand alone' SME since they also require a broader range of technologies. However, because of their size constraints, they must utilize their limited resources even more astutely to maintain their technological portfolios.

THE SECOND DYNAMIC: TECHNOLOGICAL EVOLUTION AND SME R&D COLLABORATION

Our argument thus far has illustrated that the two broad types of SMEs have markedly different objectives, given their differing external environment, and are suited to particular (and quite different) tasks. We have also outlined how (*ceteris paribus*) the nature of their R&D collaborative activities might differ. However, industries evolve over time, and this is the second dynamic that we mentioned earlier. Following Tether and Storey (1998), who have built on the work of Abernathy and Utterback (1978), Teece (1986) and

Klepper (1996), among others, there seems to be a strong correlation between industry structure and industrial evolution. However, as Tether and Storey (1998) discuss at length, while there are some regularities across industries and product classes, there are limits to generalizing using either an industrial evolution argument or a product life cycle argument. There are considerable variations in the industrial organization of firms in general, and SMEs in particular due to the level of maturity of their core technologies. It is essential to emphasize that this evolutionary process which determines the kinds of R&D collaboration is also associated with technologies, and although there is certainly a coevolutionary relationship with the product life cycle or industrial evolution, these arguments need to be tempered by an understanding of the underlying core technologies.

The ICT sector provides ample evidence for proposing our modification. This is a sector which is highly aggregated, covering both hardware and software elements, although most are defined as high-technology industries, using the rationale of R&D intensity greater than 5 per cent. Take a company engaged in the manufacture of instrument landing systems (ILS), which is a product that utilizes a wide variety of technologies. Despite its being classified as a high-technology product, it is an industry that is mature, in that all the core technologies (software, radio frequency transmission, sensors) are mature. The industry structure is concentrated and relatively stable, in that there are a few (less than ten) manufacturers worldwide, with few exits and entries, and new product ranges are introduced approximately every five years. The technologies can be said to be mature and post-paradigmatic, as dominant designs and well-established standards exist. There has been a consolidation of major players on an industry level, as firms that manufacture other aspects of aeronautic ground equipment have sought to 'widen' their product offerings. Thus the same firms design and manufacture radar equipment, non-directional beacons, rangefinders and air traffic control equipment. SMEs in ILS production are stand-alone SMEs (scale economies are unimportant, because the market is limited to large airports, and each airport needs roughly two per major runway). They tend to use collaboration mainly in manufacturing (through outsourcing) but not in R&D.

However, the production of ILS is about to change fundamentally because of a new core technology that is currently being introduced: ILS systems will gradually be replaced by satellite landing systems (SLS), which incorporate technology similar to global positioning systems (GPS). SLS systems are at a pre-paradigmatic stage, with the main players currently working on developing standards. In other words, while the industry is mature, its core technologies are about to change. SMEs in landing systems now have to seek new sources of knowledge and collaborate with larger firms and knowledge-based SMEs, because the SLS technology is highly specialized and not widely diffused. This is not a unique event: a similar reorganization occurred in the computer industry in the 1970s (at the time, dominant designs existed, and the industry was dominated primarily by large firms) with the introduction of microprocessors paving the way for a wide variety of new SMEs (Rothwell and Dodgson, 1994).

We propose that technological evolution based on a core technology approach is a more accurate way of viewing industry dynamics and collaboration, because the proliferation and involvement of SMEs change fundamentally according to the technologies in question.

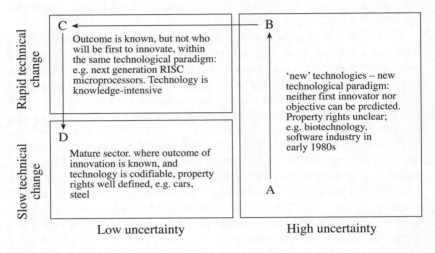

Source: Narula (2001).

Figure 8.1   Technological evolution with a given paradigm

Figure 8.1 gives a stylized presentation of the technological evolution of sectors, utilizing two basic measures, technological uncertainty and speed of technological change (Narula, 2001). Technological paradigms evolve over time, from nascent, pre-paradigmatic and highly uncertain, to mature, certain and slow-evolving. Note that, because most products and processes are multi-technology-based, we refer here to individual technologies. It should further be noted that, despite the multi-technology nature of products and processes, certain technologies are more central or 'core', while others are more marginal (Granstand *et al.*, 1997). It is possible, therefore, to argue that industries demonstrate a similar evolution. It is self-evident that the framework in Figure 8.1 is a stylized one, and that sectoral evolution is a continuous rather than discrete process. We will now discuss how the structure of industry – in terms of size of firms and, in particular, predominant type of SME – varies with the evolution in the technological characteristics of the ICT sector. Figure 8.2 illustrates, in the same context as Figure 8.1, the types of SMEs that tend to predominate during each stage of industry evolution.

Quadrant C *GPN SMEs* *Knowledge SMEs* Stand-alone SMEs	**Quadrant B** *Stand-alone SMEs* *Knowledge SMEs* GPN SMEs
Quadrant D *Keiretsu SMEs*	**Quadrant A** *Knowledge SMEs*

Figure 8.2   Types of SMEs at different stages of an industry's evolution

Quadrant A

New technologies begin from a basic idea, often a fundamental invention or technological breakthrough based on an idea, which may have been hitherto a scientific theory. However, at an early stage, the technology is impractical. Its potential use is not obvious, it is not close enough to being commercial, and/or it may still remain at an early stage of development. Current research interests in superconductors illustrate this well. Only the largest firms with large resources invested in basic research (such as Bell Labs, or IBM) are likely to be willing to invest in a project such as this, given that neither the time-horizon is practical, nor what variation in the technology is likely to win. There exist so many research trajectories and combinations of materials, from ceramics to semiconductors, that it does not serve most firms to invest in such research. Apart from large MNEs, university departments and publicly-funded facilities are likely to engage in such long-term investment. Cooperation is primarily amongst large laboratories, and mainly on a scientific level. An example of such a technology is superconductivity, which potentially has many benefits, but the technology still requires very low temperatures.

As the rate of technological innovations and breakthroughs becomes more rapid, and a commercially viable product becomes closer to reality, large firms and universities may create (or may have to create) knowledge-based SMEs as spin-offs, as important scientists involved seek more control of their inventions and the possible returns. Scientific personnel at the cutting edge of new technologies are rare, and this may be the only way to keep them. In addition, large laboratories and firms do not act as the best incubators for new, nascent technologies, which need more flexibility and a more organic organization, a primary advantage of an SME. Besides, by cooperating, the large firm is insulated from taking additional risk and minimizing investment, by allowing external agencies to share the costs. This is currently the case with much genetic research, but ICT firms in the 1980s and 1990s undertook similar alliances in Internet technologies. The SME can seek additional resources from venture capitalists and public funds. At the same time, the large firm often has an option to acquire the discoveries of the knowledge SMEs if it makes a move towards more commercializable technologies. Nonetheless, the basic nature of the research means that few such knowledge-based SMEs will exist, outside dedicated university-based research centres.

Quadrant B

Eventually, however, as innovations move towards the taking out of patents which may be commercially exploited, an increase in such knowledge SMEs may be expected. Prototypes of products now exist, and the SME needs not only technological resources but also manufacturing and managerial personnel and expertise. At this stage, the more successful knowledge-based SMEs become stand-alone SMEs, but in the early stages of quadrant B these will be an exception rather than the rule. Increased financial flows from both large firms and venture capitalists will fuel the movement of the best scientists, as there is a race to establish a dominant technology, and thus to define the paradigm. This is the situation that the biotechnology and robotics industries find themselves in today. The software industry was also at this stage in the late 1970s and early 1980s. Eventually, as the knowledge SMEs begin to grow, spin-offs from these companies will begin, creating additional knowledge SMEs. Large firms will begin to acquire the more successful companies in these sectors, attempting to internalize and apply these new technologies to their existing products and processes. Acquiring these knowledge SMEs allows the larger firm to integrate the new technology into their existing R&D activities and, it is hoped, the large resources available to the big company will help to reduce the 'distance to market'.

Towards the end of quadrant B, products based on the new technologies begin to enter the market, although they will tend to be of a specialized nature, owing to their high cost of production. There is a high concentration, as only a few firms will have the technological competences necessary. Technological change remains rapid, and leadership moves from one company to another, with no clear dominant player. Production is predominantly undertaken by stand-alone SMEs, which operate on a small scale, since competitive advantage is based on technological assets rather than price.

Quadrant C

By quadrant C, the technology will have been diffused, and the technical difficulties of large-scale production will have been overcome. Production in small batches will gradually be replaced by large-scale production: either by former stand-alone SMEs, which have rapidly expanded their operations, or by large firms that have acquired the technology from SMEs, through alliances or M&A. As the technologies become diffused and increasingly codifiable, firms will seek to outsource or engage in alliances for components and subassemblies from stand-alone SMEs and specialist supplier firms which possess the appropriate niche technologies.[2] These may develop over time into global production networks. This type of SME becomes increasingly important as the technology becomes codifiable and increasingly mature, so that large firms seek to use outsourcing. SMEs within the network undertake most, if not all, the R&D required for their niche input into the process, and this specialization leads to a co-dependence between the various firms, SME and large, in the network. The dominance of knowledge SMEs that themselves have core technologies in quadrant C gradually declines, except perhaps in niche sectors. It should be emphasized, however, that, as new technologies that are pre-paradigmatic (quadrant B) are introduced into existing (quadrant C) products, firms will need to seek alliances with them. For instance, currently substitutes for LCD displays are being developed which are less fragile and more flexible (quadrant B), and notebook computer manufacturers (a quadrant C product) are seeking to identify the most viable of the various alternatives. As technological change becomes less rapid towards the end of quadrant C, much of innovation moves towards development-type work, and incremental improvements of increasingly mature products.

Quadrant D

By quadrant D, the technology is mature. Technical change is now slow, with minor but consistent innovations over time, and can be regarded as post-paradigmatic. The technology is to a great extent codifiable, widely disseminated, and the property rights are well-defined. Innovation is rarely patentable in these technologies, where applications development accounts for most innovatory activity. Competition shifts towards price, economies of scale and downstream activities in order to add value, as the original product is priced as a commodity. SMEs simply do not have the size advantages to engage in production (except perhaps in specialized niches) and stand-alone SMEs are the exception rather than the rule. The main opportunities for SMEs are as *keiretsu*-type MNEs, acting as specialized suppliers to large firms. Collaboration tends to take the form of outsourcing. Indeed, in these technologies, large firms expect suppliers to undertake much of the investment in development of new products and processes on their behalf. This is particularly common in the case of equipment suppliers to large firms in mature sectors, who expect the suppliers (whether large or small) to invest in R&D as a substitute for their own R&D expenditures (Fritsch and Lukas, 2001). This is the case even where the supplier firms have core technologies in earlier quadrants.

SOME EVIDENCE: STAND-ALONE SMES IN THE ICT SECTOR

In this section we address the question of R&D collaboration by ICT firms, illustrating the differences between SMEs and larger firms. We focus on what we have earlier described as 'stand-alone' SMEs. Our discussion is based on data that derive from the TIK-R&D database, a larger survey being conducted on the internationalization of R&D by Europe based MNEs. The criteria for selection of these firms have been (a) that they were majority-European owned as of 1998, (b) engaged in manufacturing, (c) have annual R&D expenditures greater than (approximately) US$1 million and/or ten full-time R&D employees. Although the database consists of 110 European firms, only 47 are in the ICT sector. In order to avoid any possible bias due to industry differences, the sample is further narrowed by excluding firms primarily engaged in software and ICT service firms. Firms in the sample are engaged in the design and manufacture of electronics-based hardware, including medical electronics, avionics, scientific and measuring equipment, and industrial electronics. We have attempted to match 'similar' firms together, in terms of technology intensity and primary technologies, but not nationality, structure of ownership or age of firms. Furthermore, SMEs that act primarily as suppliers to larger firms were excluded, because they are involved in a 'keiretsu'-like symbiotic relationship. The final sample available for the analysis is 13 SMEs and 12 large firms. The UN definition of SMEs to include firms with fewer than 500 employees has been used.

The firms in our sample, like most ICT firms, can be classified in quadrant C, although certain industries have progressed towards quadrant D (PC manufacturers, hard disk technologies), where products are mature and compete mainly on price, having taken on a commodity-type nature. It is true that, while new technologies do exist that are still pre-paradigmatic (nano-electronics, artificial intelligence, neural networks), broadly speaking firms in our sample are predominantly paradigmatic. Clear dominant technologies have presented themselves, and de facto standards have been established. Unambiguous technological trajectories exist, and most innovatory activity is focused on the dominant paradigms. Technological change remains rapid, but mainly through incremental, rather than radical, innovation. Innovation also tends, for the most part, to be undertaken either in applied research or in development, and rather rarely in basic research. Since innovation is built around clear trajectories, the nature of the incremental innovation is known; what is unclear is who will be first to the market. Although property rights are clearly defined in quadrant C, the rapidity of change means that firms maintain their competitive advantage by being first to innovate and exploiting the lead time of being 'first'. In our sample, the life cycle of products averaged around 12 to 18 months, a pace usually dictated by 'major players' (that is, large firms).

Thus far, these tendencies apply universally to all firms in quadrant C. However, R&D in quadrant C (and in ICTs in particular) is resource-intensive, in terms of both capital and knowledge. Most products are multi-technology in nature, and multiple competences are needed. Figure 8.3 illustrates the kinds of technologies that a typical ICT firm may require. Few firms, regardless of size, can afford to maintain R&D facilities with world-class competences in so many different sectors. This is particularly so in the case of SMEs, which by definition have limited resources. Even if SMEs maintain twice the level of R&D intensity of a large firm in the same industry (which typically might be 5 per cent), a company of 500 employees might maintain an R&D department of about 50 people, while a large firm with 5000 employees might have an R&D facility of 250 people.

Table 8.1 gives a rough idea of the differences in size between the large firms and the SMEs. Large firms in our sample spent five times more on R&D than the SMEs. However, in terms of R&D employees, large firms were on average only three times larger. The average size in terms of R&D employees of SMEs in our sample was 42. There are only so many specializations that an SME can maintain with such a small absolute R&D headcount. There is a certain minimum threshold size of a research group within any area, and this represents a real constraint on SMEs. In addition

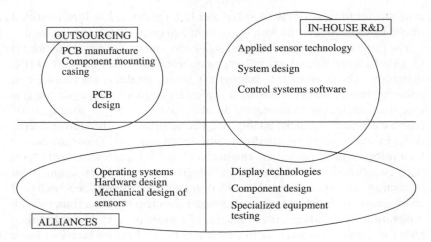

Note: No attempt has been made to locate technologies on a relative basis within any given quadrant.

Source: Narula (2001).

Figure 8.3   Distribution of competencies of an ICT firm, based on managers' perceptions

– and this is true for firms of all sizes – there is no guarantee that the research group in any given facility will in fact consistently innovate at the technological frontier, and within the dominant paradigm, even if world-class researchers are present. In other words, there are cognitive limits on what firms can and cannot do (Pavitt, 1998). Firms therefore are dependent on the 'last-best' (that is, state-of-the-art) innovation. If a firm is engaged in developing an innovation in a given technological paradigm, it must strive to improve (or at least take into account) not its own last-best innovation, but the last-best innovation that has been patented, or that is the dominant design on the market,[3] even if this was created by another firm. Thus its path dependency is always tempered by the state of the art, and this means that, roughly speaking, technological trajectories of different firms within any given technological paradigm are similar.

There are therefore two pressures on ICT firms: to maintain an equivalent breadth of R&D competences to those of other firms in the same industry, and at the same time to maintain their innovative activities at the industry rate of evolution. The benefits of smallness, which are variously associated with greater flexibility and rapid response, compensate for some of the disadvantages of size, and may allow SMEs to maintain the rate of technological change. But they do not necessarily help an SME when it comes to the absolute limit on its resources.

Table 8.1   Some basic indicators

	SMEs	Large firms
Mean R&D expenditure (US$mn)	4.15	21.54
Mean R&D employment	42	129
% of R&D in home location	90.7	57
% of firms with overseas R&D labs	36.4	77.8
Percentage of firms with R&D facilities in the USA	27.3	66.7
Average size of R&D facilities in the USA (employees)	8.2	96.5
% of R&D acquired externally	21.9	12.4
% of firms with < 20% external acquisition	28.6	10

Source: TIK-R&D database.

Keep in mind, too, that SMEs have also to devote resources to other aspects of the value chain. They must seek to achieve economies of scale in production, and also to market their products effectively, and provide support services. In quadrant C, market share considerations are at least as important as technological assets: it is insufficient simply to have the best product, if no one will buy it. More importantly, if a competitor's technology is accepted as the industry standard, it can threaten the existence of the firm.

It is impressive, nonetheless, that the SMEs in our sample employ more people relative to their R&D expenditures than large firms, and the answer lies to some extent in their greater use of non-internal R&D sources. Larger firms tend to use a smaller percentage of their R&D budgets (on average 12.4 per cent) to outsource and engage in strategic alliances than SMEs which utilize on average 21.9 per cent of their R&D budget (Table 8.1). The limitation in resources, and the need to maintain the firm's position on the technological frontier of the various technological areas that it requires, is mainly responsible for the growth in the use of non-internal R&D activities in both large and small firms. Our use of the term 'non-internal' is a deliberate one, and is intended to include both external activities (arm's-length relationships such as licensing, R&D contracts, outsourcing and other customer–supplier relationships) and quasi-external activity (such as strategic alliances, which are taken to include a myriad of organizational modes; see Narula and Hagedoorn, 1999). Non-internal activities, apart from the obvious benefits of exploring new areas and instigating radical change, have the advantage of being a 'reversible' form of investment (Gambardella and Torrisi 1998). The capital needed is smaller, and the risks are substantially reduced, and, in the case of failure or organizational crisis, limited damage is inflicted on the primary operations of the firm. Nonetheless, the tacit nature of innovation, and the risks associated with loss of technological competitiveness, encourage a high level of in-house R&D activity.

External acquisition of technology is most easily done when the technology behind the product is codifiable and standardized and for which multiple non-distinguishable sources of these inputs are available (Narula, 2001). The same argument holds true for R&D activity: R&D output is partly tacit, and therefore externalization of R&D means that the firm only gets the codified results, not the accumulated person-embodied skills. As has been noted elsewhere, even where firms outsource, they maintain a minimum level of in-house capacity in those technologies in order to decipher and utilize them (Veugelers, 1997). In other words, R&D outsourcing is only undertaken where doing so is cost-effective and does not threaten the competitive advantages of the company. Having a single source or single buyer may prove to be most cost-effective, but it is generally accepted that low costs do not always translate to the best technology.

The manner in which firms select external as opposed to internal R&D acquisitions is associated with the centrality of the technological competence to the firms' activities (Narula, 2001). Firms will, *ceteris paribus*, prefer to undertake innovative activities in their distinctive competencies through in-house R&D. Although there is considerable overlap (Figure 8.3), broadly speaking niche and marginal competences are strategically less significant, and can be undertaken through alliances. However, the strategic importance of these technologies determines to what extent their development can be externalized. This, in turn, is determined by the extent to which the technology is tacit, the extent to which collaboration is required to utilize it, and the extent to which the partner's activities need to be monitored.

Background competences are, by and large, the area where outsourcing is primarily used. In general, it would seem firms prefer to undertake research in their distinctive competencies in-house as much as possible. There is, however, considerable overlap in the use of in-house R&D and alliances for niche competencies, and between outsourcing and alliances in marginal/peripheral competencies. SMEs tend to be more concerned about their loss of technological assets than large firms. SMEs tend to use non-internal means with a great deal of care, bordering, in some cases, on paranoia. One firm said,

> Because we do not have the resources [ourselves, and have to outsource], we make sure none of our partners has enough of our technology to become a competitor. We provide the macro-specifications to one partner, which does the design. But we have a different company to do the manufacturing of the relevant sub-assembly. We make sure that no company is responsible for more than one sub-assembly, and always pick companies smaller than us.

Another manager agreed:

> We use more than one supplier, our products are based on several boards. Each supplier produces only one board, because we don't want any supplier to have access to our complete product. We might be able to get a lower price, but we don't want to be in a position that the supplier is able to become a competitor. Non-disclosure agreements aren't enough.

In general, the vulnerability due to smaller size means that SMEs have to be more wary of alliances. One of the SMEs in our sample considered alliances unacceptably risky:

> These competencies are too important to us ... we have spent many years building our strength in these sectors ... frankly we have world class competences....I am loathe to consider letting anyone near our technology. We only use alliances [in these areas] if we have to.

In general, however, SMEs use non-internal means to a greater extent than large firms, because they can maintain a sufficiently high level of in-house competence in only a few (or even a single) technological areas. This represents an advantage of the SME, according to one manager, who argued,

> We are not married to a given technology, and that is precisely why we are successful. If we did our own research, we would have a vested interest in a particular technology, even if it is not the best, and this would eventually become a problem.

Thus there are many more technologies which they have to acquire externally. The use of alliances in connection with niche sectors was, in general, associated with firms that had limited R&D facilities and/or considered that there was a large technological gap between their technological competencies and the market leaders. SMEs considered alliances as a way of extending their technological competencies more than large firms, but only when they were unable to do so through outsourcing. For instance, one medical equipment manufacturer did not have the resources to invest in the next generation of displays. Although LCD technology has become more mature over the last five years, it remains capital-intensive and proprietary technology rests with a handful of companies. It therefore sought an alliance with a US company which is a market leader in medical equipment, many times their size. The US firm did not currently compete with them in their particular product segment, and agreed to share the technology and to distribute their products in the USA. As a manager pointed out,

> It's a risk [to ally ourselves with such a large player], but the cost of developing our own display systems would use up almost our entire R&D budget for a couple of years ... and our old product range was [beginning to look] old ... [They] have the technology lying around, because they have more people in their R&D facilities than we have in our entire company ... [if they wanted to] they could buy us out, whether we had a partnership with them or not [so it doesn't matter whether or not we partner with them].

There are two points we want to make here. First, there is a limit to how much of a firm's R&D activities can be externally acquired, owing particularly to technological and strategic considerations. Second, even if costs are reduced through the use of non-internal means, they remain non-trivial and the constraints of absolute limits of resources remain.

Both large and small firms have similar motives to undertake inter-firm R&D collaboration (Table 8.2). The primary motivation for both groups of firms was not considered to be the reduction of risks or costs, but the reduction of innovation time span, and the access to complementary technologies. However, larger firms are in a better position to establish partnerships, because they have more to offer. SMEs have fewer technological assets with which to barter, while the technological portfolio of large firms is larger, and besides they can offer cooperative agreements at other levels too, from either production or their marketing and sales operations. This is apparent from Table 8.3.

Where SMEs concentrate their activities in-house, they are still forced to consider alliances with larger firms, simply as a means of getting access to marketing and sales channels. A telecommunications equipment company explained,

> Although we do not need anyone for technology, we are not able to offer a 'suite' [an integrated package of products]. The way of the future is systems integration, and it is the key. Customers want our equipment to work in tandem [with products of other manufacturers]. Our competitors are all large and can offer an integrated package, we can't. So we are looking for a partner who will sell our product, but we are faced with a dilemma, because the only companies who make [the other parts of the suite] are our competitors.[4]

In general, both large and small firms show a preference for outsourcing applied research and product development to public research institutes and universities because of the fear of giving away their technology to a competitor or potential competitor. Although our data are by no means conclusive, anecdotal evidence suggests that SMEs tend to engage in fewer strategic alliances with other firms, preferring to outsource wherever possible. It should be noted that there is a lower limit to the extent to which any firm (but particularly SMEs) can use non-internal sources as a substitute for internal R&D. Both alliances and outsourcing require complementary

Table 8.2   The importance of different R&D motivations for ICT firms

	SME % major or crucial		Large firms % major or crucial	
	mean	importance	mean	importance
Reduction of costs	2.4	40	3.0	28.6
Reduction of risks	2.5	30	2.9	14.3
Reduction of innovation time	3.4	70	3.3	42.9
Access to markets	2.4	30	2.2	33.3
Access to complementary technology	3.6	60	4.6	100
Setting standards	2.7	30	2.7	42.9

Source: TIK-R&D database.

Table 8.3   R&D activities that firms prefer to undertake with partners

What kind of research do you undertake with your partners?

	SMEs	Large Firms
	(% of firms that responded 'often' or 'most of the time')	
Basic research	0	0
Applied research	50	14.3
Development	50	71
Design	10	43
Production and marketing	20	71

Source: TIK-R&D database.

resources. Some level of in-house capacity is essential to absorb the externally acquired information. Furthermore, alliances in particular (compared to outsourcing) require considerable managerial resources, not just because of the collaborative aspect, but also because alliances tend to be used where technology is tacit. Again, limited human resources mean there is a limit to what percentage of a smaller absolute size of personnel can be devoted to managing alliances.

CONCLUDING REMARKS

This chapter has highlighted the increasing imperative of ICT firms to expand their portfolio of technological competences, and the fact that this applies to SMEs as much as it does to large firms. Fortunately, reduced costs of enforcing agreements, the decline in barriers to trade and investment and the improvements in communications have improved the efficacy of cooperative ventures, especially for R&D.

Although the analysis of the dynamics and the types of SMEs applies across all industries, the empirical evidence we have used here has focused on 'stand-alone' SMEs in the ICT sector, which are engaged in direct competition with larger firms, and broadly speaking are 'mini-large firms'. Both large firms and SMEs need roughly the same breadth of technological competencies, as multi-technology products are the norm in the ICT sector. For both groups of firms, maintaining such a large portfolio of technological competencies is difficult, but more so for the SME. The use of non-internal technology development through outsourcing and alliances has provided benefits for both types of firms, but particularly for the SME.

SMEs tend to maintain a smaller group of in-house technological competencies, and are generally able to leverage their limited R&D resources more efficiently. They tend to use almost twice as much of their R&D expenditures on R&D collaboration than large firms. However, there are cognitive limits to what SMEs can do, and how much they can use non-internal R&D, owing to their absolute size limitations. Nonetheless, the more successful SMEs have been able to maintain their competitive position through a more astute use of non-internal R&D, with less in-house R&D than larger firms.

However, collaboration has its price. First, even where non-internal means are used, some level of in-house competence must be maintained in order to understand and integrate the various technologies together. Second, most R&D alliances have a very low success rate. A failure rate of 50 per cent was judged by firms in our sample to be 'very good indeed'. For a large firm, these losses are easier to accept as they often have multiple, redundant, back-up agreements with several firms. In addition, large firms have more to offer in a partnership, and can more easily find alternative sources, compared with SMEs. SMEs are more careful about picking partners because they have limited opportunities to fail. As Beamish (1999) notes, mistakes are proportionately more expensive for an SME than for a large firm. There are also strategic reasons to be careful: partnering with a larger firm can lead to a loss of technological competence.

It seems that there is a limit to the amount of a firm's R&D activities that can be externally acquired, particularly owing to technological and strategic considerations. In addition, even if costs are reduced through the use of non-internal means, they remain non-trivial, and the constraints of absolute limits of resources remain.

We have not discussed the international dimension of collaborative activity. Firms in the ICT sector all have a growing need to monitor the innovation systems of countries other than their own, and to be located close to both their markets and their competitors to maintain their competitiveness. They need to do so both through R&D facilities abroad and through alliances. However, SMEs are again constrained by their resources. Even alliances require some level of physical presence, and the threshold level to establish such facilities is often prohibitively high for SMEs. Some aspects of the internationalization of SMEs have been evaluated by Lu and Beamish (2001), but further research on the R&D aspect is sadly lacking.

Stand-alone SMEs in the ICT sector are an endangered species. In the long run, these firms are faced with three options: expand, be acquired or specialize. This is in fact what might be predicted from our discussion of industry evolution. As technologies become more mature and diffused, competition shifts away from technological excellence per se, and towards price. Size and costs become more critical. Thus, if SMEs specialize, they can maintain their position on a technological basis where small size and flexibility allow SMEs to be at least as innovative as large firms, if not more.

NOTES

1. While some countries (for example, Norway, Denmark, Ireland) regard all firms with more than 100 employees as large, in this chapter we define SMEs as firms with fewer than 500 employees, as used by the United Nations.
2. The decision to ally or outsource depends on (a) whether the specifications for the subassembly are codifiable and multiple, substitutable sources exist, and (b) whether the technologies used in the subassembly are not central to the outsourcing firm. In general, non-internal sources are used as the technology moves towards quadrant D. That is, these technologies are rapidly becoming mature and post-paradigmatic. See Narula (2001) for further elaboration on the decision factors behind outsourcing and alliances.

3. Numerous examples of technically suboptimal innovations defining the technological trajectory exist (for example, Betamax v. VHS, Macintosh v. PC). Perhaps the best documented example is the QWERTY keyboard (David, 1985).
4. Two months after the interview, this SME was acquired by a large competitor.

REFERENCES

Abernathy, W., and J. Utterback (1978), 'Patterns of innovation in industry', *Technology Review*, **80**, 40–47.

Ahern, R. (1993), 'Implications of strategic alliances for small R&D-intensive firms', *Environment and Planning*, **25**, 1511–26.

Audretsch, D., and M. Vivarelli (1996), 'Firm size and R&D spillovers: evidence from Italy', *Small Business Economics*, **8**, 249–58.

Beamish, P. (1999), 'The role of alliances in international entrepreneurship', in R. Wright (ed.), *Research in Global Strategic Management*, vol. 7, Stamford, CT: JAI Press, pp. 43–61.

David, P. (1985), 'Clio and the economics of QWERTY', *American Economic Review*, **75** (2), 332–7.

Ernst, D. (2000), 'Inter-organisational knowledge outsourcing: what permits small Taiwanese firms to compete in the computer industry?', *Asia Pacific Journal of Management*, **17**.

Fritsch, M., and R. Lukas (2001), 'Who cooperates on R&D?', *Research Policy*, **30**, 297–312.

Gambardella, A., and S. Torrisi (1998), 'Does technological convergence imply convergence in markets? Evidence from the electronics industry', *Research Policy*, **27**, 447–65.

Granstrand, O., P. Patel, and K. Pavitt (1997), 'Multi-technology corporations: why they have "distributed" rather than "distinctive core" competencies', *California Management Review*, **39** (4), 8–25.

Hagedoorn, J. (1996), 'Trends and patterns in strategic technology partnering since the early seventies', *Review of Industrial Organization*, **11**, 601–16.

Hagedoorn, J. (2002), 'Inter-firm R&D partnerships – an overview of patterns and trends since 1960', *Research Policy*, **31**, 477–92.

Klepper, S. (1996), 'Entry, exit, growth and innovation over the product life cycle', *American Economic Review*, **86**, 562–83.

Lu, J., and P. Beamish (2001), 'The internationalisation and performance of SMEs', *Strategic Management Journal*, **22**, 565–86.

Narula, R. (2001), 'Choosing between modes of non-internal technological activities by firms: some technological and economic factors', *Technology Analysis and Strategic Management*, **13**, 365–88.

Narula, R., and J. Hagedoorn (1999), 'Innovating through strategic alliances: moving towards international partnerships and contractual agreements', *Technovation*, **19**, 283–94.

Pavitt, K. (1998), 'Technologies, products and organisation in the innovating firm: what Adam Smith tells us and Joseph Schumpeter doesn't', *Industrial and Corporate Change*, **7**, 433–52.

Rothwell, R., and M. Dodgson (1994), 'Innovation and size of firm', in M. Dodgson (ed.), *Handbook of Industrial Innovation*, Aldershot, UK and Brookfield, USA: Edward Elgar, pp. 310–24.

Santangelo, G. (2001), 'The impact of the information and communications technology revolution on the internationalisation of corporate technology', *International Business Review,* **10**, 701–26.

Teece, D. (1986), 'Profiting from technological innovation', *Research Policy*, **15**, 285–306.

Tether, B., and D. Storey (1998), 'Smaller firms and Europe's high technology sectors: a framework for analysis and some statistical evidence', *Research Policy*, **26**, 947–71.

Tidd, J., and M. Trewhella (1997), 'Organizational and technological antecedents for knowledge creation and learning', *R&D Management*, **27**, 359–75.

Veugelers, R. (1997), 'Internal R&D expenditures and external technology sourcing', *Research Policy*, **26**, 303–15.

PART III

FDI and competitiveness

9 Relational assets: the new competitive advantages of MNEs and countries

INTRODUCTION

Most paradigms and economic theories of the determinants of international business (IB) activities, and particularly those designed to explain the extent, composition and geography of foreign owned production, are essentially asset based. By assets, we mean the accumulated stock of the resources and capabilities of firms which, potentially at least, are capable of generating a future income stream and/or an augmentation to that stock.

The IB literature[1] usually distinguishes between three kinds of assets (see Table 9.1):

1. those specific and unique to particular multinational enterprises (MNEs),[2] or potential MNEs: these may be located in the home country of the MNEs, or in the countries which are host to their affiliates;
2. those which are external to MNEs, but are accessed and then deployed by them: these assets may likewise be located in the home country of the MNEs or in foreign countries;
3. those which encompass the organizational form by which these two kinds of assets are harnessed, created and coordinated by the management of MNEs, whether exercised by the parent companies or by their foreign affiliates.

As set out in Table 9.2, over the years, the content, relative significance and governance of these different types of assets have changed. Until the industrial revolution, the critical wealth-creating assets were of two kinds. The first consisted of land and property owned mainly by households, and the way in which these assets were husbanded. The second comprised the capital, entrepreneurship and markets owned, accessed or exploited by merchants, including the great trading and colonizing ventures of the 16th and 17th centuries.[3] For much of the 19th and 20th centuries, they were the physical and financial assets owned by firms, but supplemented by those of other institutions, and accessed primarily through the market. Today, the critical assets consist of a kaleidoscope of intangible resources and capabilities, especially all kinds of knowledge and information embodied in human and physical capital, both owned and accessed, from a variety of sources, and by firms.[4] Though the ownership or access to physical and financial assets remains important, particularly in the case of resource-intensive activities, such assets are increasingly playing a supportive, rather than a dominant role in the wealth creation process.[5]

Table 9.1   Three kinds of assets available to MNEs or potential MNEs

---

1. Those owned by MNEs or potential MNEs
   * located in home countries
   * located in foreign countries

2. Those external to MNEs but accessed by them
   * located in home countries
   * located in foreign countries

3. Those which relate to the organizational modality by which 1 and/or 2 above are harnessed, upgraded, coordinated and used by the management of MNEs
   * by that of the parent company
   * by that of their foreign affiliates

The last decade, in particular, has seen an escalation of the scholarly writings on the nature and significance of knowledge capital and its competition enhancing qualities for both firms and countries, and of the appropriate organizational modalities for its creation, sustenance, exploitation and diffusion.[6] Indeed, one might be led to believe that the intellectual component of human capital was now the 'be all and end all' of a firm's or nation's competitive prowess.

This, in our opinion, would be misguided. Certainly when one widens the unit of analysis from that of the firm to groups of firms or interest groups to the country, a good deal of evidence is emerging on the critical role of social capital (later to be defined) as a prerequisite for, and facilitator of the productive creation and deployment from specific tangible and intangible assets. Yet, in the business literature, apart, perhaps, from writings on industrial and/or customer relations, only scant attention has been paid to (what we shall term) 'relational assets' (R-assets), as they affect the success or failure of intra- or extra-firm associations, the latter encompassing linkages both between private and public organizations and between organizations and persons. This domain has largely been occupied by sociologists, social psychologists and, latterly, by organizational scholars.[7] Economists and

Table 9.2 The changing characteristics of (productive) assets

	1. Specific to ownership	2. Accessed by firms	3. Organized by firms
(a) Pre-industrial revolution	• Land, property • Entrepreneurship, trading/colonising experience, transport facilities	• Labour, materials • Finance capital	• Internal to households. • Elementary markets • Internal to merchants
	(Initially domestically created but wealth also increased through overseas trade and colonization)		
(b) 19th & 20th centuries	• Machines, buildings • Financial assets • Property rights	• Labour, intermediate products	• Largely hierarchical, within firms • Growth of joint ventures • More sophisticated markets
	(Mainly domestically, but increasingly foreign sourced)		
(c) 21st century	• Property rights • Intellectual assets • 'Connectivity' advantages (including R-assets)	• Leasing of property • Intermediate products • Knowledge and information • Collective (social) assets	• Heterarchical within firms • Coalitions between firms • Networks • Markets
	(Accelerated movement towards the global or regional creation, accessing and utilization of assets)		

business strategists have tended to approach the subject of R-assets hesitantly and obliquely in two ways: first, by implicitly incorporating it into their analysis of market failures and hierarchical modes of governance and, second, by identifying the critical conditions for successful inter-firm alliances, in terms of such ingredients as cultural affinity, trust, reciprocity and forbearance.

In the last decade or so, management and marketing scholars, in particular, have given more explicit attention to the role of inter- and intraorganizational relationships as affecting the competitive advantages of firms. A selection of the more important contributions are set out in Appendix 9.1 of this chapter. Kale *et al.* (2000), for example, coined the term 'relationship capital' to embrace the 'mutual trust, respect and friendship that reside at the individual level between alliance partners' (p. 221). Leana and Rousseau (2000), in their discussion of 'relational wealth', Nahapiet and Ghoshal (1998) in their analysis of the 'relational dimension' of social capital, Holm *et al.* (1996) in their construct of 'relational understanding' and Dyer and Singh (1998) in their assessment of 'relational specific assets' and 'relational rent', take a broader perspective of the gains which may arise from successful inter- and intra-firm collaboration. Hall and Soskice (2001) have averred that a firm's core competencies and dynamic capabilities are critically dependent on the quality of the relationships they establish both within their boundaries and with external institutions, including customers and governments. Morgan and Hunt (1994) have identified the main components of successful 'relational exchanges' in terms of relationship commitment and trust. Most recently of all, Choi and Ericksson (2001) have examined some of the costs and benefits of 'relational development' between domestic and foreign firms, using an internationalization process model initially devised by Johanson and Vahlne (1977).

It is the purpose of this chapter to take this discussion a little further by offering some exploratory observations on the nature, significance and governance of firm-specific R-assets and, more particularly, to examine their relevance in explaining the recent growth, structure and geography of MNE-related activity. We use the adjective 'related' advisedly, for we shall concern ourselves with not just MNE-owned activity, that is, activity financed by FDI, but with the totality of activities under the effective control of MNEs. Such activities are based not only on resources and capabilities which MNEs actually own, but also on those which they can gain access to by one means or another, and then internalize for their own use. (We shall take up the significance of an access regime of governance, in contrast to an ownership regime, to the international activities of firms later in this chapter.)[8]

THE CHARACTERISTICS OF FIRM-SPECIFIC R-ASSETS

First a working definition. We define a firm's R-assets as the stock of a firm's willingness and capability to access, create, to shape economically, and to coordinate the resources and capabilities necessary to beneficial relationships, and to sustain and upgrade the quality of these relationships. Such relationships, which may take various forms, though always conducted by and between individuals, may take place both within the confines of a particular firm or between that firm and other organizations or individuals.

This definition comes closest to that of 'relational quality' identified by Hall and Soskice (2001). It is also similar to that of Kale *et al.*'s concept of 'relational capital' and Holm *et al.*'s (1996) concept of 'relational understanding', but it embraces intra-firm as well as inter-firm associations. It is, however, somewhat narrower than the relational concepts developed by Leana and Rousseau (2000), Dyer and Singh (1998) and Nahapiet and Ghoshal (1998), in that it focuses on the willingness and ability of firms to engage in successful relationships, rather than on the overall benefit arising from these relationships.

The relationships between R-assets and other kinds of corporate assets, whether owned or exploited by firms, are set out in Figure 9.1. As can be seen, they run alongside human embodied intellectual capital, but are more empathetic and emotionally based. (This may be why economists are uneasy in dealing with them.) R-assets have a number of other distinctive qualities, but their essential uniqueness lies in the fact they can only be augmented or productively employed if they are used jointly with other R-assets, whether located within the same institution or another.

The sociologist Amitai Etzioni believes that, to be successful, partnerships, whether they be between persons, interest groups, corporations or governments, need to share a set of core values and objectives (Etzioni, 1996). R-assets are essentially facilitating assets. When properly deployed, they enhance – one way or another – virtually all functional activities of the firm possessing or using them. These include R&D, production, sourcing, personnel management, administration and marketing, as well as a myriad of transaction-specific activities.

R-assets are, then, entirely human intensive, although such assets may be embedded in, and used by, individuals or organizations. In their usage, R-assets can give rise to a plethora of inter- and intra-institutional associations, ranging from the simple, shallow and one off, to the complex, dense and continuous.

(PRODUCTIVE) ASSETS

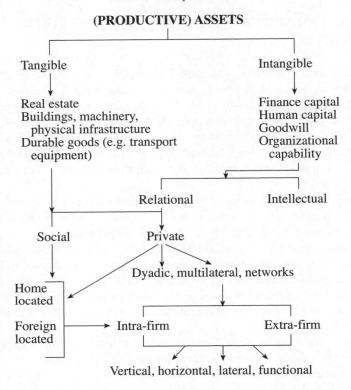

Figure 9.1   The pyramid of corporate assets (at the individual firm level)

Some other characteristics of R-assets are set out in Table 9.3. Note, for example, that they may be augmented or used by firms in the pursuance of dyadic, multilateral or network relationships. As with other resources and capabilities, R-assets need to be scarce, unique and imperfectly imitable if they are to confer a sustainable competitive advantage on the firm(s) creating, acquiring or deploying them. Unlike some other, for example tangible assets, R-assets may be of negative value (that is, a liability). On the other hand, they are not exhausted when used. Unlike physical assets they cannot be owned – only attained and then controlled or influenced in the way in which they are used and coordinated with other assets.

R-assets are likely to be tacit and idiosyncratic, and more context-specific, yet more pervasive, than most other assets. In particular, their presence, content and effectiveness are likely to vary according to the culture, values and norms of each of the countries in which they are generated or employed, and those of the firms creating or utilizing them. Most noticeably they are likely to be more embedded in firms operating in coordinated market economies than in those operating in liberal market economies.[9] Lastly, although the focus of our current interest is on the R-assets of individual corporations, the concepts of jointly held R-assets (and social capital) are no less gaining the attention of researchers. We shall give these latter concepts more attention a little later in our chapter.

Table 9.3   Some unique characteristics of firm-specific R-assets

---

A bundle of attributes, principles, values and norms
Multifaceted in origin: internally generated, externally accessed
Shallow and simple ⇔ deep and complex
Dyadic ⇔ network relationships
Like other assets, R-assets need to be scarce, unique and imperfectly
   imitable if they are to confer a sustainable competitive advantage
Vary according to function and activity of firms: they range from routine
   to highly idiosyncratic relationships
Likely to be strongly contextual (reflecting cultures, ideologies and
   economic systems which may be both country and firm-specific)
Unlike most other assets, R-assets are only of value when combined with
   those of other economic actors: the concept of shared core values
Difficult to measure as their values are not independent of other assets
   with which they combined
Value of R-assets is likely to be cumulative and path-dependent
Cannot be owned, only controlled or influenced in their deployment
Are only partially mobile across national boundaries

The Ingredients of R-assets

What then are the ingredients, as opposed to the characteristics, of R-assets? How fungible are they? What are their mediating qualities? R-assets are a composite or mixture – a salad bowl – of a complex set of principles, values and standards possessed by an economic actor, and its willingness and ability to coordinate these with those of another (or other) economic actor(s). Unlike that of tangible assets, or even knowledge capital, the value-in-use of R-assets rests in the content and structure of the relations between and among the economic actors involved.

The list of ingredients making for productive R-assets is an extremely lengthy one. Figure 9.4 identifies some of these. These range from the primary attitudinal values, such as trust, honesty and reciprocity which are critical to any relationship, to those which are more context-specific, and vary according to the values placed upon particular R-assets by the respective partners to the relationship; and its particular *raison d'etre*. For example, such shared values as enthusiasm, vision, entrepreneurship and a spirit of curiosity, adventure, risk taking and learning intent are likely to be especially important for successful innovating activities. Those such as diligence, team orientation, flexibility, reliability and quality enhancement are likely to be more important for production and subcontracting relationships. Most financial dealings place a major responsibility on the contracting parties to be honest, truthful, transparent and accountable. Harmonious and productive labour and customer relations require emotional intelligence and a strong sense of loyalty and forbearance. Trust, integrity and honesty, and the absence of opportunism and moral hazard, are at the root of successful adversarial (zero-sum game) exchange relationships. In their dealings with governments, firms need to draw upon a reservoir of R-assets including a spirit of community and a desire to protect or augment social capital. In all cross-border relationships, whether intra-firm or inter-firm, the qualities of goodwill, cultural sensitivity, flexibility, patience and respect are likely to be at a premium. And each and every one of these R-assets tends to become more important as a firm's resort to arm's length market transactions becomes less beneficial.

The Governance of R-assets

Relationships between economic actors stretch along a continuum ranging from arm's-length markets to those embedded in hierarchies. In between, there is a labyrinth of non-equity bilateral and pluralistic associations, including networks.

The economics and organizational literature is replete with explanations as to why one relationship mode is preferred to another. However, until recently, most have been couched in terms of the comparative transaction costs (TC) of a discrete exchange of intermediate products, rather than of the wider advantages of cooperation in non-exchange functions to the participating firms. Moreover, all too frequently, scholars have tended to assume there *are* alternative modes of undertaking a particular activity or task when, in practice, this may not always be so.

While, since its inception, the TC literature has always explicitly considered a range of relational specific costs and benefits, in respect of both intra-firm or inter-firm transactions,[10] it is less forthcoming in explaining the appropriate organizational vehicle for deploying R-assets to advance the learning, innovating or productive activities of firms – or indeed, the ways in which they may benefit by being part of an industrial network or spatial cluster of firms (Nahapiet and Ghoshal, 1998). Because they are often project-based and intended to promote time-limited and very specific objectives, many contemporary cross-border strategic alliances cannot be regarded as substitutes for an FDI; nor may a purely market solution be viable.

Nevertheless, some generalizations are possible which we believe could be usefully taken up by TC scholars. In the case of shallow and simple economic relationships between economic actors which have congruent goals and values, and where the value of R-assets is likely to be insignificant relative to that of other resources and capabilities, the market route or a straightforward contractual agreement may well be the most cost-effective mode of asset augmentation or usage. At the opposite extreme, in the case of thick, complex and highly idiosyncratic relationships, and/or those between economic actors who, initially at least, display a very different set of goals, values and norms, then, depending on the extent to which control over the *non*-R-assets can be exercised without ownership, either the activity or the products being traded will be internalized or an inter-firm alliance will be concluded. Since, however, by their nature, R-assets are tacit and tend to be function or project-specific, and since their deployment is being increasingly directed to learning-related activities, it follows that the alliance route is the one more likely to be preferred. However, whatever modality is chosen, the competence of a firm (or its subunits) to coordinate the R-assets involved in any cooperative intracorporate or intercorporate activity might be considered as an R-asset in its own right (Holm *et al.*, 1996, 1999). We have included such a capability alongside the more attitudinal values identified in Table 9.4.

Form of R-assets

As we have just indicated, any relationship or association forged by a firm (or individuals within the firm) may be either among its constituent units of decision taking (over which, through ownership, it has *de jure* control) or between itself (or parts of itself) and an external economic actor or actors. These actors include other private firms, a group or network of firms, private interest groups such as non-governmental organizations (NGOs), public corporations, governments and supranational agencies.

The choice between an intra-firm or inter-firm creation, protection and use of R-assets, (the 'make or buy' decision), is one decision that a firm has to make regularly. Another concerns the kind of associations to which R-assets are applied. Here the extant literature on linkages, spillovers and integration is useful. Figure 9.2 identifies the main kinds of relationships. These may be between individuals, teams, special interest groups and corporations. They may be intra-firm or extra-firm. We shall focus on extra-firm and, especially, inter-firm relationships. These, in turn, may be classified according to the

Table 9.4   Selected ingredients of R-assets; how their significance might vary according to the activities of firms

	Subcontracting	Innovation
1. Primary ingredients (→ universally acknowledged values etc.)		
Trust/trustworthiness	**	*
Honesty	**	**
Reciprocity	*	0
Respect for, and ability to handle, cultural and other differences in secondary ingredients	*	0
2. Secondary ingredients (→ context-related values etc.)		
Entrepreneurship/vision	0	*
Behavioural norms	*	*
Attitude to risk/uncertainty	0	**
Work ethic	0	0
Willingness/capability to learn/experiment	*	**
Adaptability	**	*
Forbearance	*	0
Reliability	**	0
'First-best' attitude	*	*
Commitment	*	0
Sense of fairness	0	0
Opportunism	*	0
Abuse of monopoly by another power	*	0
Moral hazard	0	0
Corruption	0	0
Free-riding	*	*
Volatility	*	0
Instability	*	*
3. Negotiating/coordinating capabilities of the firm/firms	0	*

Notes:
1. ** important, * above average importance, 0 of average or below average importance, relative to R-assets as a whole.
2. R-assets consist of a bundle of values and virtues which need to be nurtured. The 'optimum bundle' will vary according to the type of relationship being concluded and the R-assets of the partner organization, and are likely to be country- and firm-specific.

Source: Author's estimates.

Production	Labour relations	Marketing/distribution	Exchange (general)
*	**	*	**
**	**	**	**
0	*	0	0
*	**	*	**
*	0	0	0
**	**	*	*
*	0	0	*
**	*	0	0
*	0	0	0
**	*	0	*
*	**	*	0
*	0	*	0
**	0	*	0
*	*	*	0
0	*	0	*
0	*	*	*
*	*	*	**
0	*	*	*
*	*	*	*
*	0	0	0
0	0	0	**
*	0	0	**
**	*	0	*

nature of the relationship. Is it, for example, between a firm and its supplier or customer, or is it an alliance between a firm and one of its competitors? Or is it a relationship according to type of activity, production process, function or markets served? Or, in the specific context of FDI, is it of a market resource input, efficiency or asset seeking kind?

To be successful, each and every association, whatever its kind, requires a bundle of R-assets to be available to each of the economic actors involved. But how much, and what kind, and what should be the appropriate governance of these assets, is likely to be highly context-specific. The more intensive, pervasive and complex relationships (and hence the need for more or better quality R-assets) are likely to arise in coalitions between firms from different organizational or country-specific cultures, and with different competencies and experiences, which engage in joint innovatory and learning activities. The less demanding relationships (and hence the need for fewer R-assets) relate to the exchange of fairly standardized products among firms from similar economic, ideological and organizational backgrounds. It is the contention of this chapter that the R-asset-intensive activities of firms have been increasing relative to their other activities in recent years, and that an increasing proportion of the former have been taking the form

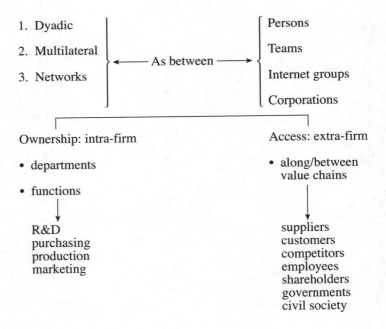

Figure 9.2   Types of R-assets

of cross-border extra-firm associations intended to gain access to new knowledge-related resources and learning capabilities.

Where do networks fit into this analysis? Consider again Figure 9.2. Unlike firms, most networks do not create wealth for themselves. According to Nahapiet and Ghoshal, networks may be considered as a form of social capital.[11] Their value is demonstrated as and when the participants in the network internalize and efficiently utilize the various benefits they offer. Frequently, these gains of networks take the form of augmented R-assets. If nothing else, networks help foster intra-network and inter-firm relational capital. From the work of Granovetter (1985, 1994), Putman (1993), Porter (1998) and Enright (2000) – to cite just four current exponents of the benefits of the spatial clustering of related activities – we are seeing a great deal of casual evidence that such networks not only offer the constituent firms knowledge and information-related externalities, but also strengthen many of the ingredients of their R-assets, notably those of trust and trustworthiness, bond building, norms and sanctions, adaptability, open communication and the promotion of shared core values and learning capabilities (Nahapiet and Ghoshal, 1998).

How does one Value R-assets?

How are R-assets measured? How does one quantify their output, or indeed their constituent inputs? The answer is, with very great difficulty. To a certain extent, similar problems beset scholars trying to put a monetary value on other forms of intangible assets, and of knowledge capital in particular. But they arise in acute form in the case of R-assets, for two reasons. The first is that there is no market, either for the inputs or for the output of R-assets, apart from that of the other assets in which they are embedded. The second is that few of the main ingredients of R-assets (as set out in Table 9.3) are themselves directly measurable, let alone marketable.

Table 9.5 summarizes some of the scholarly attempts to measure the R-assets of groups of firms and of countries (or societies). By and large, the proxies for societal R-assets, and/or their output, can more readily be identified and obtained, and are more meaningful than those for corporate R-assets. Such indices as the extent of civil litigation, crime (particularly violent crime) drugs, terrorism, truancy, divorce rates, bribery, tax evasion and corruption all testify to a degree of social dysfunction, and a breakdown of interpersonal relationships; just as others, for example, membership or participation in churches, clubs, charitable institutions and civic engagement, point to the robustness of social bonding and the moral health of the community (Putnam, 1993, Knack and Keefer, 1996, Brehm and Rahn, 1997). Some measures, for example, the size of the police force, the number of social or behavioural counsellors and the quality of property rights protection may also be regarded as positive indices in so far as their presence and action are designed to protect or improve the existing stock of social relational capital.

Indicators of the significance of micro–meso social R-assets have been developed by various scholars, for example Ariño *et al.* (2002), Chang, Singh and Lee (2000), Chen and Chen (1998), Dunning and McKaig-Berliner (2002), Dyer and Nobeoka (2000), Enright (2000), Kim (2002a, 2002b), Morgan and Hunt (1994), Tsai and Ghoshal (1998) and Zaheer *et al.* (1998). Some of the explanatory variables which have been tested are set out in Table 9.5. Broadly speaking, the empirical efforts of economists and economic geographers have been directed to evaluating the importance of spatial relational transaction costs, the external economies associated with networks, and the number, frequency and past ties of intra-network transactions.[12] Management and organizational and marketing economists have tended to focus on more socially specific micro or meso variables, including those which embrace (a) a microcosm of macrosocial goods and bads, and (b) an aggregation at a dyadic group or network level of corporate R-assets (Gomes-Casseres, 1994).

The suggested proxies for the R-assets of individuals are perhaps the least satisfactory of all. There are a few exceptions. One is firm-level data on labour turnover, industrial disputes, strikes, training and so on, but, even here, economic and regulatory, rather than social, reasons may be the main explanation for such incidences, or changes in same.[13] Other proxies include the extent of moral dysfunction in the form of corporate corruption, lack of safety standards and undesirable business practices. Recent research on inter-firm coalitions has suggested measures such as the number and frequency of past alliances concluded between any two firms, the number of cliques to which a firm belongs, reputation and status, the type of alliance and the level of mutual trust and commitment that arises out of the close interaction between the partners to the coalition. While some of these data make use of secondary and relatively objective measures, research, especially by Dyer and Chu, (2000), Holm *et al.* (1996, 1999), Kale *et al.* (2000), and Ariño *et al.* (2002) has relied on the perception of corporate executives as obtained by case study or survey data. Here we believe that, notwithstanding all the problems and deficiencies of these data, for at least the next stage for advancing our understanding about the significance of R-assets for corporate success, the field study and/or case study is likely to offer the most productive way of proceeding.[14]

Already, as documented by Daniel Coleman in his *Working with Emotional Intelligence* (Coleman, 1998) there is a good deal of casual evidence that successful corporations are identifying their possession of or access to (different

Table 9.5 Some measures of R-assets (or liabilities)

At a firm level (corporate R-assets)	At a dyadic, multi-firm or network level (micro–meso social R-assets)	At a country level (macro social R-assets)
Number, frequency and diversity of past alliances	Reduced spatial relational transaction costs	No one measure, but package of same
Number of cliques to which firm belongs	Various externalities, e.g. availability of better-quality, cheaper inputs	Number/quality of community groups
Number, duration, intensity and continuity of inter-firm linkages	Institutional/social infrastructure	Degree of civic engagement
Types of alliances (e.g. degree of complementarity/interdependence among partners)	Common innovatory/R&D capacity	(Negative) extent of crime/corruption
Survey material on significance of R-assets	Access to extra-firm institutions, universities, etc	(Negative) breakdown of personal relations/divorce
Reputation for integrity	Number of inter-firm intra network transactions	(Negative) civil litigation
Codes of conduct (how a partner or potential partner views your trustworthiness)	Number and nature of knowledge-based institutions	Radius of trust
Absence of industrial unrest: low labour turnover	Number/quality of business/social clubs and community groups	(Negative) prison population
Social responsibility	Perception of individual firms	Surveys on quality of social capital/justice systems
Negotiation outcomes		(Negative) extent and depth of tax evasion
Transparency and openness (negative).		
Termination (switching) costs (negative)		
Investment in worker training or retraining		

Note: data based on various sources: Ariño et al. (2002), Burt (1997), Brehm and Rahn (1997), Chang et al. (2000), Chen and Chen (1998), Dunning and McKaig-Berliner (2002), Dunning and Morgan (1971), Dyer and Chu (2000), Dyer and Nobeoka (2000), Enright (2000), Gulati (1995, 1998, 1999), Fukuyama (1996, 1999), Giersch (1996), Holm et al. (1996, 1999), Kim, (2002a, 2002b), Knack and Keefer (1996), Leana and Rousseau (2000), Morgan and Hunt (1994), Parkhe (1998) Putnam (1993), Rowley et al. (2000), Tsai and Ghoshal (1998), Uzzi (1997), Zaheer et al. (1998).

kinds of) R-assets as the critical distinguishing feature between themselves and their less successful competitors. Similarly, in an analysis of the distinctive qualities of star performers among 286 US and other firms in the 1990s, by Lyle Spencer Jnr, it was found that an overwhelming proportion (80 per cent) that set apart these performers from their average counterparts depended on the emotional intelligence of their senior executive and professional staff, rather than on their cognitive ability (Coleman, 1998, p. 379).

R-assets and Social Capital

What now of the relationship between R-assets and social capital (see again Table 9.2)? The term 'social capital' has a variety of meanings, as recently summarized by Adler and Kwon (2002) and Dasgupta and Serageldin (2000). At the one extreme it has been defined as that part of a country's stock of tangible and intangible assets which is socially owned or controlled. Under this umbrella, social (or societal) capital includes much of the physical, legal and commercial infrastructure critical to the competitiveness of firms. At the opposite extreme, it could be perceived as the capital available to two firms or subunits of a firm as a direct result of a dyadic relationship between them. For our purposes, while bearing in mind the more macro perceptions of social capital, we find the interpretation of Nahapiet and Ghoshal (1998) most apposite: 'the sum of the actual and potential resources embedded within, available through and derived from the network of relationships possessed by an individual or social unit. Social capital thus comprises both the network and the assets that may be mobilised through that network' (p. 243).

Francis Fukuyama puts it a little differently. He perceives social capital as 'a country's stock of informal values or norms shared among members of a group that permits cooperation between them' (Fukuyama, 1999, p. 16).[15] The value of this stock is likely to be more than the sum of its constituent parts, as a collection of connected R-assets is likely to generate its own externalities. The balance of social capital, taking the broader definition, is then made up of an infrastructure (including tangible assets and institutional structures which 'house' social R-assets, or the absence of same), such as prisons, courts of justice, religious and educational establishments, and also of societal rules, procedures, customs and routines (North, 1990).

Like firm-specific R-assets, social capital is not a single entity, but a variety of different entities. As we have seen, its content depends on the unit of analysis and the function that unit is intended to perform. Thus it inheres in both the macro and the micro structure of relations between and among actors. Whatever its coverage, social capital affects both the willingness and the capacity of its constituent firms to generate and deploy their own R-assets; and, as we shall see later, it can be a major influence on the kind and purpose of relationships, their content and form, and their location: both between and across national borders.

THE CHANGING SIGNIFICANCE OF R-ASSETS

Why is more scholarly attention now being given to R-assets? We suggest that this is primarily due to the huge increase in the extent, form and geography of economic relations between individuals and between and within organizations over two decades or so, and particularly the global spread of MNE-related activity. Stretching back much further in time, and well before the industrial revolution, R-assets, particularly in primitive (for example, tribal) societies (and some such societies still exist in the least developed countries) were a critical component of the wealth creating process. In turn, we believe that the advent of R-assets has been the direct result of five interlinked developments of alliance capitalism (Dunning, 1997) which have occurred in the world economy. These are first, a series of dramatic and, for the most part, systemic technological advances – particularly in all forms of informatics, including E-commerce; second, the widespread liberalization of markets, both domestic and cross-border; third, the growing significance of most service sectors, which tend to be more R-asset-intensive than their primary or secondary sector counterparts; fourth, the emergence of several important new players on the world economic stage, notably China and Russia; and fifth, the emergence and maturation of the global economy which is both a facilitator and an outcome of the first four factors.

Exactly how have these changes increased the significance of firm-specific R-assets, and particularly (as we shall tackle in the next section) what is their role in determining the extent, pattern and form of the cross-border activity of firms? Space permits us to highlight just seven of these, which we highlighted in Table 9.6.

1. The cutting edges of economic activity have become more idiosyncratic and innovation-driven. This has increased the need for, and the depth and complexity of, intracorporate and intercorporate relationships throughout the value chain.
2. The scope and depth of cross-border economic relationships have noticeably increased, and in doing so, have embraced a new and wider range of values, ideologies and social mores. In successfully dealing with such associations, a fund of R-assets, which acknowledges and respects

these country or region-specific differences, and promotes the wellbeing of each of the participants, is critical.

3. Societal, and to some extent business, goals have changed. Rather than concentrating on purely efficiency-related issues, the focus of interest is being increasingly directed to transforming societies and acknowledging the role of cultural values and the quality of life, for example with respect to leisure and the environment (Stiglitz, 1998; Rifkin, 2000). These changes are spawning many new coalitions, both within and among firms, and between them and other organizations, including special interest groups and governments.

4. Competitive pressures following market liberalisation have led to the shedding and/or disinternalisation of activities of firms; and, with it, an increased reliance on external suppliers and sub-contractors for the production of intermediate goods and services.

5. At the same time, the interdependence between the technologies required at different stages of the value chain, or indeed to produce any particular product, is increasing. This means that intra-firm transactions are not being replaced by arm's-length transactions but by inter-firm coalitions of one kind or another.

6. The rate of technological obsolescence is accelerating, and this places a premium on speeding up the learning and innovation process. In order

Table 9.6   Why have R-assets become more important over the last two decades?

More idiosyncratic economic activities, especially those which are knowledge-intensive

Scope and depth of cross-border relationships have increased and, with them, access to new and distinctive values, ideologies and customs

Change in societal goals: in particular the role of efficiency, the social dimension of economic activity, the ownership of (or access to) means of production

Competitive pressures leading to disinternalization/shedding of non-core activities of firms

Growing interdependence of technologies, organizational and management capabilities

Increased rate of obsolescence and rising cost of innovatory activities leading to more alliances

Move towards heterarchies and a greater decision-making role for management of MNE affiliates

---

to achieve their objectives, and as research and development (R&D) is becoming increasingly time-consuming and expensive, firms are being forced to engage in the kind of strategic innovatory alliances which demand considerable R-assets on the part of the constituent partners if they are to be successful.

7. Partly as a result of the above factors, firms have reconfigured their organizational profiles, and are increasingly substituting or augmenting their hierarchical (pyramidal) command structures with more heterarchical structures. (Hedlund, 1986, 1992; Hedlund and Rolander, 1991). These latter structures are encouraging more cooperative and deeper horizontal and vertical interpersonal relationships and, in the case of MNEs, are allowing their foreign subsidiaries greater responsibility and autonomy in their decision taking (Birkinshaw and Hood, 2000). As a result, these affilates are forming more and closer relationships with their local suppliers, customers and competitors, and also with their own workforce (Rugman and Verbeke, 2001b).

R-ASSETS AND THEORIES AND PARADIGMS OF MNE ACTIVITY

What, then, are the implications of the growing importance of both corporate R-assets and social relational capital for our theorizing about the cross-border activities of firms and, in particular, FDI and the formation of non-equity alliances? Let us tackle this question using the lens of the eclectic (or OLI) paradigm,[16] and also that of a selection (and it is only a selection) of the contextually specific theories it embraces.

The O-specific Competitive Advantages of Firms

Let us first consider the ownership (O)-specific, that is, the sustainable, unique and non-substitutable advantages of firms,[17] compared to those of their competitors. These are usually considered under two headings. The first set of advantages (Oa) embrace the specific assets or proprietary rights which are under the jurisdiction of the firm, whether this is by dint of ownership, or by leveraging and coordinating the use of resources and capabilities which it gains from the market, directly from other firms, or from the community at large. To reiterate an earlier point, firms do not own human capital or the assets of other firms, but, by a variety of means, they are able to gain access to them and exercise some degree of governance over their use. Though intangible, these assets usually enable the tangible assets owned or acquired by the firm to be created, augmented or deployed more effectively.

The second type of advantage (Ot), is that which is derived from the efficient co-ordination of the first kind of assets. *Inter alia*, this includes the capability of the firm to optimize its locational portfolio of these assets, and to choose the optimum modality of governance. It is this kind of capability which comprises of an amalgam of human and organizational intellectual and R-assets owned or used by corporations. Such a capability may be exercised at various levels, within and between firms, according to the purpose of the association and the nature of the assets, including the R-assets of the other actors participating in the activity. It may be enhanced by being part of a dyadic alliance or a network of related firms, and from the cumulative experience of past relationships (Kale *et al.*, 2000). MNEs, in particular, may be expected to augment their R-assets as a result of their value-adding activities and their access to foreign-based resources, capabilities and networks (Dunning, 1997; Doz *et al.*, 2001; Enright, 2000; Birkinshaw and Hood, 2000; Birkinshaw and Solvell, 2000). New evidence of the relative importance of foreign located R-assets has been unearthed in a recently completed survey on the internationalization of large professional service firms (Dunning and McKaig-Berliner, 2002).[18]

It is the accumulated stock of R-assets, the learning and experiences attached to them, and how these are coordinated with externally accessed resources and capabilities, which, we believe, should be more explicitly acknowledged by the three contextual theories which purport to explain the content and character of the O-specific advantages of firms. None of these has incorporated R-assets into their model building, though, as we have already mentioned, a useful start at doing just this has been made by several management scholars, and most particularly by those cited in Appendix 9.1 and by Chang *et al.* (2000). In an extension of the Uppsala internationalization model, Johanson and Vahlne (1977, 1990), and Choi and Eriksson (2001) have examined the role of relationship development of firms in assisting the access to, transfer and coordination of foreign-located knowledge, and the learning and commitment associated with this process.

R-assets may be internally or externally generated. Indeed, the ability (including the willingness and ability of firms to gain new R-assets from cross-border intra-firm and inter-firm relationships) is itself becoming an important core competence. Since the pioneering work of Johanson and Mattson (1988) and Walter Powell (1990) a decade or more ago, various attempts have been made to explore how, and in what conditions, networks may enhance the intellectual and relational capabilities of their participants.[19] A recent paper by Tai Jy Chen (2000), for example, has identified the benefits to Taiwanese electronics firms of their membership of domestic and foreign networks. These include access to more efficient production and innovatory activities, and the opening up of new cultural horizons as a direct result of relational subcontracting.

A further fascinating glimpse into the importance of such R-assets as trust, reciprocity, reputation and informal social relationships is provided by Tallman and Jenkins (2002) in their study of the agglomeration of the motor sport firms in Motor Sport Valley, a region to the west and north of London. Work by Michael Enright (2000) on clusters of both foreign and domestic firms in the Hong Kong financial district mirrors and extends earlier work by Ray Vernon (1960) and Dunning and Morgan (1971), which pinpointed the importance of such R-assets as trust, group loyalty, openness and a lack of opportunism in explaining the dense concentration of financial and other office activities in the New York Metropolitan Region, and in the 'square mile' of the City of London. Finally, a recent contribution by Rugman and Verbeke (2001b) has specifically addressed the role of MNEs as 'flagship' firms in promoting and benefiting from foreign based clusters.

For reasons already stated, technological advances and globalization underlie both the rationale for, and the benefits flowing from, dyadic alliances and network relationships. We have further suggested that, as these relationships deepen and become more complex, so the choice of partner(s) and the networks in which they participate is influenced, not only by the knowledge capital shared, but also by the ability and willingness of the partners to be empathetic towards each other. While it 'takes two to tango' (as the expression goes), the likelihood of forming and sustaining such an association does very much depend on the amount and quality of R-assets each organization is able to bring to any cooperative or exchange venture.

Three related propositions which arise from this analysis are the following:

1. R-assets are becoming a more important component of the resources and capabilities of firms engaging in cross border activity;
2. MNEs are likely to possess a greater stock of R-assets relative to non-MNEs (*inter alia* because of the greater number, more complex and wider geography of linkages with which the former are associated);
3. MNEs are increasingly likely to protect or augment their core competences as a direct result of access to, and deployment of, foreign based R-assets. Such access and deployment may be achieved as a result of both intra-firm and inter-firm associations.

A final point about corporate R-assets is that they are likely to be context-specific. Thus research has suggested that Japanese MNEs, relative to US and European MNEs, in the 1980s possessed the kind of R-assets most likely to promote efficient production and subcontracting arrangements in the motor and consumer electronics sectors (Dunning, 1994), while US MNEs in the 1990s recorded a comparative advantage in the kind of R-assets which helped encourage teamwork, entrepreneurship and R&D-type alliances. The virtues of openness, loyalty, leveraging diversity, curiosity, reliability, empathy, prudency, bond building and commercial integrity also vary considerably between national and/or corporate cultures. The extent and quality of property protection and patent systems is also likely to enhance the robustness and significance of R-assets particularly in, and among, developing countries (De Soto, 2000).

Some firms, such as the Quaker-originated UK firms of the 19th century, also paid especial attention to building R-assets, particularly of an intra-firm character (Jeremy, 1990; Marinetto, 1999; Searle, 1998). Corporate culture can, and often does, play a pivotal role in promoting R-assets (or inhibiting their promotion). The relative significance and content of R-assets is likely to vary considerably between industries and types of value-added activities. It is also likely to be more pronounced in the case of cross-border mergers and acquisitions (M&A) than in that of greenfield FDIs and asset-augmenting FDI relative to resource-seeking FDI. The contextual nature of the R-assets of MNEs or potential MNEs is further illustrated in Table 9.7.

To what extent are R-assets, which reflect the ideologies and values of a particular country, transferable across national borders? Unlike most other types of assets, for example a particular kind of technology, R-assets are not viewed as the same product by different institutions or people. Again, the experience of Japanese investors in the European and US motor industries in the 1980s and 1990s suggests that this is so. On the other hand, the literature is full of examples of the lack of sensitivity of many MNEs in seeking to impose their own R-assets rather than adapt to those valued by their foreign associates or customers. Blending R-assets from different cultures, social mores and moral ecologies is likely to be one of the most taxing challenges confronting MNEs over the next decade or more; and it is those firms which are successful in creating, sustaining and sympathetically melding such capabilities into their own organizational culture which are likely to be the future winners in the global market place.

The L-specific Advantages of Countries

The 'where to locate' decision of MNEs or potential MNEs has been extensively surveyed in the literature (Dunning, 1998; UNCTAD, 1998; Rugman and Verbeke, 2001a; Siebert, 1995). Scholarly research has revealed that the critical variables influencing this decision are likely to be both time- and context-specific, and are especially sensitive to the *raison d'être* for MNE activity. For example, is it natural resource or market seeking? Is it intended to be (existing) asset exploiting or asset augmenting? Is it directed to mainstream manufacturing or to services – and if the latter, to what kind of services? Is it part of a multi-domestic or a globally integrated strategy by MNEs?

One thing seems certain. In most industrialized countries, at least, over the last three decades or so, the most important location-bound attractions of countries have shifted from the availability, cost and quality of natural factor endowments (including unskilled labour) to created assets, notably intellectual capital, innovatory systems and institutional and communications infrastructure. As global competitive pressures and the increasing mobility of knowledge and information have brought about at least some convergence in such attractions, so attention (both by firms and by governments) is being focused on 'soft' locational variables. Of these, social capital – and more particularly social R-assets – is perhaps the most decisive. At a micro or macro level, the availability of complementary or enhancing R-assets from partner firms and networks is becoming a more important locational incentive. From a societal viewpoint, whether national or subnational level, 'quality of life' variables, including the minimization of crime, pollution, corruption, congestion and unacceptable social behaviour, are now taking pride of place as investment determinants (Wallace, 2000). And, while we would not wish to press this point too far, research by Herbert Giersch (1996) and others, for example Brittan and Hamlin (1995), is emphasizing the increasing role played by economic morality as a location-bound competitive enhancing asset.

Turning now to developing and transition economies, while the availability and quality of natural resources and low (real) labour costs continue to remain important locational attractions (particularly in the less developed and resource-rich countries), there is increasing evidence, especially from former communist countries like Russia and Cambodia, that deficiencies both in institutional infrastructure and in social relational capital are among the greatest obstacles to inward FDI (UNCTAD, 1998, 2000, and Bevan *et al.*, 2004). Business surveys on the attractiveness of both developing and developed countries to potential investors (such as those reported by the Economist Intelligence Unit, the World Competitiveness Forum and the European Round Table of Industrialists) are consistently putting the quality of social capital, and the R-assets of organizations with which they have (or wish to have) associations, at or near the top of their locational preferences. It may be further inferred that MNEs that can optimize their global portfolio of location-specific R-assets while, at the same time, judiciously adapting their own and their affiliates' R-assets to local requirements, are likely to be among the winners in an increasingly integrated, yet multicultural, world.

From this brief analysis we would offer two further propositions. First, spatially specific R-assets are becoming a more important influence on the location choices of MNEs, both between and within countries; second, the global locational portfolio of assets of MNEs, chosen on the above criteria, and the interaction between their own R-assets and those of the institutions and the individuals of the countries in which they operate, is becoming a more significant determinant of their global competitiveness.

Once again, however, we would stress that the form, content and relative significance of L-specific R-assets is likely to be context-specific. Table 9.7 sets out some of the country, industry or activity and firm specific factors likely to influence the locational decisions of MNEs. Clearly the distance (physical, psychic or cultural) between investing and potentially recipient countries of MNEs is likely to have an effect, as is the accumulated experience of actually producing in the countries.

Knowledge, service and transaction-intensive industries are more sensitive to specific differences in the presence and quality of social capital than others, while the degree of comparability between the economic systems, cultural mores and moral sensitivities of the home and host countries are likely to be a key factor explaining the organizational mode by which the R-assets of investing firms are augmented or exploited (Hill, 1995). Recent work on networks is also identifying country-specific characteristics which are affecting the locational choice of MNEs from and to those countries (Ozawa, 2001, Dicken *et al.*, 2001). As to the *raison d'être* of FDI, strategic asset-seeking firms are likely to be more sensitive to the location of enhancing R-assets than are those engaged in (natural) resource seeking, or those whose subsidiaries produce fairly standardized products.

The Organization of R-assets: the I Component of the OLI Paradigm

As we have already observed, a good deal of both internalization and network theory, which was initially designed to explain the organizational mode (or modes) of IB activity, can be used to explain that specifically relating to the creation and use of R-assets. This is because each approach focuses on the motives for, and the content of, human relationships, at both an individual and an organizational level. Indeed, in their attempts to identify the reasons for market failure, TC scholars have pinpointed not only knowledge-related deficiencies of arm's-length exchanges, for example information symmetry and bounded rationality, but also relational deficiencies, notably those arising from a lack of trust between the participants, opportunism and moral hazard. Much of the literature on alliance performance, both domestic and cross-border, also explicitly acknowledges the contribution of many of the ingredients of R-assets, as set out earlier (Barney and Hansen, 1994; Parkhe, 1998; Tsai and Ghoshal, 1998; Dyer and Singh, 1998; Chen *et al.*, 1998).

However, what is relatively new in the last decade or so, and is increasingly engaging the attention of scholars researching networks and alliances, is the emphasis now being given, first to the character and content of intra-firm and inter-firm relationships as assets in their own right, and second, to the ways in which their creation, access and use are organized.

Let us elaborate on these last two points by offering just three examples. First, the flattening of decision trees and the movement towards heterarchical organizational structures (Hedlund, 1986, 1992; Hedlund and Rolander, 1991; Bartlett and Ghoshal, 1989) have (a) reduced the role of the 'command' route of generating intra-firm R-assets and replaced that with a visionary, strategic guidance and decision-sharing route, and (b) fostered an appreciation of the fact that the managers of MNE subsidiaries, relative to their counterparts in the parent companies, are often better informed of the asset-augmenting and learning opportunities offered by the institutions of the country or countries in which they operate, and also of the needs and competences of local suppliers and customers, the strategy of indigenous competitors and the policies of host governments (Birkinshaw and Hood, 1998; Rugman and Verbeke, 2001b, 2001c). Both these developments have led to a re-examination of the governance and geographical locus of intra-firm activities throughout the value chain, and this has occurred precisely because of the newly perceived importance of R-assets as a created competitive advantage.

Second, the choice between cross-border intra-firm and alliance relational activities is being fundamentally affected by the reduced role of transnational ownership (via FDI), and the increasing importance of access in obtaining and controlling the use of competitivity enhancing resources and capabilities. We have already alluded to the fragmentation and disinternalization of the value chain of many firms, which is occurring despite, or in conjunction with, the M&A boom of the mid-to-late 1990s (UNCTAD, 2000). There are many reasons for favouring a more market-oriented route of resource acquisition and subcontracting, which has been aided and abetted by the advent of e-commerce (Zaheer and Manrakhan, 2001; Dunning and Wymbs, 2001). But knowing where and how to harness resources and capabilities you do not own (or wish to own), and how best to coordinate these with your own core competencies, requires a series of interinstitutional relationships which, to be successful, need a fund not only of intellectual capital, but of R-assets as well.

Table 9.7 R-assets, OLI and some contextual situations

	Industry/activity	Country
O	Knowledge content, complexity of idiosyncrasy of products/ processes Transaction intensity (c.f. processing with fabricating activities) 'Service' composition of value-adding activity	Stage of development, size, culture, moral ecology, goals of economic transformation Liberal, c.f. with coordinated market-oriented economic system Formal property/patent systems
L	Some industries/activities more locationally footloose than others Need to have access to complementary resources and capabilities located in foreign countries	Physical, psychic, cultural distance an important variable, in particular, whether there is a complementary infrastructure of social capital, e.g. norms, values and standards, or one which reflects differences in the identity and content of R-assets
I	Importance of R-assets and the need to protect them via the internalized route will vary according to the idiosyncrasy of products and processes; opportunities for relationship damaging	Nature of organizational culture, both at a country and firm level, which affects governance of the creation, access to and use of R-assets

Firm	Type of FDI
Size of firm Organizational structure, e.g. whether heterarchical or hierarchical Degree of disinternalization along value chain(s) Product/process diversification Need to have access to external assets Past experience with alliances Degree of multinationality	Mostly high-technology manufacturing/market/efficiency- seeking and strategic asset-seeking FDI FDI in R&D activities
Location portfolio of existing assets, and alliance ties, their embeddedness, and performance Psychic, cultural, language, etc ties between investing firms and institutions and individuals in potential host locations	Efficiency-seeking FDI less location bound, but needing more complementary resources and capabilities than market or asset- seeking FDI
Extent to which existing R- asset-related activities are market/contract-governed and based on a synergy of agreed values and norms Organizational culture and evaluation of R-assets in both home and foreign countries Foreign value-adding experience Product composition of home and foreign ventures	As for 'O' above, but particularly relevant in explaining asset augmenting by way of M&A I route more likely in case of 'sequential' rather than 'greenfield' route Degree of multinationality

We will not labour this point further, save to point out that since R-assets are often directed to achieving very specific objectives, and these objectives are frequently geared to optimally restructuring the value activities of firms rather than increasing the efficiency of asset usage, received internalization theory needs revisiting.

Third, it is here, too, that we believe the network approach comes into its own. As is generally acknowledged, firms participate in networks because of the economics and social externalities they are perceived to confer. In as much as these benefits have to be internalized by the participating firms if they are to be realized by them, there is no conflict between the network approach and internalization theory. But internalization in this case is based not on the ownership of assets, but on the governance over those which are externally accessed. Moreover, since the intra-network connections are usually non-contractual and frequently idiosyncratic and value-laden, the willingness and ability of firms to seek advantage from any exchange of knowledge, ideas or contacts is likely to be strongly dependent on the R-assets they possess, and how these interact with those of the network as an entity in its own right.

These thoughts can be reiterated in the form of three related propositions. First, access to resources and rights rather than ownership of resources and rights is likely to increase the value of R-assets of firms used in conjunction with those of other organizations. Thus one might expect cross-border M&A and asset-seeking alliances to play a more important role in the future portfolio of MNE activity.

Second, because of learning *et al.* and relational enhancing benefits generated by networks, it may be predicted that the participation by MNEs and/or their affiliates in cross-border networks will increase, relative to purely dyadic associations with foreign firms.

Third, the contribution of the R-assets of the foreign affiliates to those of the MNEs of which they are part is likely to increase. Partly this is the result of flatter intra-MNE organizational structures; and partly that of the closer and deeper linkages between the affiliates and indigenous firms. Such linkages are themselves fostered by the added relational space generated by networks.

As with the previous two components of the eclectic paradigm, the extent to which firms may wish to internalize the generation or use of R-assets is strongly contextual. For example, one might expect MNEs from coordinated market economies (or erstwhile collectivist economies) contemplating FDI in other coordinated market economies to prefer to engage in cooperative agreements and/or give their subsidiaries more decision-taking autonomy than those from liberal market economies investing in other liberal economies. Similarly, firms with a hierarchical organizational structure and an experience of contract-based relationships are more likely to choose the internalized route of augmenting and deploying R-assets. Firms which produce standardized products involving few R-assets are likely to favour a straightforward FDI or licensing route. The greater the cultural distance between the home country of the MNE and the country or countries in which it intends to augment or exploit its R-assets, the greater the probability it will choose to do so via an alliance or shared equity route rather than by setting up a *de novo* 100 per cent-owned affiliate.[20]

RECONFIGURING THE OLI PARADIGM

Putting these thoughts together, what are the implications of explicitly incorporating R-assets into the eclectic paradigm of MNE activity? At this exploratory stage of thinking we would offer just four further general propositions.

1. The ability to create and sustain firm specific R-assets, and to coordinate these efficiently across national boundaries, both within their own organizations and between their and other organizations, or networks of organizations, will increasingly influence the extent and pattern of MNE activity.
2. The presence or absence of networks of related activities is likely to be a more important determinant of the geography of MNE activity in the next decade or more.
3. The increasing significance of cross-border R-assets as generating and sustaining the competitive advantages of firms is likely to lead to an increase in MNE-related activity, relative to that which otherwise would have occurred.
4. Though FDI will probably continue to be the main modality of the territorial expansion of firms, the rising importance and need to tap into extra-firm R-assets is likely to lead to a higher proportion of the global sales of MNEs being accounted for, or sold to foreign organizations with whom they have a non-equity economic linkage, and over whose resources and capabilities they have some continuing governance or influence.

IMPLICATIONS OF THE RISING IMPORTANCE OF R-ASSETS

There are several implications of the growing significance of R-assets. Table 9.8 offers some bullet points for (a) IB theory, (b) policy makers (c) business and (d) supranational agencies. These are largely self-evident and are, in fact, being increasingly acknowledged by both scholars and practitioners. In the case of IB theory, the presence and content of R-assets require modifications to the extant theories of the O-specific advantages of firms, the L-specific advantages of countries and theories of the organization of business activity which purport to identify and evaluate the explanatory variables determining the extent to which MNEs or potential MNEs will internally coordinate the first two sets of advantages, or choose to augment or exploit these by way of non-equity alliances of one kind or another.

For policy makers, the chief implication of our analysis is for them not only to better appreciate the importance of the presence and quality of their location-bound assets for attracting and retaining mobile investment, but also to devise the most cost-effective policies to upgrade these assets. In the pursuance of this objective, governments of coordinated market economies are likely to depend on more non-market policies, for example, with respect to education, innovation, environment and social policies, while those of liberal market economies are likely to depend on market-based incentives and penalties of one kind or another.

As far as businesses are concerned, the more successful and socially responsible MNEs already fully recognize the need to pay more attention to upgrading both their internal and their external relational capabilities. Some examples of the ways in which this might be achieved are set out in Table 9.8. At the same time, as Henderson (2001) has cogently pointed out, businesses also need to recognize that not all forms of corporate social responsibility (which might be perceived as an R-asset) work to the long-term benefit either of its practitioners or of society as a whole.

Lastly, supranational agencies have a very real responsibility to better identify and enhance their understanding and appreciation of the R-assets not only of the institutions and countries which they represent, and/or in whose discussions and deliberations they participate, but of the special interest groups that are no less concerned with the issues being debated.[21] Again, however, the same caveat which Henderson voices about the tasks and responsibilities of firms could equally apply to such organizations as the World Bank, the International Monetary Fund and the World Trade Organisation.

We do not imagine any of these tasks will be easy to tackle or resolve in the short run. Very real problems and challenges abound. Perhaps the most daunting of these are (a) the reconciliation of different cross-cultural perspectives on at least some of the ingredients of R-assets and hence the willingness and ability of firms to create, sustain and upgrade the quality and effectiveness of intra-firm and extra-firm cooperative arrangements; and (b) provision, by national and/or subnational governments, of the appropriate

Table 9.8   Implications of the growing significance of R-assets

1. *For IB theory*

Access to competitivity-enhancing assets, including R-assets, is becoming as important, if not more important than ownership

More explicit acknowledgment of R-assets – both in themselves and as enhancing the value of non R-assets – as determinants of IB activity

In embracing R-assets, more attention needs to be paid to cooperative modes of business relationships, and particularly to networks, as aids in upgrading and sustaining both firm-specific R-assets and the social capital of interorganizational associations

The presence and use of R-assets need to be more explicitly identified and evaluated in explaining the performance of MNEs

There is a need for a more systemic, holistic approach to understanding the determinants of IB activity while, inter alia, specifically acknowledging the role of networks in affecting the OLI configuration facing firms

2. *For policy makers (at a national or regional level)*

A better acknowledgment of the role of intangible social capital (e.g. total macro R-assets) as a location-specific competitive asset

To seek ways of improving social (relational) capital and encouraging virtues making up R-assets (through example, the media, exhortation, legislative policies towards crime/social dysfunction)

3. *For businesses*

To recognize the need to create, gain access to and sustain unique R-assets through appropriate search and training methods

To re-examine the role and content of ethical conduct and social responsibility, and to foster relation-enhancing skills and attitudes among employees

To upgrade and encourage codes of behaviour focusing on, and recognizing the principles of, beneficial intra- and interorganizational relationships

4. *For supranational agencies*

To foster international acceptance and respect for the key (and universal?) R-assets (e.g. trust, truthfulness, reciprocity)

To promote open and harmonious relationships among individuals and organizations across national boundaries, and particularly between developed and developing countries

To fight against socially dysfunctional R-assets, e.g. drugs, terrorism, pornography, social dysfunction, especially those which arise from economic poverty

To respect cross-cultural *et al.* differences in the significance, content and prioritization of the lesser R-assets

To be more empathetic to the views of NGOs and other interest groups, without necessarily agreeing with them social capital for FDI and MNE activity to perform both profitably and in the interest of their constituents.

CONCLUSIONS

In conclusion, in this chapter we have sought to do three things. First and foremost, we have attempted to give a sense of the importance of a hidden asset available to corporations but not often explicitly identified – much less rigorously analysed – in the literature, namely that of the R-assets which they have the power to use, internally create, sustain and utilize.

Second, we have suggested that R-assets are becoming, and have become, a more important part of the portfolio of competitivity enhancing assets of MNEs; and we have explained why the characteristics of the 21st-century innovation-driven global economy are demanding that more attention be paid to them.

Third, we have identified some of the ways in which extant IB theories and paradigms may need to be modified to better incorporate both firm- and country-specific R-assets. In particular, we have suggested that the growth of networks has provided additional insights into (a) the way in which industrial *et al.* clusters might augment the competitive advantages (and especially the R-assets) of the participating firms, (b) the content and value of their locational portfolios, and (c) the ways in which they may best relate their own R-assets to those of other firms and network of firms, to advance their own efficiency and learning capabilities.

This contribution has been an exploratory one. We would be the first to admit that it has raised more questions than it has answered. In particular, it has not attempted to tackle the question, 'Under what circumstances is an investment R-asset creation or sustenance economically worthwhile to a firm?' For example, there may be several ways in which a firm may minimize or counteract the negative effects of market transactions or cooperative ventures: such as, opportunism or moral hazard. When is an investment in upgrading mutually acceptable norms and high-quality decision taking likely to be preferred to other deterrence mechanisms such as the threat of retaliation, increased monitoring or additional resource commitments?[22] Moreover, while fully acknowledging all the difficulties inherent in measuring R-assets, we have sometimes tried 'to square the circle'. Finally (to the disappointment of some readers, no doubt) this chapter has not offered a single explanatory statistical equation. But, while we would be the first to point out these lacunae in the work of one of our PhD students, we would like to think that experience offers us some privileges, including the luxury of getting away with a less than rigorous analysis while still making a useful contribution to a relatively unexplored area of research.

NOTES

1. See, for example, Caves (1996), Dunning (1993, 2002) and Rugman and Brewer (2001). For a resource-based perspective on MNE activity, see, for example, Helleloid (1992), Fladmoe-Lindquist and Tallman, (1994), Peng (2001) and Madhok and Phene (2002).
2. Throughout this chapter, we shall take a threshold definition of an MNE as a firm which engages in foreign direct investment.
3. Going back much further in history, many of the earliest MNEs took the form of Assyrian, Greek and Roman trading and land exploratory companies (see Moore and Lewis, 1999).
4. One writer (McPherson, 1973) regards 'the right not to be excluded' from the access to the productive resources of society as one of the key emerging competitive advantages of firms.
5. As shown, for example, by the declining proportion of material to total costs in the production of most tangible products. However, in many poorer developing countries, a high proportion of gross national product is still accounted for by primary and elemental secondary activities.
6. For some contributions from economists and management scholars, see Teece (1992, 2000), Quinn (1992), Kogut and Zander (1993), Nonaka and Takeuchi (1995), Boisot (1998) and Burton-Jones (1999) and various articles in a special issue of the *Strategic Management Journal*, **17** (52), 1996.
7. See particularly the writings of Burt (1992, 1997), Granovetter (1985, 1994), Coleman (1988) and Portes (1998). A useful summary of the evolving views of these and other scholars is contained in Adler and Kwon (2002). One exception is Mark Casson's incisive study on the economics of business culture (Casson, 1991). Another is Knack and Keefer's examination of the economic returns to social capital (Knack and Keefer, 1996).
8. For an exposition of the growing importance of the former regime in our contemporary knowledge-based economy, see Rifkin (2000).
9. Hall and Soskice (2001) delineate coordinated market economies as those in which 'firms coordinate their activities primarily by way of hierarchies and competitive market arrangements' and coordinated market economies as those in which 'firms depend more heavily on non-market relationships to coordinate their endeavours with other actors and to construct their core competences' (p. 8).
10. Hall and Soskice (2001).
11. Defined as 'the sum of the actual and potential resources embedded within, available through, and derived from the network of relationships possessed by an individual or social unit. Social capital thus comprises both the network and the assets that may be mobilised through that network' (Nahapiet and Ghoshal, 1998, p. 243). For the purposes of this chapter we shall treat this definition as a micro or meso interpretation of social capital. See pp. 214–5.
12. One of the earliest studies of this kind sought to identify and measure the relational ties between financial and other institutions in the 'square mile' of the City of London (Dunning and Morgan, 1971).
13. As, for example, in the case of the dramatic reduction of strikes in the UK in the 1980s.
14. For a recent case study approach which seeks to evaluate the importance of relational quality as a measure of corporate success see Ariño *et al*. (2002).
15. As most noticeably articulated by Oliver Williamson and Jean François Hennart in their various writings. See, for example, Williamson (1979, 1985) and Hennart (1988, 1999).

16. A definition which is also quite apposite to describe more meso or micro concepts of social capital. See too Adler and Kwon (2002) who define social capital as 'a resource for individual and collective actors located in the network of their more or less durable social relations' (p. 3).

17. In identifying and evaluating these advantages, the eclectic paradigm draws upon various intellectual strands, but most particularly those of industrial organization theory, resource-based theory and the evolutionary theory of the firm. In the last two decades, we have found the resource-based theory, particularly when it acknowledges the role of institutional capital (Oliver, 1997), most useful in identifying the source and content of such advantages, and the conditions for their sustainability; and evolutionary theory for emphasizing the path dependency and cumulative features of these assets. For an application of the resource-based theory to our understanding of MNE activity, see Helleloid (1992), Fladmoe-Lindquist and Tallman (1994) and Peng (2001). For a recent attempt to integrate strategic management theory and the eclectic paradigm, and to present a more firm-specific approach to MNE activity, see Madhok and Phene (2002).

18. In this survey, access to R-assets was ranked the seventh most important of some 26 competitive advantages identified by professional service firms. They were also ranked the sixth most likely to be derived from foreign operations. Among the most multinational and largest of these firms, this advantage was ranked first or second. Network-related benefits, particularly for clients, customers and suppliers, were generally ranked between third and fifth in order of significance (Dunning and McKaig-Berliner, 2002).

19. See especially the writings of Gulati (1998, 1999) Holm *et al.* (1996, 1999), Uzzi (1997), Chen and Chen (1998) and Tsai and Ghoshal (1998).

20. As was found, for example, by the Hennart and Larimo (1998) study of the impact of culture on the comparative strategy of Japanese and Finnish MNEs.

21. We might add that such interest groups, particularly some of the more vociferous NGOs, need also to upgrade their own R-assets if their views (whether correct or not) are to be taken seriously.

22. Some of these avenues, with illustrations of their effectiveness, are set out in two recent papers by Das and Rahman (2001, 2002). See also two related papers, one by Zaheer and Venkataram (1995) that compares the transaction cost and sociological approaches as alternative ways of maintaining the value of relation-specific assets, and another by Zaheer *et al.* (1998) that examines the influence of interorganizational and interpersonal trust on corporate performance.

REFERENCES

Ariño, A., J. de la Torre and P.S. Ring (2001), 'Relational quality managing trust in corporate alliances', *California Management Review*, **44**, 109–31.

Barney, J.B., and M.H. Hansen (1994), 'Trustworthiness as a source of competitive advantage', *Strategic Management Journal*, **15**, 175–90.

Bartlett, C., and S. Ghoshal (1989), *Managing Across Borders: The Transnational Solution*, Boston, MA: Harvard Business School Press.

Birkinshaw, J., and N. Hood (1998), 'Multinational charter subsidiary evolution: capability and charter change in foreign owned subsidiary companies', *Academy of Management Review*, **23** (4), 713–95.

Birkinshaw, J., and N. Hood (2000), 'Characteristics of foreign subsidiaries in industry clusters', *Journal of International Business Studies*, **31** (1), 141–54.

Birkinshaw, J., and O. Solvell (2000), 'Leading-edge multinationals and leading edge clusters', *International Studies of Management and Organisation*, **33** (2).

Boisot, M.H. (1998), *Knowledge Assets: Securing Competitive Advantage in the Information Economy*, Oxford: Oxford University Press.

Brehm, J., and W. Rahn (1997), 'Individual-level evidence for the causes and consequences of social capital', *American Journal of Political Science*, **41**, 999–1023.

Brittan S., and A. Hamlin (eds) (1995), *Market Capitalism and Moral Values,* Aldershot, UK and Brookfield, USA: Edward Elgar.

Burt, R. (1992), *Structural Holes: The Social Structure of Competition*, Cambridge, MA: Harvard University Press.

Burt, R. (1997), 'A note on social capital and network content', *Social Networks*, **19**, 355–73.

Burton-Jones, A. (1999), *Knowledge Capitalism*, Oxford: Oxford University Press.

Casson, M. (1991), *The Economics of Business Culture*, Oxford: Oxford University Press.

Caves, R. (1996) *Multinational Enterprise and Economic Analysis*, Cambridge: Cambridge University Press.

Chang, S., H. Singh and K. Lee (2000), 'Complementarity, status, similarity and social capital as drivers of alliance formation', *Strategic Management Journal*, **21**, 1–22.

Chen, C.C., X-P. Chen and J.R. Meindl (1998), 'How can cooperation be fostered? The cultural effects of individualism/collectivism', *Academy of Management Review*, **23** (2), 285–304.

Chen, H. and T-L. Chen (1998), 'Network linkages and location choice in foreign direct investment', *Journal of International Business Studies*, **29**, 445–69.

Chen, T.J. (2000), 'Network resources for internationalization. The case of Taiwan's electronics firms', mimeo, National Taiwan University, Taipai.

Choi, S-G., and K. Eriksson (2001), 'Knowledge transfer through relationship development', paper presented at the conference on 'Cooperative Strategies and Alliances', I.M.D., Lausanne, July.

Coleman, J. (1988), 'Social capital in the creation of human capital', *American Journal of Sociology*, **94**, 5095–110.

Das, R.K., and N. Rahman (2001), 'Opportunism dynamics in strategic alliances', paper presented at the conference on 'Cooperative Strategies and Alliances', I.M.D., Lausanne, July.

Das, R.K., and N. Rahman (2002), 'Partner misbehaviour in strategic alliances: guidelines for effective deterrence', *Journal of General Management*, **27** (1).

Dasgupta, P., and I. Serageldin (2000), *Social Capital: A Multifaceted Perspective*, Washington, DC: The World Bank.

De Soto, H. (2000), *The Mystery of Capital*, London and New York: Bantam Press.

Dicken, P., P.F. Kelly, K. Olds and H.W-C. Yeung (2001), 'Chains and networks, territories and scales: towards a relational framework for analysing the global economy', *Global Networks*, **1** (2), 89–112.

Doz, Y., J. Santos, and P. Williamson (2001), *From Global to Metanational,* Boston: Harvard Business School Press.

Dunning, J.H. (1994), 'The strategy of Japanese and US manufacturing investment in Europe', in M. Mason and D. Encarnation (eds), *Does Ownership Matter?*, Oxford: Clarendon Press, pp. 59–86.

Dunning, J.H. (1997), *Alliance Capitalism and Global Business*, London and New York: Routledge.

Dunning, J.H. (1998), 'Location and the multinational enterprise. A neglected factor?', *Journal of International Business Studies*, **29**, 67–83.

Dunning, J.H. (2002), *Theories and Paradigms of International Business Activity. The Selected Essays of John Dunning*, vol. 1, Cheltenham, UK and Northampton, MA, USA: Edward Elgar.

Dunning, J.H., and A. McKaig-Berliner (2002), 'The geographical sources of competitiveness of professional business firms', *Transnational Corporations*, **11** (3), 1–38.

Dunning, J.H., and E.V. Morgan (1971), *An Economic Study of the City of London*, London: Allen and Unwin.

Dunning, J.H., and C. Wymbs (2001), 'The challenge of electronic commerce for international business theory', *International Journal of the Economics of Business*, **8** (2), 273–302.

Dyer, J.H., and W. Chu (2000), 'The determinants of trust in supplier–automaker relationships in the US, Japan and Korea', *Journal of International Business Studies*, **31** (2), 259–85.

Dyer, J.H., and H. Singh (1998), 'The relational view: cooperative strategy and sources of interorganisational competitive advantage', *Academy of Management Review*, **23** (4), 660–79.

Enright, M.J. (2000), 'Globalization, regionalization and the knowledge based economy in Hong Kong', in J.H. Dunning (ed.), *Regions, Globalization, and the Knowledge Based Economy*, Oxford: Oxford University Press, pp. 131–69.

Etzioni, A. (1996), *The New Golden Rule*, New York: Basic Books.

Fladmoe-Linquist, K., and S. Tallman (n.d.), 'Resource-based strategy and competition advantages among multinationals', CIBER Brigham Young University/University of Utah working paper series no. 1, Salt Lake City and Provo, Utah.

Fukuyama, F. (1996), *Trust*, London: Penguin Books.

Fukuyama, F. (1999), *The Great Disruption*, New York: The Free Press.

Giersch, H. (1996), 'Economic morality as a competitive asset' in A. Hamlin, H. Giersch and A. Norton (eds), *Markets, Morality and the Community*, Melbourne, Australia, Centre for Independent Studies, occasional paper, no. 65.

Gomes-Casseres, B. (1994), 'Group versus group. How alliance networks compete', *Harvard Business Review*, July/August, reprint no. 94402, 1–11.

Granovetter, M.S. (1992), 'Problems of explanation in economic sociology', in N. Nohria and R. Eccles (eds), *Networks and Organisations: Structure, Form and Action*, Boston, MA: Harvard Business School Press, pp. 25–56.

Granovetter, M.S. (1994), 'Business groups', in N. Smelser and R. Swedberg (eds), *Handbook of Economic Sociology*, Princeton, NJ: Princeton University Press, pp. 453–75.

Gulati, R. (1995), 'Does familiarity breed trust? The implications of repeated ties for contractual choice in alliances', *Academy of Management Journal*, **38**, 85–112.

Gulati, R. (1998), 'Alliances and networks', *Strategic Management Journal*, **19**, 293–317.

Gulati, R. (1999), 'Network location and learning; the influence of network resources and firm capabilities on alliance formation', *Strategic Management Journal*, **20**, 397–420.

Gulati, R., N. Nohria, and A. Zaheer (2000), 'Strategic networks', *Strategic Management Journal*, **21**, 203–15.

Hall, P.A., and D. Soskice (eds) (2001), *Varieties of Capitalism*, Oxford: Oxford University Press.

Hedlund, G. (1986), 'The hypermodern MNC – a heterarchy', *Human Resource Management*, **25**, 9–25.

Hedlund, G. (1992), *Transnational Corporations and Organisations,* London and New York: Routledge.

Hedlund, G., and D. Rolander (1991), 'Action in heterarchies – new approaches to managing the MNC', in C.A. Bartlett, Y. Doz and G. Hedlund (eds), *Managing the Global Firm*, London and New York: Routledge.

Helleloid, D. (1992), 'A resource based theory of the multinational enterprise', mimeo, University of Washington, Seattle.

Hennart, J.F. (1988) 'A transaction costs theory of joint ventures', *Strategic Management Journal*, **9**, 361–74.

Hennart, J.F., and J. Larimo (1998), 'The impact of culture on the strategy of multinational enterprises: does national origin affect ownership decisions?', *Journal of International Business Studies*, **29** (3), 515–38.

Hill, C.W.L. (1995), 'National institutional structures, transaction cost economizing and competitive advantage: the case of Japan', *Organizational Science*, **6** (1), 119–31.

Holm, D.B., K. Eriksson and J. Johanson (1996), 'Business networks and cooperation in international business relationships', *Journal of International Business Studies*, **27** (5), 1033–53.

Holm, D.B., K. Eriksson, and J. Johanson (1999), 'Creating value through mutual commitment to business network relationships', *Strategic Management Journal*, **20**, 467–86.

Jeremy, D.J. (1990), *Capitalists and Christian Business Leaders and the Churches in Britain 1900–60,* Oxford: Oxford University Press.

Johanson, J., and L-G. Mattson (1988), 'Internationalization in industrial systems – a network approach', in N. Hood and J-E. Vahlne (eds), *Strategies in Global Competition*, London: Croom Helm, pp. 287–314.

Johanson, J., and J-E. Vahlne (1977), 'The internationalisation process of the firm – a model of knowledge development and increasing market commitments', *Journal of International Business Studies*, **8** (1), 23–32.

Johanson, J., and J-E. Vahlne (1990), 'The mechanism of internationalisation', *International Marketing Review*, **7** (4), 11–24.

Kale, P., H. Singh, and H. Perlmutter (2000), 'Learning and protection of proprietary assets in strategic alliances: building relational capital', *Strategic Management Journal*, **21**, 217–37.

Kim, Chang-Su (2002a), 'Absorptive capacity and learning. The role of prior knowledge and experience in learning alliances', mimeo, Rutgers University, Newark.

Kim, Chang-Su (2002b), 'Socio-technical relatedness and learning in cross-border R&D alliances', PhD thesis, Rutgers University, Newark, May.

Knack, S., and P. Keefer (1996), 'Does social capital have an economic payoff? A cross-country investigation', *Quarterly Journal of Economics*, **112** (4), 1251.

Leana, C.R., and D.M. Rousseau (eds) (2000), *Relational Wealth*, Oxford: Oxford University Press.

Madhok, A., and A. Phene (2002), 'The co-evolutional advantage: strategic management theory and the eclectic paradigm', mimeo, Salt Lake City: University of Utah.

Marinetto, M. (1999), 'The historical development of business philanthropy: social responsibility in the new corporate economy', *Business History*, **41** (4), 1–20.

McPherson, C. (1973), *Democratic Theory: Essays in Retrieval*, Oxford: Clarendon Press.

Moore, K., and D. Lewis (1999), *Birth of the Multinational*, Copenhagen: Copenhagen Business School Press.

Nahapiet, J., and S. Ghoshal (1998), 'Social capital, intellectual capital and the organisational advantage', *Academy of Management Review*, **23** (2), 242–66.

Nonaka, L., and H. Takeuchi (1995), *The Knowledge Creating Company*, Oxford: Oxford University Press.

North, D.C. (1990), *Institutions, Institutional Change and Economic Performance*, New York: Cambridge University Press.

Oliver, C. (1997), 'Sustainable competitive advantage combining institutional and resource-based views', *Strategic Management Journal*, **18** (9), 697–713.

Ozawa, T. (2001), 'Japan's outward capitalism in evolution', paper presented at 27th EIBA Conference in Paris, (ECCP/EAP); mimeo, Colorado State University, Fort Collins.

Parkhe, A. (1998), 'Building trust in international alliances', *Journal of World Business*, **33** (4), 417–37.

Peng, M. (2001), 'The resource-based view and international business', *Journal of Management*, **27**, 803–29.

Porter, M. (1998), *On Competition*, Boston, MA: Harvard Business School Press.

Portes, A. (1998), 'Social capital, its origins and applications in modern sociology', *Annual Review of Sociology*, **24**, 1–24.

Powell, W. (1990), 'Neither markets nor hierarchy: network forms of organization', in L.L. Cumming and B.M. Straw (eds), *Research in Organizational Behavior*, vol. 12, Greenwich: JAI Press, pp. 295–336.

Putman, R.D. (1993), *Making Democracy Work: Civic Traditions in Modern Italy*, Princeton, NJ: Princeton University Press.

Quinn, J.B. (1992), *Intelligent Enterprise*, New York: Free Press.

Rifkin, J. (2000), *The Age of Access*, London: Penguin Books.

Rugman, A., and A. Verbeke (2001a), 'Location and the multinational enterprise', in A. Rugman and T. Brewer (eds), *Handbook of International Business*, Oxford: Oxford University Press.

Rugman, A., and A. Verbeke (2001b), 'Multinational enterprises and clusters', paper presented at the conference on 'Cooperative Strategies and Alliances', I.M.D., Lausanne, July.

Rugman, A., and A. Verbeke (2001c), 'Subsidiary specific advantages in multinational enterprises', *Strategic Management Journal*, **22** (3), 237–50.

Stiglitz, J. (1998), 'Towards a new paradigm of development', The Prebisch Lecture for 1998, Geneva: UNCTAD.

Tallman, S., and M. Jenkins (2002), 'Alliances, knowledge flows and performance in regional clusters', in F. Contractor and P. Lorange (eds), *Cooperative Strategies and Alliances*, Oxford: Elsevier Science.

Teece, D.J. (1992), 'Competition, cooperation and innovation', *Journal of Economic Behaviour and Organisation*, **18**, 1–25.

Teece, D.J. (2000), *Managing Intellectual Capital*, Oxford: Oxford University Press.

Tsai, W., and S. Ghoshal, (1998), 'Social capital and value creation: the role of intra-firm networks', *Academy of Management Review*, **41** (4), 464–76.

UNCTAD (1998), *World Investment Report. Trends and Determinants*, New York and Geneva: UN.

Uzzi, B. (1997), 'Social structure and competition in inter-firm networks: the paradox of embeddedness', *Administrative Science Quarterly*, **42**, 35–67.

Vernon, R. (1960), *Metropolis 1985*, Cambridge, MA: Harvard University Press.

Wallace, L. (2000), 'The United States', in J.H. Dunning (ed.), *Regions, Globalisation and the Knowledge-Based Economy*, Oxford: Oxford University Press.

Williamson, O. (1985), *The Economic Institutions of Capitalism: Firms, Markets and Relational Contracting,* New York: Free Press.

Zaheer, A., and S. Manrakham (2001), 'Concentration and dispersion in global industries: remote electronic access and the location of economic activities', *Journal of International Business Studies*, **32** (4), 667–86.

Zaheer, A., and N. Venkataram (1995), 'Relational governance as an interorganisational strategy. An empirical test of the role of trust in economic exchange', *Strategic Management Journal*, **16**, 373–92.

Zaheer, A., B. McEvily, and V. Perrone (1998), 'Does trust matter? Exploring the role of inter-organisational and interpersonal trust on performance', *Organisational Science*, **9**, 141–59.

APPENDIX 9.1 SOME CONCEPTS RELATED TO R-ASSETS

We refer to the mutual trust, respect and friendship that reside at the individual level between alliance partners as 'relational capital', which as defined, rests upon close interaction at the personal level between alliance partners (Kale *et al.*, 2000, p. 221).

'According to the *Concise Oxford Dictionary* (fifth edition 1964) cooperation is "working together to the same end". In business relationships between suppliers and customers "working together to the same end" can ... basically be regarded as mutual understanding in coordinating exchange activities in the relationship. This presupposes that the partners are able to handle unforeseen issues that may arise. We call this basic quality of cooperation in business relationships *relationship understanding'*, (Holm *et al.*, 1996) p. 1037).

'Relational wealth' is 'the value created, by and for a firm, through its internal relations among and with employers, as well as external alliances and reputation' (Leana and Rousseau, 2000, p. 278). 'Relational wealth is an intangible asset that successful firms optimise and leverage' (ibid. p. 6).

'We define a *relational rent* as a supernormal profit jointly generated in an exchange relationship that cannot be generated by either firm in isolation and can only be created through the joint idiosyncratic contributions of the specific alliance partners ... A firm may choose to seek advantages by creating assets that are specialized in conjunction with the assets of an alliance partner' (Dyer and Singh, 1998, p. 662).

'We use the concept of the *relational dimension* of social capital to refer to those assets created and leveraged through relationships. This concept focuses on the particular relationships people have, such as respect and friendship that influence their behaviour' (Nahapiet and Ghoshal, 1998, p. 243).

'Relational embeddedness' describes the kind of personal relationships people have developed with each other through a history of interactions (Granovetter, 1992).

'Our conception of the firm is *relational* [our italics]. We see firms as actors seeking to develop and exploit *"core competences"* or *dynamic capabilities* ... We take the view as critical to these is the *quality of the relationships* [our italics] the firm is able to establish, both internally with its own employees, and externally, with a range of other actors that include suppliers, clients, collaborators, stakeholders, trade unions, business associations, and governments' (Hall and Soskice, 2001, p. 6).

'Relational quality' is 'the extent to which the partners (to an exchange) feel comfortable and are willing to trust in dealing with one another ...

relational quality is a broader concept than trust. It involves factors such as the degree of compatibility of corporate cultures and decision-making styles, a convergence of world views and other organizational characteristics' (Ariño *et al.*, 2002).

'Relational marketing' refers to all marketing activities directed towards establishing, developing and maintaining successful relational exchanges (Morgan and Hunt, 1994, p. 22).

10. Regaining competitiveness for Asian enterprises

INTRODUCTION

I address this distinguished audience with mixed feelings. On the one hand, it is my immense privilege to share with you some thoughts on the subject of the competitiveness of Asian enterprises. On the other hand, I do so with a real sense of reticence, and, indeed, unease. This unease stems from the fact that, as little as a decade ago, rather than someone like myself standing here before you, it would have been much more appropriate for an Asian economist or business scholar to be addressing a Western audience on the regaining of competitiveness by US or European enterprises. For at that time, you well know, it was towards Japan, and to some of the newly industrializing Asian economies – notably Singapore and Hong Kong – that occidental observers and practitioners were looking to tap into the secrets of high and increasing productivity, good labour and government–firm relations, and resounding export successes.

What, then, has happened over the last ten years or so, during which time the USA and, to a lesser extent, European firms have not only recaptured much of their earlier competitiveness, but are now leaders in the innovation of an impressive range of cutting-edge technologies, especially bio- and information–related technologies?

Essentially, I would suggest that the rejuvenation of the US economy (and I will concentrate on the US economy if I may) reflects four things. Credit for the first three, a market-friendly institutional and commercial infrastructure, well conceived and efficiently implemented macroeconomic policies, and an innovatory educational and fiscal environment favourable to human resource development and continual product improvement, rests primarily with the US government. Credit for the fourth, the willingness and ability of US corporations, not only to learn from the successes of their Far East competitors – for example, in respect of cost reduction, quality control and manpower management – but to restructure their businesses and upgrade their entrepreneurial management in the light of the demands of global capitalism, rests with many thousands of individual firms.

There is little question that, while foreign competition, particularly from Japanese firms, was the initial impetus compelling US firms to reappraise their competitive positions, the recent upsurge in consumer spending, of US industrial productivity, of all kinds of innovating activities and of the seemingly unbounded confidence displayed by savers and investors in the US stock market, have all combined to sustain the longest and most impressive peacetime boom in modern US history.

These remarks should not be taken to infer that I believe US-style capitalism is necessarily 'first-best practice', and even less that it should be slavishly copied. I, for one, have several misgivings about some of its social consequences and moral underpinnings, and about the business practices of some of its corporations. One thing is certain: crony or casino capitalism is by no means the monopoly of Eastern countries. (Only recently I discovered that Americans spend more on gambling in casinos than on any other leisure pursuit.)

But economic events today are, I think, demonstrating three things. First, the prerequisites for national economic success in the global economic village at the turn of the millennium are very different from those of even a decade ago. Second, the role of national governments in creating and sustaining the appropriate economic and institutional environment for markets to operate efficiently and responsibly remains of critical importance, not least as it affects the locational attractiveness of the indigenous resources and capabilities within its jurisdiction to foreign investors. Third, these events demonstrate the need for flexibility and the readiness of firms of all nationalities to take on board the challenges of change, and embrace the many uncertainties and volatilities of the emerging knowledge-based global economy.

I would further add that, although it is one of the largest trading and investing nations of the world, the vast internal resources and capabilities of the USA have allowed US businesses to take in their stride the vagaries and traumas of the international and financial system, and particularly those which have beset the Asian economies over the last three to four years.

WHAT ASIAN COUNTRIES MIGHT DO

With the current US macroeconomic strategies and business practices in mind, let me now turn to what I perceive needs to be done if Asian enterprises are to recapture the kind of growth and success they enjoyed in the 1970s and 1980s. Clearly, my remarks must be very general, although I fully recognize the dangers of generalizing when the 15 or so Asian countries participating in this mart are so different in their stages of development, size, economic structures, modes of governance, cultures and so on.

In the short time available, let me consider just three groups of factors likely to influence the future well-being of Asian enterprises. And, being aware of the particular interests of this audience, let me concentrate on how these factors can and do affect the ability of Asian countries to meet the needs of foreign direct investors, and also the capabilities of indigenous Asian enterprises to compete in the global market place.

Extra-Asian Factors: the Global Economy

It almost goes without saying that the economic prosperity of Asian economies, and particularly those dependent on foreign markets, is affected by the health of the world economy, and especially that of the larger trading nations. By themselves, the smaller Asian countries may be able to do little to affect the prosperity of their larger neighbours (China, Indonesia or Japan) and even less those in Europe and North America. At the same time, just as the Asian crisis quickly spread from one part of East Asia to engulf the whole region, so recovery in one major Asian country may spark off a cycle of renewed growth elsewhere in the region.

Moreover, with the experience of the European Community to draw upon, I would also emphasize the benefits which could arise from closer Asian regional integration. These benefits not only lower cross-border transport and communication costs but, more importantly, increase the gains which arise from the specialization of economic activity, including innovatory activities, in accord with the principle of dynamic comparative advantage. Certainly, a good part of the regained competitiveness of European companies in the last two decades has come directly from the removal of intra-European trade and investment-related barriers.

Yet, even if it were possible to get rid of most intra-Asian obstacles to closer economic integration, there are other impediments which face Asian countries and firms, which arise from the actions of the wider economic community. These especially relate to the conditions in which trade and FDI are conducted, and the governance of the international movement of intangible assets, particularly financial assets. Here the reform of the international trading and financial systems, both of which were set up prior to the advent of flexible exchange rates and electronic commerce, seems long overdue. Second, there is need for a more realistic recognition of the fact that the merits of free and unimpeded cross-border flows of capital rests on two conditions being achieved. The first is that the institutional and banking infrastructures and the exchange and non-financial markets of recipient countries are such as to be able to absorb and efficiently utilize foreign capital. The second is that the cost of imprudent actions by financial speculators are borne primarily by them, and not by innocent parties adversely affected by their actions.

Such constraints on the upgrading of the competitiveness of Asian countries (and, indeed, of other countries and regions in the world) are well known and are often vociferously stated around international negotiating tables. Equally important, however, is the need for the larger trading importers to reduce barriers to trade and/or discriminatory treatment against Asian exporting countries.

In general, I am cautiously optimistic about the external economic and political environment for the recovery and upgrading of competitiveness of Asian firms, although I believe it will take several years for the full effects to be worked out. Indeed, I believe recent economic events in Asia have not only sounded a salutary warning to the international community on the unpredictability and fragility of the world economy, but have made its leading participants more aware of their responsibilities as fashioners and monitors of the global economic system. It has certainly caused several distinguished economists and policy advisers to revise their opinions on the unalloyed benefits of free markets – and particularly free capital markets – in a world riddled with all kinds of structural distortions and institutional rigidities. Hopefully, the lessons learned will prompt the relevant international institutions to devise and implement a more stable, yet flexible, global economic and institutional environment, and one in which all the nations of the world and their enterprises will avoid at least some of the instabilities they have recently experienced.

Asia-specific Factors

Let me now turn to the main focus of my presentation. What can Asia and Asian enterprises do to regain their earlier competitiveness? Can they in fact do so? The answer to the second question is a qualified 'yes'. It is qualified for two reasons. First, there is a lot more (and tougher) competition in the world than there was even five years ago. In the high-tech and information-intensive sectors, US enterprises, in particular, are leaner, fitter and more entrepreneurial than they used to be. At the other end of the value chain, Central and Eastern European countries, as well as third and fourth generations of Asian tigers – not to mention India – are improving their productivity in leaps and bounds.

Second, the focus and quality of competition faced by most of the countries represented here today are undergoing a major shift. In the 1970s and 1980s, it was primarily geared towards minimizing real labour, material and transport costs. In the 1990s, the competitiveness of firms is increasingly reflecting their willingness and capabilities, first to engage in product improvement and innovation, and, second, to harness resources and capabilities from throughout the world and to integrate these with their home-based competencies.

Hence my first conclusion on the future of the competitiveness of Asian firms is that it largely rests on their ability, and that of their home governments, to recognize the ingredients and form of the new competition, and to upgrade and/or reorganize their resources and capabilities to meet the demands made by it. How might they do this? Let me turn first to the role and responsibilities of governments and then to those of enterprises. And let me repeat that I am being forced to generalize and that, in practice, the menu of measures which need to be taken to raise competitiveness will vary between the countries, regions within countries, industries, and even between firms. Nevertheless, I believe some useful generalizations can be made, if for no other reason than that the great majority of Asian countries represented here today are committed to upgrading their competitiveness by democratic means and by pursuing market-based objectives, and that all want to benefit from their full participation in the global market place.

The role of governments
My first point – and I cannot stress it too strongly – is that, despite the widespread trend towards the deregulation and liberalization of markets and the advent of global capitalism, the role of national and, indeed, subnational governments in promoting a competitivity-enhancing economic system remains a critical one. But, second, it is no less important to recognize that this role is constantly changing. What was appropriate to Japan or Korea in the early stages of their economic development is no longer appropriate today. Following the emergence of the European Union's internal market, the competitivity-enhancing policies of the member states have had to be completely reconfigured. The advent of electronic commerce is dramatically realigning the boundaries of economic exchange vis-à-vis those of political jurisdiction. And most developing countries in the late 1990s are pursuing export-led development strategies, in marked contrast to the import substitution strategies they practised twenty years ago.

It is, I think, helpful to distinguish two roles which democratic governments may play as competitivity-enhancing organizations. The first, and this is a unique role, is as creators and sustainers of the economic system which governs the allocation of resources under their jurisdiction, and the rules underpinning that system. The second, which is shared with private firms, is as a participator or operator in that system. As to the first role, this primarily takes the form of the provision of the appropriate legal, institutional, regulatory and ethical framework aimed at facilitating the efficient and socially responsible workings of the market place, in respect both of the production of existing goods and services, and of the innovation of new goods and services. Let me elaborate by referring to the particular locational needs of inbound foreign direct investors.

All studies on the locational preferences of foreign direct investors I have come across emphasize the importance of three groups of factors: the national policy framework, economic determinants and business facilitation. These are set out in Table 10.1. By their macroeconomic and micromanagement policies, governments may affect each of these factors. In today's knowledge-based economy, the extent and quality of government-sponsored educational programmes, innovatory systems and physical infrastructure are critical in ensuring that inward investors have access to the kind of immobile assets they consider necessary to complement and/or upgrade their core competencies. Similarly, governments, by a variety of means (not least by competition and taxation policies), can provide the right 'sticks' and 'carrots' for firms to be efficient, for domestic investment and entrepreneurship to be encouraged, for workers to upgrade their skills and talents, and for consumers to be discriminatory in their buying habits. By their social policies, they can aid the movement of workers from less to more productive activities or locations, help enterprises and households to adjust to the imperatives of technological progress, and provide a safety net to counter at least some of the adverse affects of economic change.

Governments can also foster a competitivity-conducive ethos or mindset of their constituents: the dramatic changes in UK economic fortunes following Margaret Thatcher's accession to power in the 1980s demonstrates what can be done in this respect. They can help, by education, by example and by the appropriate incentives and regulatory measures to ensure that the ethical underpinnings of the institutions and that the behaviour of economic entities within their jurisdiction, are such as to foster such virtues as civic responsibility, honesty, flexibility, trust, reciprocity, loyalty and forbearance. For these are (just some of) the critical ingredients of economic morality, which, itself, is becoming an increasingly sought-after competitive asset in the locational portfolio of foreign investors.

More particularly, in their policies to attract FDI, I see governments needing to devise a set of micromanagement strategies which will be customized or tailor-made to their perceived dynamic comparative advantage and also to the specific needs of the major foreign investors they wish to attract. While it is inevitable that most countries which are similar in size, stage of development and factor endowments should want to engage in the same kinds of economic activities and, therefore, compete with one another for FDI, there is no such inevitability about the manner in which they compete; that is, how they organize and implement their

Table 10.1 Host-country determinants of FDI

Host-country determinants

I. Policy framework of FDI
Economic, political and social stability
Rules regarding entry and operations
Standards of treatment of foreign affiliates
Policies on functioning and structure of markets (especially competition
    and M&A policies)
International agreements on FDI
Privatization policy
Trade policy (tariffs and NTBs) and coherence of FDI and trade policies
Tax policy

II. Economic determinants

III. Business facilitation
Investment promotion (including image-building and investment-
    generating activities and investment facilitation services)
Investment incentives
Hassle costs (related to corruption, administrative efficiency, etc)
Social amenities (bilingual schools, quality of life, etc)
After-investment services

Source: UNCTAD, *World Investment Report 1998*, Geneva and New York: UN.

economic strategies. Neither does a certain similarity in what is produced
deny the value of a selective, or niche, industrial or innovatory strategy,
which not only differentiates between the particular competitive advantages
of countries (for example, one country may produce one range of car, textile,
pharmaceutical and food products, and another quite a different range) but
helps lock in valued foreign investment, that is, making it more location-
bound, while fostering the continual upgrading of its activities. Here the
Singaporean economy offers a classic example of what can be done.

Successful and dynamic product specialization, in accordance with the
needs of domestic and global consumers, still remains the key to advancing
national economic prosperity but, to achieve this, careful thought and
planning, and cooperation between the public and private sector, are called
for. Not least, this is because governments and markets need to better
recognize the close interdependence between various economic activities

Type of FDI classified by motives of MNEs	Principal economic determinants in host countries
A. Market-seeking	Market size and per capita income
	Market growth
	Access to regional and global markets
	Country-specific consumer preferences
	Structure of markets
B. Resource/asset-seeking	Raw materials
	Low-cost unskilled labour
	Skilled labour
	Technological, innovatory and other created assets (e.g. brand names), including as embodied in individuals, firms and clusters
	Physical infrastructure (ports, roads, power, telecommunication)
C. Efficiency-seeking	Cost of resources and assets listed under B, adjusted for labour productivity
	Other input costs and costs of other intermediate products
	Membership of a regional integration agreement conducive to the establishment of regional corporate networks

(along and across value chains) and, inter alia, this frequently means they need to be in close geographical proximity to each other. The work of Michael Porter (1998a) and others has quite clearly shown that countries which nourish the spatial clustering of related activities are those which have historically recorded the most impressive performances in the sectors comprising those clusters. Well-known examples include the agglomeration of high knowledge-intensive industries in Massachusetts, the watch industry of Switzerland, tomato canning in Naples, the cork industry in northern Portugal, the motion picture industry in Hollywood, the horse-breeding industry in Cambridge in New Zealand, and the computer software cluster in Bangalore.

Other research has also revealed that, providing the conditions are right, foreign investors may, and often do, play an important role in promoting, developing and upgrading these clusters. The success of the Venezuelan oil and petroleum cluster, the Canadian telecommunication and aluminium cluster, the financial services cluster in Hong Kong, the electronics cluster in Singapore and the pharmaceutical cluster in New Jersey (USA) are cases in point (see, for example, Enright, 1998 and 2000).

This brings us to the role of subnational governments in their actions to upgrade the competitiveness of the resources and firms within their jurisdiction. Here I would like to make two observations. The first is that the motors of economic growth, although being spread across an increasing number of countries, are, at the same time, becoming more and more spatially concentrated within countries. Yet, like an archipelago of islands, these small concentrations are closely linked to each other, frequently so through the modality of foreign direct investment and cross-border inter-firm activities. The point I want to make is that the governments of these subnational economies, through a variety of policy instruments,[1] will as much determine the upgrading of the competitive advantages of their constituent firms as any actions taken by their national counterparts. This opinion is also shared by McKinsey's Kenichi Ohmae (1995), who views microregions and smaller nation states as gateways linking larger spatial areas to the rest of the global economy.

The second observation, which follows from the first, is that it is increasingly the promotional efforts of regional investment agencies and the incentives offered by regional governments, rather than the policies of national administrations, which are becoming the decisive factors influencing the location decision of MNEs. Certainly, this is the case in both Europe and the USA. It would appear that, apart from those of the small and least developed economies, national governments are becoming much more neutral towards inbound FDI than they used to be. At the same time, they need to be mindful of the ways micromanagement policies affect, for good or bad, the competitive advantages of particular regions within their domain, and particularly those sought after by foreign investors.

I would briefly make one other comment about the changing role of Asian governments. I introduce it by referring to the changing characteristics of the competitive advantages of enterprises. Business scholars are generally agreed that the unique and critical competencies of today's successful corporations are not primarily the technological assets they own, nor their capabilities to deploy or upgrade these assets effectively (important as both of these may be), but reside in their ability to seek out, harness and leverage the human, physical and financial resources they need from throughout the world and to motivate their stakeholders – alliance partners, for example, workers, consumers and suppliers alike – to be efficient, yet socially responsible and accountable, in the way they do this. This suggests a holistic and integrated approach to management. It also suggests that the main function of top management is less to control or formally direct the use of the resources and capabilities under their governance, and more to set goals and targets to inspire and to encourage delegated entrepreneurship. It suggests a less hierarchical and pyramidal, and a more cooperative and multidirectional, strategy to decision taking. It suggests that there need not be any conflict between their economic objectives and their corporate citizenship. For example, some of the most environmentally sensitive MNEs in the world are also the most productive, while others are recognizing that their reputation as socially responsible employers is directly correlated to their long-term profitability.

Now, apply, if you will, those same criteria to governments. I firmly believe that, if it is to remain the dominant wealth-creating mechanism of the 21st century, global capitalism needs to be socially responsible and accountable for its workings. I also believe that democratic governments have a mandate for ensuring that this is the case and persuading all its constituents to act accordingly.

Consider, for a moment, how, at the turn of the millennium, social and economic objectives are becoming increasingly interdependent. Thus an innovating and efficient economy needs an educated, well motivated and contented workforce, a social goal in its own right. It needs an assimilation of unemployed and underemployed workers into the productive labour force; one of man's greatest needs is to gain fulfilment by the work he does. It needs to foster the virtues of creativity, partnership and a respect for human rights. It needs low levels of pollution (as pollution is a sign of unproductive use of physical resources). It needs to minimize the output of 'bads' such as drugs, crime and terrorism, all of which are social, as well as economic, disbenefits. It needs an efficient and inclusive health service, and the provision of adequate safety standards. It needs comprehensive and clearly defined competition policies, which help protect the weaker members of society from the unacceptable behaviour of the strong. It needs a strong and effective legal system, transparent accounting practices and a vibrant ethical code or set of regulations, to minimize unacceptable business behaviour, moral hazard and opportunism.

All these are socially worthwhile goals, and they are entirely consistent with, if not supportive of, upgrading competitiveness. Others may involve some kind of trade-off, at least in the short run, namely a more egalitarian distribution of income with the necessary incentives to innovate and create more wealth. Yet current events are reminding us that, unless democratic capitalism can be seen to advance the aspirations of the majority of the electorate, and especially those who perceive they are disadvantaged by it, it will eventually collapse. To avoid this happening, all constituents of society need to play their part, but especially it is the task of governments to resolve the paradox between the unevenly distributed consequences of the global market place and the demands of social justice.

This task, along with a streamlining and integration of the various government departments responsible for economic matters (this, I admit, is much easier said than done) and a real and continuing dialogue with the private sector to reduce inefficiencies and promote innovation, will do much, I believe, to provide the right institutional framework for the capitalism of the early 21st century. This, in turn, will both raise the competitiveness of its own firms and provide the kind of locational advantages necessary to attract foreign direct investment. If the recent economic crisis does nothing other than to cause Asian governments to reappraise their own role in affecting the competitiveness of their resources and that of their firms, it will not have been in vain.

To summarize some of the points I have made on the role of Asian governments in affecting the competitiveness of Asian firms, let me draw upon some data recently published by the IMD[2] in its 1997 *World Competitive Yearbook*. In it, the authors identify eight broad criteria and 279 individual competitive indices likely to affect the competitiveness of business enterprises, be they domestic or foreign-owned, in 46 countries. Each country is ranked in respect of each index and then the indices are averaged to obtain an overall index of national competitiveness.

In Table 10.2, I have compared the strengths and weaknesses of the ten most competitive Western industrialized nations,[3] with ten East Asian countries. I have broken the latter into two groups, based on their overall rankings (which is closely related to their GNP per head). Group 1 Asian countries consist of Singapore, Hong Kong, Japan, Taiwan, Malaysia and Korea, and Group 2 of Thailand, China, the Philippines and Indonesia.

The conclusions are, I think, very revealing. In the mid or late 1990s, the main weaknesses of Group 1, the middle- to high-income Asian countries, taken as a whole and relative to those of Western nations,[4] appeared to be in seven main categories: high youth unemployment, quality of legal and administrative systems, innovating capacity, improper practices, above-average international telephone costs, restrictions on FDI and inadequate competition laws. Group 2 Asian countries also demonstrated these weaknesses, but, in addition, they scored, relative to both Group 1 Asian countries and Western nations, low capital availability, undemanding markets to replace demand conditions, insufficient protection of intellectual property rights, lack of local competition and inadequate information technology.

More generally, in his comments on some other data on the micro competitiveness of countries, Porter (1998b) has observed that, for low- and middle-income countries such as Group 2 Asian countries to improve their competitive position, they should concentrate on reducing corruption,

Table 10.2 Relative strengths and weaknesses of Asian and Western countries over which governments may have some influence

	Group 1	Group 2	Western Countries
Strengths	Open (or opening up) economies	Low unemployment	Property rights well protected
	Good domestic savings	Long working hours	High percentage of educational enrolment
	Good airport facilities	Low central government expenditure	Strong competition laws
	Value traded on stock market	Low personal taxes	Low cost of capital
	Government/private enterprise relationships	Low labour costs	Adequate venture capital
	Regulation of banking institutions	Fewer investment disputes	Increasing role of SMEs and start-up firms
Weaknesses	Administrative centralization	Administrative centralization	Above average unemployment
	Restrictions on FDI and cross-border ventures	Insufficient protection of property rights	People not flexible to change
	Lack of regional integration	High youth unemployment	Inadequate domestic savings
	High youth unemployment	Low public expenditure on education	Bureaucracy
	Improper business practices	Improper business practices	Past expectancies of people and institutions of welfare state
	Inadequate consumer protection	Lack of computer power	Protectionism (e.g. EU's agricultural policies)
	Price controls	Inadequate information technology	
	Inadequate competitive laws	High international telephone costs	
	Inadequate internet connections		
	High international telephone costs		

Source: World Competitive Year Book, Geneva: World Economic Forum, 1997.

raising regulatory standards, improving information and communication infrastructures, promoting more cluster development and local competition and upgrading the quality of domestic consumer choice. It is his belief that the main factors constraining an improved economic performance were the insufficient local competition, an unacceptably high administrative-cum-regulatory burden, and an inadequate or unsuitable physical or administrative infrastructure.

The role of Asian enterprises

I have suggested that the main and unique role of governments, whether they be local, national or supranational, is to provide the economic, legal and political framework, and the institutional infrastructure, which enables private markets to work effectively and in a socially acceptable way. They are also setters of the 'rules of the game' and the boundaries of acceptable market behaviour; and also of guarantees that, as far as possible, these rules are adhered to.

But in democratic capitalism it is the thousands of individual firms, guided by the wants of millions of consumers, who are the real wealth creators. What should be their role in regaining their competitiveness? It is an unfortunate fact of life that it sometimes takes a crisis or a disaster for one to know or evaluate properly one's strengths and weaknesses, particularly where the strengths are the result of, or exaggerated by, institutional rigidities, overexuberant financial markets and inadequate or inappropriate accounting procedures. And there can surely be no question that the pre-crisis strengths of many Asian enterprises were overplayed by Western observers, and their weaknesses underestimated. It was only when the full force winds of competition were felt, and when the fragility of the institutional infrastructure of many Asian countries was exposed, that these weaknesses were fully brought to light.

As you will gather from my opening remarks, I feel very reluctant to suggest, in any detail, ways and means by which the competitiveness of Asian enterprises in international markets might be regained. In any case, apart from anything else, so much will depend on factors specific to particular countries, activities and firms. But, perhaps, to conclude my presentation, a few 'key points' may be in order. These draw less on the recent experiences of Asian enterprises, taken as a whole, in the 1980s and early 1990s, and more on the evolving competitiveness of the world's more successful leading MNEs, including some of Asian origin.

However, to start with, let me turn to some findings of the *World Competitive Yearbook* with respect to the category of 'management'. Here some 20 indices of competitiveness were pinpointed. Taking the two groups of Asian countries earlier identified, Table 10.3 sets out the strengths and weaknesses of Asian enterprises relative to those of Western origin.

The conclusions are again very interesting. The main weaknesses of the higher income Asian enterprises would appear to be the (lack of) competence of their senior managers, their lack of transparency and/or accountability, low innovating capability and a too complex and/or rigid organizational structure or system. Their comparative advantages include their lack of industrial disputes, in total quality management and the ability to bring new products speedily to market. For middle- to lower-income countries, the weaknesses were similar, but, in addition, their inexperience in tapping into international markets was considered a major drawback to their overall competitiveness. At the same time, the countries enjoyed several unique strengths (see Table 10.3), although, in general, their competitive prowess was shifting from that based on cheap labour and natural resources to one based on product improvement, building international distribution systems and broadening markets.

Now for my key points. I put these in the form of questions which I believe senior managers of Asian enterprises should be asking themselves.

1. Given a more open, competitive and innovation-driven economic environment, to what extent are our existing competitive assets suited to the needs of our existing or potential customers? Should we pay more attention to product innovation and improvement; should we step up our investment in human resource development?

2. Is the organizational structure of our enterprise best suited to the needs? Is it too hierarchical? Does it encourage the initiative, entrepreneurship and far-sighted decision taking of managers? How can the various parts of the organization be better integrated? As Asian managers, we observe that, in the last decade, several Western enterprises have drastically and successfully restructured their organizations to make them more visionary and to encourage more subsidiarity in decision taking. Are these successes a reflection of Western culture? Can they be assimilated by our organizations and adapted to our cultural and other specific needs? (I believe the answer to this last question is 'yes', at least in respect to globally oriented enterprises, as there is a distinct set of 'best practices' evolving which are designed to meet the needs, not of a single culture, but of a cosmopolitan culture.)

3. Are we giving sufficient attention to the range and composition of our products and production processes? Should we not be doing more downsizing and/or outsourcing of some of our non-core activities? Are we sufficiently differentiating our products, and the services which we

Table 10.3 Relative strengths and weaknesses of management as identified by World Competitive Yearbook

	Group 1	Group 2	Western Countries
Strengths	Time-to-market for a new product Total quality management (Lack of) industrial disputes	Companies enjoy public trust Worker motivation Total quality management (Lack of) industrial disputes Sense of social responsibility	Quality management Efficient in generating shareholder value Entrepreneurship and growth of start-up firms
Weaknesses	Competence of senior managers Price/quality ratio of products Overall productivity Cost inefficiencies and managerial slack Below average innovating capacity Top/heavy administrative structure	Overall productivity Labour productivity Price/quality ratio of products Lack of experience in international business Below average innovating capacity	Unit labour costs Time-to-market for a new product Industrial disputes

Source: World Competitive Yearbook, Geneva: World Economic Forum, 1997, IMD (1997).

provide to our domestic and international customers, from those of our competitors?

4. Should our locational strategy be reconfigured? Are we taking advantage of (do we help promote) clusters? Are we part of a 'learning' micro-region? Is our liaison with our suppliers, customers and advanced educational providers all that it should be? Are we exploiting all the benefits we should from regional integration schemes?

5. Are we exploring all the avenues for identifying and tapping into the resources, capabilities and markets of foreign countries? How far might outbound FDI, or the conclusion of strategic alliances with foreign firms, further the upgrading of our competitive advantages?

6. Are we paying sufficient attention to integrating the social and economic objectives of our enterprises, especially in the areas of working conditions, creative learning, safety, the environment and product standards?

CONCLUSIONS

I am confident that most Asian enterprises can, and most likely will, regain much of their past competitiveness, and that Western enterprises would be ill-advised to think otherwise. But how quickly this will occur, what particular form the 'new' competitiveness will take and how it will affect the traditional organizational and financial structures of Asian firms remain to be seen. Much will obviously depend on confluence between the *reaction* of individual Asian countries and enterprises to changes in the global economic and institutional environment, and the *proactive* policies and strategies pursued by these same enterprises and national governments.

One thing is certain. The core competitive advantages of both countries and firms are becoming increasingly knowledge-intensive and dependent on much more inter-firm, and firm–government cooperation. As for locational competition, I sense that, as the economic structures of countries, especially industrial or industrializing countries, begin to converge, such competition will be based less on traditional factors such as labour and material costs, market size and transport costs, and more on the institutional infrastructure, the presence of clusters and the behavioural mores of governments, individuals and firms.

I believe very strongly that, if it is to succeed – not only in Asia but in the world as a whole – global capitalism must embrace more fully than it has so far done such civic virtues as honesty, trust, forbearance, diligence, an entrepreneurial spirit and a sense of community spirit. This can only be achieved through education, example and the appropriate coercive (for example, regulatory) measures.

In the past, Asian countries have set a good example of many of these virtues. But the recent crisis has also brought to light the absence of others, and, indeed, some dis-virtues which themselves helped contribute to the crisis. I do not believe a morally weak society, be it developing or developed, from the East or the West, the North or the South, can survive the twin demands of global capitalism and social justice. Indeed, it may well be that, in the future, economic progress is dependent not only on the acknowledgment of people's social needs, but on their adherence (and that of both private and public institutions) to a strong and, if possible, a universally accepted ethical code. I would like to think that this will be the case.

NOTES

1. Such as those relating to firm strategy and rivalry, acting as a buyer for the cluster's products, the creation of specialized education programmes and local university research efforts, establishing cluster-oriented free trade zones and industrial or supplier parks (see Porter, 1998a and 1998b; Enright, 1998 and 2000).
2. International Institute for Management Development.
3. USA, Netherlands, Denmark, Norway, Finland, Switzerland, Canada, Ireland, Luxembourg and UK.
4. We would stress the phrase 'taken as a whole'. In fact, there were as many differences in the competitiveness indices among Asian countries (for example, Singapore and Korea; China and Indonesia) as there were between Asian countries as a group and Western countries, also as a group.

REFERENCES

Adler, P.S., and S.-W. Kwan (2002), 'Social capital prospects for a new concept', *Academy of Management Review*, **27** (1), 17–40.

Bevan, A., S. Estrin and K. Meyer (2004), 'Foreign investment, location and institutional development in transition economies', *International Business Review*, **13** (1), 43–64.

Coleman, D. (1998), *Working with Emotional Intelligence*, New York: Bantam Books.

Dunning, J.H. (1993), *Multinational Enterprises and the Global Economy*, Wokingham: Addison-Wesley.

Dyer, J.H. and K. Nobeoka (2000), 'Creating and managing a high-performance knowledge-sharing network. The Toyota case', *Strategic Management Journal*, **21** (Special Issue), 345–67.

Enright, M.J. (1998), 'Regional clusters and multinational enterprises: independence, dependence, or interdependence?', *International Studies of Management & Organization*, **30** (2), 114–38.

Enright, M.J. (2000), 'Globalization, regionalization and the knowledge-based economy in Hong Kong', in J.H. Dunning (ed.) *Regions, Globalization and the Knowledge Based Economy*, Oxford: Oxford University Press, pp. 381–406.

Granovetter, M. (1985), 'Economic action and social structure: the problem of embeddedness', *American Journal of Sociology*, **91**, 481–510.

Henderson, D. (2001), *Misguided Virtue*, London: Institute of Economic Affairs.

Hennart, J.F. (2000), 'Transaction costs theory and the multinational enterprise' in C. Pitelis and R. Sugden (eds), *The Nature of the Transnational Firm*, London and New York: Routledge 72–118.

Huang, Y. (2003), *Selling China: Foreign Direct Investment During the Reform*, New York: Cambridge University Press.

IMD (1997), *World Competitiveness Yearbook 1997*, Lausanne: IMD.

Kogut, B. and U. Zander (1993), 'Knowledge of the firm & the evolutionary theory of the multinational corporation', *Journal of International Business Studies*, **24**, 625–45.

Morgan, R.M. and S.D. Hunt (1994), 'The commitment–trust theory of relationship marketing', *Journal of Marketing*, **58** (July), 20–38.

Ohmae, Kenichi (1995), *The End of the Nation State*, New York: The Free Press.

Porter, M.E. (1998a), *On Competition*, Cambridge, MA: Harvard Business Review Press.

Porter, M.E. (1998b) *The World Competitive Yearbook 1998*, Geneva: World Economic Forum.

Rugman, A.M. and T. Brewer (eds) (2001), *The Oxford Handbook of International Business*, Oxford: Oxford University Press.

Searle, G.R. (1998), *Morality and the Market in Victorian Britain*, Oxford: Clarendon Press.

Siebert, H. (ed.) (1995), *Locational Competition in the World Economy*, Tübingen: JCB Mohr.

UNCTAD (2000), *World Investment Report: Cross-Border Mergers and Acquisitions and Development*, New York and Geneva: UN.

Wei, Y. and X. Liu (2001), *Foreign Direct Investment in China: Determinants and Impact*, Cheltenham, UK and Northampton, USA: Edward Elgar.

Williamson, O. (1979), 'Transaction-cost economies: the governance of contractural relations', *Journal of Law and Economics*, **22**, 233–61.

11. The role of foreign direct investment in upgrading China's competitiveness

INTRODUCTION

The accession of China to the World Trade Organization (WTO) brings with it huge opportunities, challenges and responsibilities. The opportunities are largely self evident, notably for Chinese businesses to participate freely in an expanding global market, and to help shape the future structure, content and terms of world trade and investment agreements.

The challenges are no less demanding. To exploit fully these opportunities, China must raise the productivity and export competitiveness of its industries, enhance the skills of its labour force, upgrade its legal and institutional infrastructure, and reconfigure its economic activities. And it must do this in a way which promotes its comparative dynamic advantage, so enabling the country and its citizens to be beneficial participants in the global economy.

Over the past 30 years, the overwhelming consensus of scholarly research has shown that, provided the appropriate institutional framework is in place and the correct macroeconomic policies are followed, trade, foreign direct investment (FDI) and cross-border information and technology flows can play a critical role in advancing such goals.

In this chapter, we examine some of this evidence, and then present a sample of the more recent research findings on ways in which governments have sought to reconstruct their economic and industrial strategies in the light of the demands of the new global economy. More particularly, we propose to centre our remarks on three observations, each of which is supported by extensive empirical research.

RAISING PRODUCTIVITY

Our first observation is that inbound foreign direct investment raises the competitiveness of the host country industries, provided it is in response to appropriate economic policies on the part of the host government.

Nearly 50 years ago, as a young university lecturer, I was asked to document and evaluate the impact of US-owned firms in British manufacturing industry on the productivity of their indigenous competitors and on the UK's export performance. The contents of this study (Dunning, 1958) which was reissued in 1998, and some related research undertaken 20 years later, may seem far removed from China's current economic needs and aspirations. But, in fact, there are several similarities, not least that, in the 1950s, the UK, like China today, after a period of turmoil and social upheaval, was struggling to re-energize its industrial machine and regain some of its earlier economic stature. Moreover, these findings have been repeated in many subsequent studies of inward FDI in respect of both developed and developing countries.

Let us consider a few key conclusions.

1. In whatever industrial sector they produced, US manufacturing subsidiaries recorded superior levels of productivity and profitability than did their UK counterparts. Why was this? Primarily because, at the time, they were more entrepreneurial, more technologically competent, and possessed a greater fund of managerial and organizational expertise. By their presence in the UK, they also helped inject a new and welcome mentality of competitiveness and entrepreneurship into the business environment.

2. But, no less interesting, between the first study in 1958 and the later one in 1976, the productivity and profitability gap between the US affiliates and their UK competitors narrowed considerably (Dunning, 1976). This was almost entirely due to the knowledge transferred, examples set and competitive stimuli provided by the US affiliates. In addition, the spillover effects they had on the competitiveness of their UK suppliers and industrial customers were wholly positive.

3. The US affiliates tended to be concentrated in high-growth, technology-intensive and export oriented sectors. They supplied products with a high income elasticity of demand. Over time, as the UK improved its innovatory infrastructure, they undertook more research and development activities in the UK, and gradually helped to upgrade the UK economy in a way which was consistent with its long term comparative advantage. Britain today is one of the most prosperous countries in Europe, and much of this it owes to inbound FDI and the global operations of its own firms.

4. For several years after the Second World War, the UK economy had been cushioned by protectionism and the UK consumer had become accustomed to inferior quality standards. Not so the US consumer. One important consequence of the entry of US firms into the UK market,

then, was that the higher norms expected of them were transferred to a UK environment. This not only benefited the UK consumer, it better enabled indigenous UK producers to penetrate more demanding consumer markets. Thirty years later, the arrival of Japanese motor and consumer electronic firms had an even more salutary effect in raising UK quality standards and consumer expectations. Indeed, Japanese foreign investors have been largely responsible for resuscitating a dying auto industry in the UK.

5. Backed by UK regional policy, the US subsidiaries found it in their own interests to establish networks of related activities in particular regions of the UK, notably in the less prosperous areas and districts of above-average UK unemployment. Indeed such clusters, with all the benefits now acknowledged by geographers and economists, were among the first to emerge in the postwar international economy.

6. The accession of the UK to the European Common Market in 1971, and the subsequent completion of the internal market of the European Union in 1993, led to a substantial increase of US direct investment in the UK, and particularly that of a high quality and export-oriented variety.

In short, then, the exposure of the British economy to US inward FDI in the early postwar period (and, incidentally, such investment accounted for 90 per cent of all inward investment until 1960) was most wholly beneficial to its industrial regeneration. What lessons might China draw from that experience?

Those who are familiar with Michael Porter's 'diamond of competitive advantage' will recognize the contents of Figure 11.1, which seeks to link the role of FDI to each of the main facets of competitive advantages just described. But outside the diamond, and depicted by a series of circles, is the role of governments and investment promotion agencies (IPA), and two other 'external' influences, namely, FDI and the mentality of competitiveness. We will return to consider these influences a little later.

Over the past 50 years, the UK experience with inbound FDI has been repeated many times over in the case of other developed and developing countries, both small and large, both liberal and coordinated market economies. In the case of China, a recent study conducted for the IMF has shown that, in the 1990s, inbound FDI accounted for 2–2.5 per cent of GDP growth; and, in the year 2000, foreign affiliates were estimated to have been responsible for no less than 48 per cent of Chinese industrial exports (*IMF Survey*, 2002). The study also revealed that the labour productivity of these same affiliates was twice that of state-owned enterprises (for a more

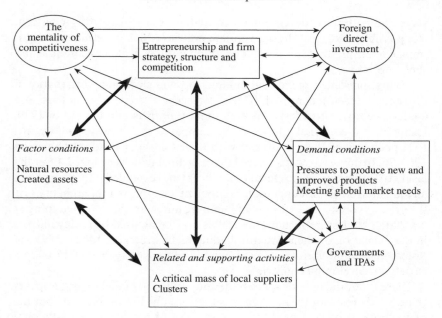

Figure 11.1   Linking the role of FDI to the main facets of competitive advantages

extensive examination of the recent growth or economic implications of inward FDI into China, see Wei and Lin (2000) and Huang (2003).

Of course, there have been exceptions. Not all countries have always sought inward FDI. For example, for most of the postwar period, both Japan and India have stringently limited the participation of foreign-owned firms. But with the advent of the global economy, and as technology now moves more freely and speedily across national boundaries, both countries have stepped up their welcome to foreign investors. Between 1997 and 2002, for example, Japan attracted seven times and India four times the FDI flows that they did in the previous five years. Central and Eastern Europe is another region of the world where FDI inflows have risen, from an annual average of $3.4 billion in the early 1990s to $23.2 billion between 1998 and 2000 (UNCTAD, 2001).

THE INVESTMENT DEVELOPMENT PATH

We now turn to our second theme. Put briefly: the role FDI plays in upgrading the competitiveness of an economy is strongly related to that economy's stage and pattern of development. Indeed, on the basis of this assertion, it is possible to suggest the appropriate policies which governments might pursue to ensure that this role is consistent with its broader economic and social objectives.

We first presented the idea about and the evidence for, an international investment development path (IDP), in respect of some 67 countries, at a conference on Third World Multinational Enterprises in Hawaii in 1979. Using a cross-sectional approach, we compared the outward and inward FDI positions of these countries with their GDP per head in the period 1967–75. In doing so, we discovered that a distinct pattern emerged. Over the last two decades, we have refined this concept and extended it to incorporate an industrial structural upgrading component (see the first three chapters of the present volume; Narula, 1996; Dunning and Narula, 1996; Dunning *et al.*, 2001). No less important, the IDP is now being used by policy makers in the formation of their structural adjustment strategies. It has also been tested, and found useful, by investment development agencies (IDAs) in a variety of developing countries.

There is not the time or space to develop fully the model (which appears to be highly relevant to the Chinese situation) but Figure 11.2 sets out the main contents of four of its five stages. (The fifth stage is currently only relevant to developed industrial countries, although the advent of internet-driven communications is reducing the time scale of development quite considerably.)[1]

Stage 1 typifies the situation for low-income developing countries (or regions within developing countries). In this scenario there is likely to be only a modest amount of inward FDI because of the lack of indigenous resources and capabilities and/or markets, and little outward FDI. Exports will consist of resource and/or low-skilled, labour-intensive products. Imports will mainly be made up of fairly standardized manufactured goods. Government policy is likely to be confined to providing the basic legal and commercial infrastructure and incentives (or protection) to local producers and foreign investors (particularly in respect of resource-based activities).

Stage 2 is the stage in which most developing countries find themselves today (although, in larger countries, the income of GNP per head may be greater or lesser in particular regions). Domestic incomes are now high enough and rising to attract some market-seeking FDI, particularly that of an import-substituting kind, while, as a result of an improved institutional infrastructure and the upgrading of indigenous capabilities, there is also likely to be some export-oriented FDI, mainly of processed primary products or technology and light manufactures. Partly as a result of this type of inbound FDI, the composition of the exports of recipient countries is likely to shift towards labour-intensive intermediate or final products, while that of its imports is likely to include a higher proportion of more sophisticated capital and consumer goods. There may also be some outward FDI to adjacent regions, or to the more advanced industrialized countries, as a means of acquiring new competitivity-enhancing assets or market access. In Stage 2, government policy is normally concentrated on upgrading the quality of indigenous labour and managerial capabilities; on creating an active capital market and an effective (and accountable) banking system; and on ensuring a favourable business environment for both domestic and foreign investors.

Stage 3 is perhaps the most interesting one and, taken together with Stage 4 (for at least parts of the economy), is likely to be the most relevant one for the future of the Chinese economy, particularly in the larger cities and coastal areas. What we see here is a large and increasing domestic market which draws in market-seeking FDI to supply those products which the investing country or countries earlier had a comparative advantage in supplying. At the same time, because of enhanced indigenous skills and managerial talent, there is an increasing tendency of foreign firms to engage in the higher-value stages of export-oriented activities. Because of the upgrading of domestic resources and capabilities, indigenous firms are now beginning to exploit their foreign markets by outbound FDI and/or cross-border cooperative ventures, as well as seeking new outlets for increasing their own competitive advantages. An increasing proportion of exports now consist of medium to high technology-intensive goods and services.

In these stages too, and especially in large countries like China and India, there is likely to be increasing regional specialization of economic activities, with agglomerations or networks of related activities such as the Bangalore cluster of software firms (in India) and the Hong Kong cluster of financial services (in South East Asia), as described in some detail by Balasubramanyam and Enright (2000). In Stage 4, too, there is likely to be a sharp increase in innovation-related activities. Often foreign-owned firms play a critical role in fostering such activities, particularly as part of their global or regional strategies. But so can (and do) national and regional governments, partly by their willingness to upgrade the supporting infrastructure for higher-value activities, partly by the framing of a positive FDI policy, and partly by offering the appropriate tax and other incentives for their indigenous firms to be more innovative and seek out new markets, and for individuals to be more entrepreneurial and to upgrade their native skills.

Regrettably, there is not the time or space to pursue these thoughts, or the contents of Figure 11.2, further, but the idea of the IDP has relevance not only for national governments but for subnational administrations and investment promotion agencies. Of course no one region or district – let

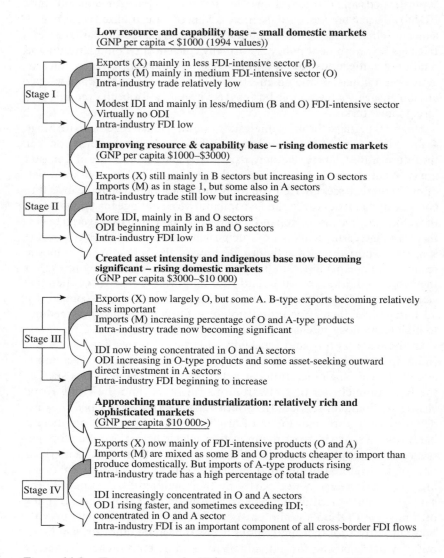

Low resource and capability base – small domestic markets
(GNP per capita < $1000 (1994 values))

Stage I

Exports (X) mainly in less FDI-intensive sector (B)
Imports (M) mainly in medium FDI-intensive sector (O)
Intra-industry trade relatively low

Modest IDI and mainly in less/medium (B and O) FDI-intensive sector
Virtually no ODI
Intra-industry FDI low

Improving resource & capability base – rising domestic markets
(GNP per capita $1000–$3000)

Stage II

Exports (X) still mainly in B sectors but increasing in O sectors
Imports (M) as in stage 1, but some also in A sectors
Intra-industry trade still low but increasing

More IDI, mainly in B and O sectors
ODI beginning mainly in B and O sectors
Intra-industry FDI low

**Created asset intensity and indigenous base now becoming
significant – rising domestic markets**
(GNP per capita $3000–$10 000)

Stage III

Exports (X) now largely O, but some A. B-type exports becoming relatively
less important
Imports (M) increasing percentage of O and A-type products
Intra-industry trade now becoming significant

IDI now being concentrated in O and A sectors
ODI increasing in O-type products and some asset-seeking outward
direct investment in A sectors
Intra-industry FDI beginning to increase

**Approaching mature industrialization: relatively rich and
sophisticated markets**
(GNP per capita $10 000>)

Stage IV

Exports (X) now mainly of FDI-intensive products (O and A)
Imports (M) are mixed as some B and O products cheaper to import than
produce domestically. But imports of A-type products rising
Intra-industry trade has a high percentage of total trade

IDI increasingly concentrated in O and A sectors
OD1 rising faster, and sometimes exceeding IDI;
concentrated in O and A sector
Intra-industry FDI is an important component of all cross-border FDI flows

*Figure 11.2   Four stages in the IDPs and TDPs of industrializing
developing countries*

alone one country – is precisely like another, and the shape and character of the IDP, and the speed by which one moves from one stage to the next is likely to be strongly contextual. But it does have general applicability, in so far as the form, extent and content of FDI and its impact on a nation's competitive position are likely to vary as development proceeds. So, indeed, will that part of the development process and the strategies of foreign investors which it is within the power of host governments and IPAs to influence. And it is to this latter question that the third part of our presentation will turn.

CHANGING LOCATIONAL NEEDS OF FOREIGN INVESTORS

The third theme may be expressed as follows: the advent of the global economy and, in particular, the reduction in all kinds of spatially related costs, the growing importance of information and knowledge as the key components of the wealth creation process, and the emergence of cooperative alliances as a major form of cross-border economic organization, are critically affecting both the locational strategies of business corporations and those of governments of countries (and regions) as they seek to attract and retain the kind of value-added activity best suited to their needs and capabilities.

It is sometimes said that globalization is reducing the role and authority of national governments, and particularly so in the case of smaller nation states which are part of a regional union (for example, Belgium in the EU). On the one hand, supranational entities, for example, the WTO and the World Bank, seem to be taking over some of the responsibilities previously assumed by national administrations. On the other hand, in large or medium-size countries like the USA, China and the UK, one sees an increasing devolution or decentralization of (some kinds of) economic decision taking to subnational authorities. In the European Union too, 'subsidiarity' is very much the name of the game.

At the same time, there is a general consensus among international business scholars that it is not so much that the economic tasks of national governments have become less extensive or important, but that the contents and prioritization of these tasks have changed. This view is based on the fact that it is increasingly the case that the attractions of countries to inbound foreign investors rest mainly in the possession of resources, capabilities and markets which are (a) location-bound, that is, immobile across national borders, and (b) which critically affect the ability of domestic and foreign-owned corporations, whose own resources and capabilities tend to be mobile, to combine the two sets of assets in the most productive way.

And the critical point here is that it is governments, whatever their political shade, which bear the major responsibility for creating and enhancing the value of these immobile assets, an increasing proportion of which are public goods. Even in such liberal market economies as the USA, federal or state governments control expenditure on education, pre-industrial R&D, transport and defence, health services and the environment.[2] By such expenditures and by their monetary and trade policies, they can and do critically affect the locational attractiveness of the USA (or parts of the USA) to foreign investors (see Doremus *et al.*, 1998). And, perhaps most important of all, as the experience of Japan clearly shows, is the culture or mentality of a country's people and institutions towards the dynamics of market forces and technological change, and the demands of the global economy.

There is also accumulating evidence that the state of personal morality and the ethics of institutions has recently become an important locational determinant of firms (see, for example, Giersch, 1996). Consumers are now becoming increasingly critical of dubious business practices: investors are becoming more environmentally conscious; civil society, in the guise of a plethora of NGOs, is forcing both national governments and supranational agencies to think again on the 'rules of the game' underpinning global capitalism, and particularly on its implications for democratic governance and social inclusivity.

Many empirical studies, including one recently carried out by the (London based) Economist Intelligence Unit (2002), are now suggesting that FDI inflows are extremely sensitive to the policy framework and the business environment of host countries. Among the positive variables identified by the EIU in its 2002 survey are the degree to which private property rights (including intellectual property rights) are safeguarded, the consistency, transparency and fairness of the legal, financial and tax system, the quality of the institutional infrastructure, 'one-stop' shopping for potential foreign investors, and a positive and welcoming attitude by IPAs. Among the significant negative factors listed, that is, those deterring FDI, are social unrest, the extent of crime and economic immorality, the level of corruption,[3] the risk of expropriation of foreign assets, exchange controls and an unfavourable macroeconomic environment. The value of each of these factors is primarily within the domain of government to influence; and such responsibilities, far from being diminished by the access of China to the WTO, have been considerably heightened.

So, turning to Table 11.1, we can see that foreign investors are concerned, not only with the economic characteristics of host countries, which are, as indicated, often specific to the particular kinds of FDI (set out to the right of the figure) but also with the policy framework and business environment.

Table 11.1 Relating host country determinants to motives and determinants of FDI

Host country determinants	Type of FDI by motives of TNCs	Principal economic determinants in host countries
Policy Framework for FDI • Economic, political and social stability • Rules regarding entry and operations • Standards of treatments of foreign affiliates • **Policies determinants and structures of markets (especially competition and M&A policies)** • International agreements on FDI • **Privatization Policies** • Trade policy (tariffs and NTBs) and coherence of FDI and trade policies • Tax policy (including tax credits) • **Industrial Regional Policies** I. **Economic determinants** II. **Business facilitation** • **Investment incentives and promotion schemes** • **Reduced information costs** • Local amenities (bilingual schools, quality of life, etc.) • Pre-and post-investment services (e.g. one-stop shopping) • **Good infrastructure and support services e.g. banking, legal accounting services** • Social capital economic morality • **Region-based cluster and network promotion**	A. Market seeking B. Resource seeking C. Efficiency seeking D. Asset seeking	• Market size and per capita income • Market growth • Access to regional and global markets • Country-specific consumer preferences • Structure of markets • Land and building costs, rents and rates • Cost of raw materials, components, parts • Low-cost unskilled labour • **Availability and cost of skilled labour** • Cost of resources and assets listed under B adjusted for productivity of labour inputs • Other input costs to and from and within host economy • Membership of a regional integration agreement conducive to promoting a more cost-effective inter-country division of labour • **Technological managerial relational and other created assets** • **Physical infrastructure (ports, roads, power, telecommunications)** • **Macro innovatory, entrepreneurial and educational capacity/ environment**

Source: Adapted and expanded from Table 10.1, p. 248–9.

Of those identified, those in bold type have become more important over the past decade. Most of the determinants apply, to a greater or lesser extent, to all countries and regions, but some, such as the extent and content of privatization schemes and the quality of the institutional infrastructure, are particularly critical to transition economies and to developing countries or regions in the earlier stage of the IDP.

One final point should be made. In a very real sense, governments of countries and regions are like business corporations. They are continually attempting to identify and upgrade their unique and sustainable competitive advantages. Moreover, in the light of frequent technological change and the demands of a dynamic, uncertain global economy, they are regularly needing to reappraise and reconfigure their modes of governance. In the case of global business corporations this, for example, has involved a reorientation of their governance profiles, as their ownership of non-core resources and capabilities has become less important than their access to them (Rifkin, 2000) and as they have pursued more holistic and integrated product and investment strategies. But also involved is a greater delegation of decision taking from the parent company to its subsidiaries to meet the specific needs of the local market place.

In the case of national governments, this has meant a reappraisal not only of the means by which the indigenous resources and capabilities for which it is responsible can be better deployed and upgraded, but also of the best ways to design and implement policy within a new global framework of shared sovereignty and intergovernmental alliances. And, as the Japanese business consultant Kenichi Ohmae has observed (Ohmae, 1995), it is leading to a more active role being played by subnational authorities in their efforts to attract inward FDI, most noticeably, as we suggested earlier, to fostering clusters of related value-added activities.

It is such opportunities and challenges as these which are facing China as it seeks to move along and up its IDP and TDP. We are fully confident that its people and institutions will readily rise to these opportunities and challenges and, in so doing, will use all their considerable skills, wisdom and determination to turn these to their own – and to the global economy's – lasting benefit. I wish them well in this daunting, but worthwhile, task.

NOTES

1. For a further elaboration of this thesis, see Ozawa *et al.* (2001).
2. For the part played by state governments affecting the location of FDI in the USA, see Donahue (1977).
3. On corruption, see a very interesting paper by Shang Jin Wei (2000).

REFERENCES

Balasubramanyam, V.N., and Michael J. Enright (2000), in J.H. Dunning (ed.), *Regions, Globalization and the Knowledge-Based Economy*, Oxford: Oxford University Press (paperback edition 2002).

Donahue, J.D. (1977), *Disunited States*, New York: Basic Books.

Doremus, P.N., W.W. Keller, W. Pauly and S. Reich (1998), *The Myth of the Global Corporation*, Princeton, NJ: Princeton University Press.

Dunning, J.H. (1958), *American Investment in British Manufacturing Industry*, London and New York: Allen & Unwin; rev. edn (1998), London and New York: Routledge.

Dunning, J.H. (1976), 'US Industry in Britain', *Financial Times*, London.

Dunning, J.H., and R. Narula (eds) (1996), *Foreign Direct Investment and Governments*, London and New York: Routledge.

Dunning, J.H., Kim Chang-Su and Lin Jyh-Der (2001), 'Incorporating trade into the investment development path. A case study of Korea and Taiwan', *Oxford Development Studies*, **29**(2), 145–54.

Economist Intelligence Unit (2002), *World Investment Prospects: The Next Investment Boom,* London: EIU.

Giersch, H. (1996), 'Economic morality as a competitive asset', in A. Hamlin, H. Giersch and A. Norton (eds), *Markets, Morals and Community*, St. Leonards: Australia Centre for Independent Studies, pp. 19–42.

IMF Survey (2002), 'For China, foreign direct investment translates into higher productivity growth', 27 May, pp. 174–6.

Narula, R. (1996), *Multinational Investment and Economic Structure*, London: Routledge.

Ohmae, Kenichi (1995), *The End of the Nation State*, New York: The Free Press.

Ozawa, T., S. Castello and R.J. Phillips (2001), 'The internet revolution, the "McLuhan" stage of catch up and institutional reforms in Asia', *Journal of Economic Issues*, **35** (2), 289–98.

Rifkin, J. (2000), *The Age of Access*, London: Penguin Books.

UNCTAD (2001), *World Investment Report: Promoting Linkages*, New York and Geneva.

Wei, Shang Jin (2000), 'How taxing is corruption on international investors?', *Review of Economics and Statistics*, **LXXXII**, February, 1–11.

Index